The Economy as a Polity: The Political Constitution of Contemporary Capitalism

T0304078

The Economy as a Polity: The Political Constitution of Contemporary Capitalism

Edited by

Christian Joerges, Bo Stråth and Peter Wagner

Routledge
Taylor & Francis Group

LONDON AND NEW YORK

First published 2005 by UCL Press

Published 2017 by Routledge
2 Park Square, Milton Park, Abingdon, Oxon OX14 4RN
711 Third Avenue, New York, NY 10017, USA

Routledge is an imprint of the Taylor & Francis Group, an informa business

British Library Cataloguing in Publication Data
The economy as a polity: the political constitution of
contemporary capitalisation
1 Capitalism 2 Globalization – Economic aspects
3 Monetary policy
I Joerges, Christian II Strath, Bo, 1943– III Wagner, Peter, 1956–
330.1'12

Library of Congress Cataloguing in Publication Data
Data available

ISBN 13: 978-1-84472-069-9 (pbk)
ISBN 13: 978-1-84472-070-5 (hbk)

ACKNOWLEDGMENTS

This book is the result of research pursued at the European University Institute (EUI) from 2001 to 2004 in the framework of the working group 'The economy as a polity', established and convened by the editors. Most of the contributors to the volume participated in the weekly working group meetings during the academic year 2002–03. Before and after this intense phase of work, seminars and workshops were held with numerous other speakers – Eve Chiapello, Marcello de Cecco, Peter Hall, Robert Salais, David Soskice, Laurent Thévenot among others – whom we would like to thank for their contributions to the intellectual milieu in which the analyses presented in this volume could flourish. Thanks are also due to Angelos Mouzakitis and Vasia Tsakiri for help with editing the contributions. Financial support from the Jean Monnet Fellowships at the Robert Schuman Centre for Advanced Studies made the stays of some contributors at EUI possible; support for organising the workshop and seminar series was provided by the EUI Research Council. Sometimes we were made to feel that we were seen as straying too far away from the disciplinary core of law, history, sociology, political science and economics or from any direct usefulness of our thoughts for policy-making. Overall, however, EUI has provided a very conducive environment for our multi-disciplinary work, and we would like to express our thanks to all those who made this possible.

San Domenico di Fiesole
November 2004

LIST OF CONTRIBUTORS

David M Andrews is Associate Professor in the Department of Politics at Scripps College, adjunct professor at the Claremont Graduate University, and founding Director of the European Union Center of California. His research focuses on Atlantic political and economic relations and on international monetary affairs.

Johann P Arnason is Professor Emeritus of Sociology in the School of Social Sciences at La Trobe University and currently a Visiting Professor of Sociology at the University of Leipzig. His research focuses on questions of social theory, theories of modernity, and the comparative study of civilisations. His most recent book is *Civilizations in Dispute* (2003).

Fred Block is Professor of Sociology at the University of California, Davis, and member of the Board of the Karl Polanyi Institute of Political Economy. His numerous publications include *The Vampire State and Other Myths and Fallacies About the US Economy* (1996) and *Postindustrial Possibilities: A Critique of Economic Discourse* (1990).

Giuseppe Bronzini is a judge at the Court of Appeals of Rome. Author of numerous essays in political theory and European and labour law, he is editor of the journal *Rivista Critica di Diritto del Lavoro*. Most recently, he has edited *Europa, Costituzione, Movimenti Sociali* (2003) and authored the book *I Diritti del Popolo-mondo* (2004).

Pepper D Culpepper is Associate Professor of Public Policy in the John F Kennedy School of Government at Harvard University. His research focuses on the role of employers in politics and on the politics of institutional change in the advanced industrial democracies, particularly in Europe. His publications include *Creating Cooperation* (2003) and *The German Skills Machine* (co-ed, 1999).

Michelle Everson is Jean Monnet Lecturer in European Law at Birkbeck College, University of London. She has researched widely in the field of European law and has particular interests in the areas of European regulatory law, European administrative and constitutional law and European citizenship.

María Gómez Garrido is a researcher in the Department of Social and Political Sciences of the European University Institute. Her work focuses on changing conceptions of work and unemployment in Europe from the late 19th century to the present.

Christian Joerges is Professor of Economic Law in the Department of Law of the European University Institute and currently works on issues of transnational and European governance, risk regulation and standardisation, and the history of concepts of integration.

Feriel Kandil, economist and philosopher at the research group *Institutions et Dynamiques Historiques de l'Economie* (IDHE) at the Ecole normale supérieure de Cachan, has published numerous articles on the philosophy and economy of the welfare state in Europe.

Peter Lindseth is Associate Professor of Law in the School of Law at the University of Connecticut. His research focuses on the historical evolution of the administrative state in the 20th century as well as the relationship of administrative governance to the process of European integration.

Bo Stråth is Professor of Contemporary History in the Department of History and Civilization of the European University Institute, where he has directed the research programme *The modernity of Europe: towards a comparative-historical and politico-philosophical re-assessment*, together with Peter Wagner.

Peter Wagner is Professor of Social and Political Theory in the Department of Social and Political Sciences of the European University Institute, where he has directed the research programme *The modernity of Europe: towards a comparative-historical and politico-philosophical re-assessment*, together with Bo Stråth.

TABLE OF CONTENTS

PART III
RE-EMBEDDING CAPITALISM: TWO PERSPECTIVES

INTRODUCTION

THE POLITICAL CONSTITUTION OF CONTEMPORARY CAPITALISM

Peter Wagner

The debate about so-called economic globalisation has reached a new phase. For some time during the 1990s even critics had been convinced that neo-liberal thinking had achieved such a hegemony that nothing stood in the way of the further dismantling of all kinds of 'barriers to trade' and of the creation of an effective world-market for all commodities, including labour and capital themselves. In the meantime, however, both the increased and increasingly effective resistance to the social consequences of neo-liberal market-making – rising inequality and insecurity throughout the world – and the visibly dysfunctional effects of lack of regulation – currency and stock market crashes, among others – have changed the politico-intellectual climate, even among economists and market-oriented policy-makers. It seems as if a new round in the debate about the respective roles of states and markets has been inaugurated. The story about 'the rise and fall of market society', which was first told in these terms by Karl Polanyi (1984 [1944] *The Great Transformation*, Boston, MA: Beacon Press) 60 years ago, is about to receive a new chapter.

This book is itself a contribution to this new chapter. However, it insists that this chapter cannot be written by merely compiling its ingredients from the earlier episodes. It has long been recognised that there is, ever since market forces had been unleashed, a struggle between regulators and deregulators of economic activity. Much intellectual energy has been devoted to trying to determine the appropriate boundary between the work of the market logic and the one of state intervention. The 'arguments for capitalism before its triumph' (Albert Hirschman (1977) *The Passions and the Interests*, Princeton, NJ: Princeton University Press) that were made in the 17th and 18th centuries optimistically suggested that the rise of commerce on its own would lead to a new and better society. It was hoped that the expansion of trade could enhance domestic and international peace as well as increase the wealth of nations. The rise of this kind of reasoning, however, coincided with – similarly Enlightenment-based – the rise of the call for popular sovereignty, for collective autonomy. From the French Revolution onwards, and increasingly from the middle of the 19th century onwards, it became clear that the workings of the market would increase social inequality and that the collective will, wherever it was permitted to express itself, requested measures to 'protect society' (Polanyi) from the dangers of the market. In the clash of these two principles, the idea arose that, under democratic conditions, states would eternally be put against markets.

While broadly agreeing with this basic analysis, the contributors to this volume consider it to be insufficient to understand the interaction between these two 'logics' – and this for two reasons: a theoretical and a historical one. First, the idea of opposed principles suggests that they are in equal measure potentially constitutive of social order. In contrast, we hold, with Polanyi, that markets cannot even be consistently thought of as self-regulating. Markets are always constituted by framework conditions that cannot be set by the markets themselves. It was an error of much social and political theory, including critical theory, to accept the postulate of market self-regulation as a theoretical possibility. In contrast, one needs to think of 'market society', or capitalism, as always being politically constituted. The range and scope of market rules requires some agreement, or at least acceptance, for economic exchange to be working at all; in democratic societies, therefore, these rules are, at least theoretically, always subject to political debate and decision. To put the issue in theoretical terms: even the most pure version of economic liberalism always entails at the same time a political philosophy. This volume thus proposes to understand contemporary capitalism by regarding the economy as a polity, as an arrangement that is always constituted by some collective agreements about its mode of operation.

Such insight clearly was present in all major contributions to the analysis of capitalism – from Adam Smith's wealth of nations to Karl Marx's critique of political economy to Max Weber's protestant ethic to Karl Polanyi's great transformation, to mark only the most crucial steps. However, it is not only this insight that seems to have been largely forgotten. There also appears to be some need more clearly to spell out the ways in which the economy can fruitfully be analysed as a polity, as politically constituted. For this reason, the first part of this volume is devoted to a retrieval of the theoretical resources that are available to us for the analysis of capitalism and to the elaboration of a novel view on that basis. Setting the tone for the volume, Chapter 1 – by Fred Block – draws its inspiration from Karl Polanyi but develops further Polanyi's theory of the fictitious commodities for the analysis of the contemporary constellation of capitalism. Polanyi had underlined in general that market society tended to consider commodities as 'goods' that had not been provided by market action, and he singled out land, labour and money as those three fictitious commodities. In his analysis of the fall of market society, he emphasised the latter two: the movement for the protection of labour had transformed market society from the late 19th century onwards; and, under the conditions of democratic mass society in the early 20th century, the rigid mechanism of the gold standard for the regulation of international finance turned out to be the main element in the collapse of the 19th century order. Block adds knowledge and competition to the list of fictitious commodities and shows how contemporary capitalism is, for the provision of those goods, dependent on means that it cannot itself provide.

In his later anthropological writings, Polanyi broadened his perspective on the embeddedness of the economy, and it is to this cultural or civilisational approach to the analysis of capitalism that Johann Arnason turns in Chapter 2. Civilisational approaches to capitalism challenge the notion that capitalism is a self-contained economic system or a functioning machine (Fernand Braudel) by thematising the cultural and political premises of capitalism as an economic regime – or, to put it another way, the underlying constellations of meaning and power. Arnason's analysis pays particular attention to the recent revival of interest in the concept of 'spirit of capitalism', made famous by Weber, but already used by Werner

Sombart, by distinguishing three approaches: the 'new spirit of capitalism' (Luc Boltanski and Eve Chiapello); nationalism as the cultural force behind capitalist development (Liah Greenfeld); and capitalism as a religion (Christoph Deutschmann).

The civilisational frame of reference is being developed in a situation where the more specific and established versions of the critique of capitalism seem inadequate. Chapter 3 – by Peter Wagner – is precisely devoted to a review of the tradition of critical theory. Selecting Theodor W Adorno's work as a key example, the chapter shows how the place of political philosophy was evacuated in critical theory in favour of a reasoning that emphasised epistemic obstacles towards analysing capitalism instead. From such an angle, then, any embedding of capitalism appeared impossible, and the well-known apocalyptic tendency of critical theory emerged forcefully. Not content with this finding, however, the chapter in a second step proceeds to demonstrate that the dimension of political philosophy in the critical analysis of capitalism can be restored. If Adorno and other critical theorists are read in this light, their observations on developmental tendencies of capitalism gain new meaning and provide insights that cannot be found, for instance, in current debates about 'varieties of capitalism'.

The work at theoretical retrieval in the first part of the volume is not meant to lead towards the comprehensive theory that will, once and for all, explain the workings of capitalism. Indeed, all three authors underline that the historical experiences with capitalism lead to transformations that in turn will require new angles of analysis. It is in the nature of the struggles over the embedding of markets that their outcomes are subject to historical contingency and cannot be completely known beforehand. Beyond a review of the theoretical tools at hand, therefore, the analysis of the contemporary constellation thus also requires an understanding of the recent transformations of capitalism. The second part of the volume is devoted to this task.

This second part is organised along two lines. Three chapters are devoted to analyses of the current state of regulation of the two fictitious commodities that were central to Polanyi: labour and money (Chapters 4, 5 and 6). Three further chapters deal with the historical development and novel forms of the mode of embedding markets (Chapters 7, 8 and 9).

Writing during the Second World War, Polanyi had concluded that the protection of labour had indeed been rather successfully accomplished, but that this achievement had at the same time indirectly led to the collapse of the international monetary order and to the domestic endangerment of liberty through the rise of fascism. At the end of that war, fascism was defeated and the reconstruction effort was devoted to the rebuilding of a world trade order on the basis of a new international monetary regime and to the maintenance of the protective shield for labour by extending national welfare state measures. In Chapter 4, Bo Stråth reconstructs the long-term history of international monetary regulation and demonstrates how the forms of embedding markets through the provision of money have changed historically with the alternating fate of world trade and with the increasing degree of dependence of national policy-making on the electorate under conditions of universal suffrage.

In a companion chapter (Chapter 5) on money as a fictitious commodity, David Andrews shows in more detail how the so-called Bretton Woods system tried both to enhance and stabilise world trade, while at the same time granting national governments policy autonomy for the development of their domestic welfare arrangements. These objectives could not be reconciled by any master-plan and the history of the Bretton Woods system, Andrews insists, should indeed not be read as the story of the establishment of a coherent arrangement and its breakdown under adverse circumstances, but rather as some ground rules and commitment that were in need of constant reinterpretation to satisfy all objectives. During the early 1970s, no common interpretation could be reached any longer, and national governments needed to find their own ways to manage their currencies under conditions of fluctuating exchange rates. The collapse of global rules was the moment for the preparation of regional arrangements, based on the insight that national states would most often be too weak to build effective protection but that supranational co-operation could provide a satisfactory answer to this problem. In this light, Stråth's chapter moves towards reconstructing the history of European monetary integration from the ambitious Werner plan of the 1970s, which did not materialise, to the current Eurozone – the capacity of which for effective re-embedding is much more doubtful – even though it is not yet fully tested.

Turning towards labour, Chapter 6 – by María Gómez Garrido – starts out from an historical reconstruction of the protection of this 'commodity' through the creation of compulsory national unemployment insurance arrangements. This reconstruction is necessary because it shows how the achievement was conditional upon the conventionalisation of wage-labour which, furthermore, occurred in national form and on the basis of the male breadwinner view of the household. In this light, it can be shown that the recent conceptual move from employment to employability is much more than an adaptation of the established arrangements to novel conditions. Rather, it breaks fundamentally with the concept of unemployment as it was consolidated during the '30 glorious years' of post-war economic growth. Given this radical challenge, Gómez suggests, a whole new understanding of work is required that may need to go beyond the national form and can take inspiration from the broader feminist rethinking of the nature of work in society.

Overall, the model of policy-making prevalent during the Keynesian interventionist welfare state of that period was national in scope and bureaucratic-hierarchical in form. There was little question about national governments' capacity – at least in the highly industrialised countries – to insulate somewhat their economies against external shocks and to regulate them internally. Current debates, in contrast, suggest that these two capacities are precisely what is put into doubt during the recent changes in the way in which market societies are politically constituted. The first change has become associated with the topic of the 'decline of the nation-state'; the second one with the rise of the concept of 'governance'. The contributors to this volume remain sceptical about the full validity of the former theorem, and they retain doubts about the fruitfulness of the latter concept. Nevertheless, these topics can fruitfully be seen as constituting the axes around which the second set of chapters in this part of the volume is organised.

By 1960, there was broad agreement about the democratic state of law being the site of public action, and about policy-making and policy implementation as law-based public administration, instructed by theories of hierarchy and bureaucracy, being the form of public action. From the 1970s onwards, however, 'implementation problems' moved into the centre of attention of policy analysts, and the failure of the Keynes-inspired growth policies of the first Mitterrand government in France during the early 1980s suggested strongly that national economies could no longer be managed by national policies alone. Against this background, Chapter 7 – by Peter Lindseth – offers a comparative history of the embeddedness of public administration itself; Chapter 8 – by Pepper Culpepper – analyses the emergence of novel forms of politico-economic co-ordination 'below' the national level; and Chapter 9 – by Christian Joerges and Michelle Everson – focuses on 'governance' as a mode of co-ordination 'above' the national level in the European Union.

Drawing inspiration from a rather marginal remark by Polanyi, Peter Lindseth turns Polanyi's basic question around. Rather than asking how public action can embed the economy, he investigates how public action itself can be – and needs to be – embedded in the larger framework of politics and society. Providing a long-term comparative perspective on France and Britain, he demonstrates how a need for public administration to be embedded itself arose ever more strongly in the context of the increasingly interventionist states. Given the highly different legal and political histories – France having an interventionist policy legacy and a Roman law tradition and Britain having a liberal policy legacy and a common law tradition – the debates took highly different shapes. In both cases, however, it became clear that normative justification from political and legal theory was increasingly required, and adequate institutional arrangements were to be developed, to sustain the legitimacy of public action.

Pepper Culpepper's comparative analysis of decentralised co-operation between political and economic actors – unions, employers and local and regional government – in France and Italy is set in the 1980s and 1990s, that is, after considerable doubts had arisen about both the efficiency and the legitimacy of national policy-making. He demonstrates how the decrease – partly intended, partly incurred involuntarily – of national intervention capacity in matters such as professional education, economic development and employment creation does not necessarily lead to a disembedding of markets. Co-operation at local or regional level can lead to new forms of embedding, even though their success is highly dependent on organisational structures and capacities of the actors involved.

While Culpepper thus indirectly explores new modes of governance at the subnational level, Joerges and Everson move the governance debate to the supranational arena. They analyse the rise of the concept of governance as a response to the declining capacity of national governments to set rules for economic actors, but they also make a direct connection to the rising expectations for more efficient regulation at the supranational level, as expressed in many contributions from political science during the 1990s. 'New modes of governance', in which a broad range of governmental and non-governmental, politically accountable and non-accountable actors co-operate are, in their view, a functionally necessary response to failures of traditional legal interventionism in general and to the limited competences and resources of the EU in particular. However, 'governance' is a response which challenges important achievements of constitutionalism. Their contribution is a search for a constructive defence of this heritage, in particular of the idea that law should discipline political processes and ensure their legitimacy. After the turn to governance, the defence of this heritage has become dependent on processes of generation of societal law ('societal constitutionalism'), on the one hand, and on constitutionalisation strategies which ensure the deliberative quality of governance in postnational constellations through indirect legal and political controls, on the other hand.

All of the chapters in this volume contain elements of reconstruction that are meant to enhance the current debate about the political constitution of capitalism, in both theoretical and political terms. The nine chapters discussed so far, however, focus on the renewal of analysis and only point to fruitful directions of institutional or policy change. Indeed, even though the volume as a whole cannot offer a map for the way out of the current transformation of capitalism, the two chapters in Part III will at least explore – in very different ways – perspectives for political renewal.

Directly linking up to the analysis of governance in the EU in Chapter 9, Chapter 10 – by Giuseppe Bronzini – discusses the prospects for the further elaboration of the 'European social model' in the light of the debates that led to the new – yet to be ratified – constitutional treaty of the European Union. The question of regional integration, and in particular the case of Europe, was touched upon in several of the preceding chapters; it now becomes the central topic in Bronzini's analysis. Turning away from the long-dominant view of European integration as pure market-making and, thus, disembedding, Bronzini explores critically the potential of Europe to become a new site for the embedding of the economy. Bronzini discusses both the difficulties of arriving at a truly supranational capacity for re-embedding and the innovative elements contained in the recent events – placing emphasis on the legal dimension through the Charter of Fundamental Rights and the work of the European Court of Justice.

Finally, Chapter 11 – by Feriel Kandil – returns to the theoretical issues raised in the first part of the volume, but does so with a deliberate emphasis on the normative tradition of political philosophy. Acknowledging the fact that recent debate has cast considerable doubt on the legitimacy of public action to give direction to the polity, she first discards the economic, ethical and political objections to public action and then, in a second step, she develops a concept of prudential public action oriented towards solidarity as a mode of intervening into society towards an enhancement of the common good that is acceptable to all members of society. Kandil concludes her reasoning by showing how the approach of prudential reason to public action could be translated into European policies towards labour, money and a more democratic governance, thus linking back to the contributions in the second part of the volume and to Bronzini's preceding analysis of the embedding potential of European integration in terms of constitutional law.

PART I

THE ANALYSIS OF CAPITALISM: WORK AT THEORETICAL RETRIEVAL

CHAPTER 1

TOWARDS A NEW UNDERSTANDING OF ECONOMIC MODERNITY

Fred Block

> Too often the writings of ... Polanyi have been ravaged like the carcasses of dead bodies – the most useful parts ripped from their meaning-giving integument and transplanted into ailing theories. (Michael Burawoy 2003)[1]

This chapter argues that a reconstruction of Karl Polanyi's social theory can provide contemporary scholars with powerful tools for analysing the last two centuries of capitalist development and for understanding the prospects and possibilities in the current historical moment. Polanyi is similar to his two great predecessors – Karl Marx and Max Weber – in that his writings do not yield their secrets easily for a range of different reasons. All three bodies of work are marked by internal theoretical tensions, shifting positions over time, and the absence of a final synthetic statement (Block 2001 and 2003; Block and Somers 2003). Moreover, our readings of all of these figures are encrusted with sedimentary layers of earlier interpretations and misinterpretations that make it difficult to recapture the 'meaning-giving integument'.

The goal here is not to provide a definitive interpretation of Polanyi's writings, but to elaborate a set of Polanyi-inspired concepts that provide leverage for the analysis of contemporary market societies. Developing such concepts is an urgent task because the critique of capitalism has reached an impasse in recent years. Other chapters in this volume, particularly by Wagner and Arnason, provide rich accounts of the analytic difficulties and intellectual dead ends that have plagued theories of capitalism. From the Enlightenment onwards, there has been a deep conflict between the project of political modernity defined as collective self-determination and economic modernity defined as the autonomous determination of the ways in which human needs are satisfied. Polanyi is one of the few thinkers who allows us to envision how this fundamental conflict could be overcome.

---

1   Burawoy's quote refers to both Gramsci and Polanyi, but the present chapter's focus is on Polanyi alone. The author is grateful to Margaret Somers, the other participants in the 'Economy as Polity' workshop, and to Peter Evans, Ana Celia Castro, and the students who participated in the class on 'The Problem of Governability in a Global Political Economy', Rio de Janeiro, July 2004.

THE DOUBLE MOVEMENT

Polanyi's masterpiece, *The Great Transformation*, was written between 1941 and 1943 – the same period in which JM Keynes and Harry Dexter White were working on post-war international monetary plans (Andrews, in this volume). Polanyi was also hoping to influence the post-war settlement; he wanted to avert the disastrous restoration of the Gold Standard that had occurred after the First World War. He believed that Gold Standard restoration had occurred then because policy-makers across the political spectrum failed to understand the deep flaws in market liberalism – the idea that society should be organised around an integrated set of self-regulating markets for commodities, land, labour and money. Polanyi's core project was to show that market liberalism was utopian, impractical, and produced horrendous unintended consequences.

Polanyi's book begins with the audacious claim that the Second World War was caused by the peculiar economic theory elaborated in England by Thomas Robert Malthus and David Ricardo in the period from 1798 to 1817. These two architects of Classical Economics provided the theoretical justification for organising society around self-regulating markets. As England became the dominant global power over the course of the 19th century, Malthus's and Ricardo's theoretical system provided the blueprint for organising the global economy around free trade and the Gold Standard. In Polanyi's view, entrusting either national economies or the global economy to market self-regulation was internally contradictory and unsustainable. The crisis-prone project of organising a self-regulating global economy finally resulted in its collapse in the 1930s. That collapse, in turn, brought fascism to power in several countries and made a Second World War inevitable.

To flesh out his analysis, Polanyi argued that European societies in the 19th century were marked by a double movement of conflicting pushes and pulls. On the one side, inspired by Malthus and Ricardo, was the movement of *laissez-faire* – the effort to eliminate barriers to the growth and integration of markets. This movement was given powerful intellectual legitimation by the Classical Economists' vision of self-regulating markets automatically establishing equilibrium between supply and demand. It was under the banner of this movement that the New Poor Law was passed in England in 1834 to create a national labour market in which wages would be the only source of income for prime age workers other than incarceration in a workhouse (Block and Somers 2003). The movement went on to abolish the Corn Laws in 1846 and to campaign for international free trade and global adoption of the Gold Standard.

Almost immediately, however, a counter-movement began to form. The purpose of this second movement was to protect society from the expansion of markets. However, in contrast to the first movement, this counter-movement lacked a unified theory; it was driven instead by the practical need of different groups to place limits on markets. One of its first victories was the passage of the Factory Acts in the 1840s to place some restraints on the exploitation of workers in the Satanic Mills of early industrial England. At the same time, the Chartist agitation by an emergent working class opened up a second front of this counter-movement. Polanyi argued that, by the 1870s and 1880s, the protective counter-movement was able to win increased regulatory interventions in virtually every country of Europe across a variety of policy areas. Hence, protective tariffs, social insurance, legalisation of trade unions, and other government initiatives insulated the citizenry from the impact of market forces.

Three things separate Polanyi's account from conventional narratives of 19th century class struggle. First, Polanyi insisted that the staffing of these two conflicting 'movements' was highly heterogeneous. The movement of *laissez-faire* was sometimes driven by capitalists, but the initiatives of intellectuals, politicians, and bureaucrats were also important. Moreover, at key junctures the movement was able to win support from coalitions that crossed class lines. The counter-movement was even more diverse; it sometimes included workers, the old landowning class, other agrarian interests, bureaucrats, politicians, intellectuals, the clergy, and capitalists who found themselves threatened by excessive market uncertainties.

Secondly, Polanyi exposes the fundamental paradox that the movement for *laissez-faire*, despite its deep hostility to 'state intervention', consistently relied on the systematic and continuous use of state power to achieve its objectives. The pattern was set with the 1834 New Poor Law. In order to create a 'free labour market', the state had first to strip the English poor of rights to assistance that they had enjoyed for more than two centuries. Then the state created a new set of disciplinary institutions – the local workhouses – to administer poor relief in a way that made it less attractive than paid employment. Finally, a new centralised Poor Law Administration was established to force local parishes to abandon their previous relief-giving practices. Even simpler *laissez-faire* victories such as establishing agricultural free trade involved the state in repressing the protests of marginal farmers and in developing alterative revenue sources to substitute for the government funds that had earlier been raised by tariffs.

Thirdly, Polanyi suggests that 'actually existing' capitalist societies are constituted by this double movement – by both the drive to expand the scope of markets and by the counter impulse to place limits on the market. Polanyi explicitly states that the idea of a self-regulating market economy was utopian in the sense of utterly unrealisable. Hence, the existence of sustainable market societies was the result of the two conflicting movements reaching some state of balance or compromise. The protective counter-movement, in effect, saved capitalists from themselves. Polanyi's analysis, however, is not functionalist. He recognises that the two movements can produce periods of dangerous stalemate in which no compromise seems possible. That was, in fact, central to his account of the rise of fascist movements starting in the 1920s. However, there is also the suggestion that certain periods of great capitalist advance, such as German industrialisation from the 1870s to the First World War, was linked to a productive, albeit shifting and conflictual, balance between these two multi-dimensional movements. (For a powerful argument along similar lines, see Swenson 2002.)

From this mutual constitution of actual capitalism by the two conflicting movements, we get the idea of the 'always and everywhere embedded market economy' (Block 2003). The key idea is that there is no such thing as a disembedded and fully autonomous economy; all market economies are constrained and shaped by non-market institutions and non-market values. This builds on two key Polanyian insights. First, the creation of market economies depends critically on the continuous exercise of governmental power. *Laissez-faire* is always an internally contradictory policy; it cannot do without the state. Secondly, without the assistance of the protective counter-movement, societies built around the free market vision would self-destruct. Their only opportunity to be viable depends upon a broad range of social practices designed to constrain and limit the play of market forces. This includes widespread adherence to values or orientations that are in deep conflict with the values of the marketplace (see Arnason, in this volume).

To be sure, market societies experience disembedding projects – systematic efforts to dismantle existing limits on market forces. The effort to create a common European market can be understood as involving such a disembedding project (see Joerges and Everson, Bronzini and Stråth, in this volume). However, there are still no disembedded economies; the disembedding projects are combined with re-embedding projects (Vogel 1996). In some cases, such as European fascism or Pinochet's Chile, the 'freeing' of the market occurs simultaneously with a systematic expansion of the state's repressive role. In other instances, disembedding projects are combined with the development of new institutions of social protection or the shift of protectionist measures from one scale of governance to another. There is no guarantee, of course, that these new protections will emerge automatically or will be as effective as those they replace. However, the inherent instability of markets means that disembedding projects will always provide opportunities for new forms of social protection.

SCALES OF GOVERNANCE

Polanyi's framework for analysing market societies was explicit in recognising five distinct levels of action. The first level of action is the mobilisation of social actors as part of these two great conflicting movements for *laissez-faire* and for social protection. These efforts tend to begin in local contestations that often make claims on local or sub-national states – the second level of action. However, as tensions intensify, demands often come to be focused on the decisions and policies of national states – the third level of action. The movements fight, for example, for and against tariff protections, new regulatory initiatives, or new forms of social insurance. Actions by national states are sometimes further constrained by regional blocs or multi-national empires – a fourth level of action. Having spent his formative years in Hungary which was then part of the Austro-Hungarian Empire, Polanyi was acutely aware that ethnicity, nationhood, boundaries, and sovereignty often do not coincide. Finally, all of these entities operate in a global environment that often constrains and limits the actions that can be taken at lower levels. Starting after 1870, when English hegemony established the combined imperatives of free trade and adherence to the Gold Standard, there has been the beginning of a global polity that establishes rules that it is costly to defy.

For Polanyi, the existence and coercive pressure of this global scale of governance is a variable that depends on shifts in the global balance of power and the relative stability of the global economy. Hence, in the 1920s when there was an international consensus for the restoration of the Gold Standard, the global rules meant that national governments were forced to resist the powerful pressures of the movement for social protection both inside and outside of the legislatures. In the 1930s, however, governments gained greater policy autonomy as the global governance mechanisms lost legitimation, enforcement mechanisms, and the institutional support of powerful governments.

This part of Polanyi's argument anticipates the contrast between the post-Second World War era of 'embedded liberalism' from 1945 to 1973 and the period of reascendant market liberalism from 1983 onward (Ruggie 1982; Stiglitz 2002; see also Stråth and Culpepper, in this volume). In the 'embedded liberalism' period, the global regime afforded governments of developed nations considerable policy autonomy which made possible the successful pursuit of 'full employment' as a policy goal and allowed the full flowering of social welfare spending (Esping-Andersen 1990; Hicks 1999). While poorer nations had considerably less scope to protect their populations from the ups and downs of the business cycle, there was still tolerance for a range of government initiatives to foster economic development.

However, all of this changed dramatically in the period of reascendant market liberalism after 1983 (Blyth 2002; Scharpf 1991). The pressures of the global regime placed increasingly restrictive limits on policy autonomy for both developed and developing nations. Governments no longer had the option to pursue 'full employment'; they were forced to tolerate unemployment in order to avoid inflation, government budget deficits, and speculative assaults on their currencies. The upward trend in welfare provision came to an end and even the most generous welfare states were forced to place limits on future spending increases. Most developing and transitional nations were pressured to abandon a range of active government development policies and to pursue instead privatisation, deregulation, and limits on government spending (Friedman 1999; Kay 2003; Stiglitz 2002).

However, in analysing the sea change between these two periods, it is easy to overdraw the contrast. While governmental policy autonomy declined considerably, it hardly disappeared (Mosley 2003). As in Polanyi's description of the workings of the 19th century Gold Standard, people and governments still found numerous 'under the radar' methods to provide protection against the tides of global market forces. For example, while the ideological claim in the 1980s and 1990s was that international trade had come to be organised on 'free market' principles, the departures from those principles were widespread. Developed nations continued to use agricultural support policies to limit access to their domestic markets. Europeans found numerous formal and informal means to limit the flow of cheap Chinese industrial exports. Most importantly, the most powerful corporations in the developed nations continued to rely on a variety of governmental supports – from direct lobbying to export credits to 'intellectual property' protection – to increase their export success in foreign markets.

FICTITIOUS COMMODITIES AND THE CO-ORDINATION PROBLEM

The great strength of Polanyi's analysis is that he demonstrates concretely why markets cannot be self-regulating and why they must be socially, politically, and ideationally embedded. He does this through his distinction between fictitious commodities and true commodities – those things that are produced for sale on a market. Polanyi argues that human labour power, land, and the supply of money must be understood as fictitious commodities because they were not produced to be sold. However, the theory of a self-regulating market system requires that society pretends that these fictitious commodities will behave like other commodities where the price mechanism produces a rapid balancing of supply and demand. When the price of a true commodity rises, producers have a strong incentive to increase the supply and consumers have good reason to shift to other products, and the reverse happens when prices fall. However, with fictitious commodities, supply side adjustments are likely to be very limited, so the speed with which supply and demand are balanced is greatly diminished. To make matters worse, disequilibrium between supply and demand for these particular economic inputs create acute difficulties for the functioning of economy and society.

In the case of labour, insufficient demand produces unemployment and a potential threat to social order when the unemployed have no other way to feed their families. Insufficient supply of labour also can be disruptive because it increases the relative bargaining power of employees who might well want to challenge the existing distributional rules. With land, the key problems are boom and bust in land markets, environmental degradation, and whether farming will remain viable as compared to other types of land use. In the case of money, a sustained shortfall in the money supply tends to be deflationary while too rapid an expansion tends to produce inflation.

Polanyi uses the fictitious commodity concept to identify three key co-ordination problems that cannot be solved by markets operating on their own. Every market society has to develop some set of institutional arrangements to manage these fictitious commodities. Labour unions, unemployment insurance and other welfare policies, education and training programmes, policies to encourage or discourage immigration and emigration, and in some places, centralised systems of wage bargaining have been part of the standard repertoire for co-ordinating supply and demand in the labour market. In the case of land, co-ordination involves zoning laws, environmental regulations, and a broad set of policies designed to protect agricultural producers from both market and weather related contingencies. In the case of money, the key co-ordinating role is played by central banks and regulatory agencies that oversee financial institutions.

Polanyi's framework can be expanded by adding two additional co-ordination problems that require institutional solutions. The first of these is yet another fictitious commodity – knowledge – a category that includes both the systematic research produced by scientists and scholars as well as the more concrete results of 'learning by doing' within organisations (Jessop 2001). There are some forms of knowledge, such as self-help books, that are produced just to be sold on the market, but this purely commodity knowledge represents only a small proportion of all knowledge production. There are two reasons for this. First, most scholars and scientists would starve if they were completely reliant on selling their ideas in the marketplace. Hence, they sell their labour power like other workers and are offered specific incentives to increase their production of knowledge. Secondly, the knowledge that firms need to solve production problems is often too specific to purchase on the market. Whether we are talking about research scientists in corporate laboratories or skilled workers and management consultants trying to improve the production process, knowledge production is a by-product of their efforts to solve specific problems in bringing products to market. Sometimes this by-product is then sold on the market, but it is a stretch to say that it was produced for that purpose.

However, if knowledge is mostly a fictitious commodity, this means that market societies must solve the co-ordination problems involved in producing a reliable flow of new types of knowledge. However, if market exchange is a highly imperfect mechanism for expanding the supply of knowledge, so, also, is hierarchy. Knowledge production and evaluation is inherently a social process that depends on co-operation and reciprocity. Moreover, subordinates are unlikely to transmit valuable knowledge upwards simply because that is what their bureaucratic superiors expect. Hence, solving this co-ordination problem depends on creating institutional environments that facilitate co-operation among peers, encourage communication across organisations, and provide employees with a combination of pecuniary and non-pecuniary incentives for developing and sharing knowledge. For this reason, all contemporary market societies increasingly rely on non-market institutions such as universities, scientific and professional communities as well as less hierarchical forms of work organisation that provide special incentives to knowledge workers.

The fifth co-ordination problem cannot properly be termed a fictitious commodity because it is not something that is ultimately sold on the market. However, market competition itself is similar to the fictitious commodities in that it is a key economic input that cannot be produced by the market alone. Effective market competition requires both multiple buyers and sellers and limits on the ability of market participants to shift costs on to others. However, since these conditions are continually being undermined by two separate and interrelated mechanisms, the maintenance of market competition represents an enormous co-ordination problem for all market societies. The first mechanism is the threat that some competitors will be too successful and will eliminate all – or almost all – of their rivals. This is the problem that antitrust legislation is intended to solve and which some societies have handled by legitimating cartel arrangements that reduce the intensity of interfirm competition (Fligstein 1990). The second is that the pressure of competition encourages firms to find ways to make money by imposing costs on others. This production of externalities or 'public bads' includes mistreatment of employees, cheating customers and investors, marketing unsafe products and degrading the environment. When unconstrained, this cost-shifting can destroy the health of the labour force, wreck the environment, and even undermine the viability of industries. The financial sector, for example, is continually at risk of meltdowns resulting from the temptation to prioritise profits over prudence.

These two mechanisms can produce 'negative market cascades' – processes through which market competition creates a dynamic that is increasingly costly to society. In the United States in the last decade of the 19th century, collusion among a handful of railroad barons made it possible to extract enormous rents from both farmers and industrialists who had no other way to ship their products to market (Dobbin 1994). More recently, the obesity epidemic in the United States appears to represent an instance in which fierce competition among fast food restaurants and other food retailers led to a massive shift in consumer preferences towards nutritionally dangerous eating patterns. Estimates of the public health costs of this increase in obesity are staggering (Nestle 2002).

Prevention of these negative market cascades poses additional co-ordination issues. Institutional solutions include government regulatory and legal initiatives, the strengthening of a variety of groups in civil society that are able to exert countervailing pressures, and the embedding of belief systems that emphasise the dangers of unrestrained competition. In fact, virtually all market societies rely on communities of professionals in civil society who are supposed to be insulated from pecuniary pressures to help avert these cascades. Medical personnel and public health workers are supposed to detect new market-driven threats to the population's health. Similarly, accountants and journalists are a first line of defence to detect corporate managers who are 'cooking the books' to cheat investors.

THE VARIETIES OF CAPITALISM AND THE OBSTACLES TO CONVERGENCE

The argument is that each market society must develop a complex system of institutions to solve the co-ordination problems posed by the fictitious commodities and the need to sustain market competition. This institutional complexity makes it unlikely that market societies would converge towards one institutional form. In fact, many of the scholars who have developed the 'varieties of capitalism' perspective (Crouch and Streeck 1997; Hall and Soskice 2001; Hollingsworth and Boyer 1997) have been explicit in drawing on Polanyi for inspiration in developing their ideas. However, there are two distinct ways in which Polanyi's analyses diverge from views that are widely held among contemporary analysts of capitalist variation.

First, the influential analysis developed by Hall and Soskice (2001) draws a contrast between Liberal Market Economies (LMEs) and Co-ordinated Market Economies (CMEs) by starting at the level of the business firm. They argue that firms face five basic co-ordination problems – industrial relations, vocational training and education, corporate governance, interfirm relations and relations with their own employees. In constructing their ideal types, they argue that in LMEs, firms characteristically handle these problems through hierarchy and competitive market relations, while in CMEs firms are much more likely to use non-market arrangements to solve these co-ordination problems. This argument is an effort to synthesise earlier work that has highlighted the contrasts between the Anglo-American model and European varieties of capitalism in the organisation of corporate finance, labour relations, and social welfare.

However, there are several significant difficulties with this formulation. It ignores the more macro-economic forms of co-ordination that occur across all varieties of capitalism, particularly the management of the fictitious commodities of labour and money. Moreover, it also ignores the substantial role that governments play in structuring particular industries. In both LMEs and CMEs, the government is integrally involved in regulating and shaping such industries as telecommunications, finance, transportation, energy, arms production, health care and housing, which cumulatively represent a substantial share of GDP.

The Soskice-Hall framework exaggerates the degree to which LMEs rely on market co-ordination. If one thinks of firms in the United States, for example, there are abundant examples of their dependence on non-market institutions and relationships that are neither arms' length contracting nor simple hierarchy. In the computer and biotechnology industries, there are networks of extremely complicated collaborations with university-based scientists that have fuelled the innovation process. Moreover, the critical role of venture capitalists in nurturing start-up firms is also something that cannot be understood in terms of impersonal market transactions. In addition, while there are important differences between stock market-centred and bank-centred systems of finance, the former still depend on very particular types of institutions such as the investment banking houses that oversee new issues of stocks and bonds and the specialist firms who maintain markets. In short, LMEs are also heavily dependent on complicated interfirm relations to solve a whole series of co-ordination problems, especially those that involve the fictitious commodity of knowledge.

Most importantly, the Hall-Soskice formulation fails to challenge the claim of market liberals that LMEs are closer to the ideal of a fully self-regulating market economy and hence are likely to be both more efficient and better able to preserve the liberty of their citizens. In contrast, the concept of the always and everywhere embedded market economy directly attacks the core postulates of market liberalism. It insists that there is no natural state in which individuals freely contract, but that the emergence and spread of market institutions depends critically on the continuous exercise of governmental power. Moreover, it insists that since four of the key inputs needed by market societies are fictitious commodities, the idea of extracting the state from the economy is inherently ludicrous.

A second and separate issue in the 'varieties of capitalism' literature has been a tendency by some analysts to anticipate that market societies would converge towards the Anglo-American variety. This argument was developed most systematically by John Gray whose 1998 book, *False Dawn*, was a powerful polemic against market liberalism. Gray, a former Thatcherite, drew heavily on the arguments of Karl Polanyi to point to the enormous dangers involved in the United States' effort to reorganise the global economy on a free market basis. One important piece of Gray's argument was his discovery of a new Gresham's Law in which 'bad capitalism tends to drive out good'. He argued explicitly that the advancing integration of global markets sponsored by the United States would undermine the varieties of capitalism that had flourished in Europe and Asia, leading to a global convergence around the highly problematic US variety of capitalism. Gray was hardly alone in making this argument; many of us worried that social scientists had discovered the 'varieties of capitalism' just in time to display relics of the non-liberal varieties in museums devoted to lost forms of social organisation.

Gray's argument was, of course, a mirror image of the arguments of market liberals who have long predicted that Europeans would be forced to abandon their expensive and wasteful welfare states in favour of the US model. However, after more than 20 years of aggressive pursuit by the United States of the global, free market vision, there is considerable evidence that convergence has not occurred. The most recent studies that we have – such as Huber and Stephens (2001) based on data through 1997 – find little change from the distinct patterns of welfare spending that were first identified by Esping-Andersen (see also Swank 2002; Wilensky 2002). Data from the Luxembourg Income Study show that the gap between the United States and both Social Democratic and Christian Democratic welfare states remains large when poverty is measured as a percentage of the population falling below 50% of median income. Moreover, Yamamura and Streeck (2003) have recently compiled a powerful set of papers arguing that the Japanese and German varieties of capitalism are not converging on the liberal model.

It is, of course, still possible that convergence will occur over the next several decades. However, the fact that it did not happen during a period when the ideology of market liberalism appeared to be globally hegemonic suggests that the obstacles to convergence will be even greater now that market liberalism seems to have lost much of its lustre beyond the borders of the United States. However, a deeper understanding of Polanyi's perspective leads to significant scepticism about the prospects for convergence.

The central problem is the issue of 'convergence to what?'. Both the US and the UK economies are far from being close to some pure model of market liberalism; they are instead complex amalgams of market and non-market elements. Moreover, the claims of political leaders notwithstanding, the role of some non-market elements has been expanding in recent years. One of the economy's key sectors – the computer industry – for example, has come to rely increasingly on a form of non-market co-ordination, such as open source software to overcome problems created by proprietary software. Moreover, in a number of key manufacturing industries, firms have shifted from arms' length contracts with suppliers to more Japanese-like long-term relationships. In short, if there is convergence across economies, it is not to any simple model, but towards complex combinations of market and non-market institutions.

The arguments about convergence also rely for their persuasiveness on a misleading conception of the world market as a rigorous Darwinian selection mechanism that forces societies to weed out less efficient enterprises and less efficient practices. However, just as Polanyi leads us to rethink our assumptions about national economies, he also suggests that we see the global economy as a more complex and politically-structured entity. For example, the weight of undifferentiated commodities, such as corn or widgets or crude oil, in international trade has been declining for years. Nowadays, most international trade revolves around highly differentiated products such as machine tools, pharmaceuticals, apparel, automobiles, aeroplanes, and entertainment products. Since being the lowest cost producer is only one of a number of distinct strategies for gaining advantage in this type of global marketplace, there is actually less pressure on nations to converge towards one way of doing things. For example, Nokia's success in global markets provides a powerful vindication for Finland's relatively generous system of welfare provision, while a number of US industries depend heavily on the political and military clout of the US Government to preserve their strong position in the global economy.

The point, in sum, is that there has been and there is likely to continue to be great variety in the institutional structures of market societies because their economies have never conformed to the abstract models of economic theory. Managing the fictitious commodities requires both an ongoing and active involvement of the state and complex combinations of market and non-market elements. This insight suggests that much of our historical understanding of economic modernity is inadequate and misleading.

THE HIDDEN HISTORY OF MODERNITY

The major theories of modernity – including market liberalism and Marxism – have agreed that there is a deep conflict between economic modernity and political modernity. Market liberals have always feared that democratic self-government would interfere with the necessary autonomy required for market economies to function. This was the key to their advocacy of *laissez-faire* and for a strict institutional separation between the sphere of politics and the sphere of the market. Contemporary thinkers in this tradition continue to search for institutional mechanisms such as independent central banks and budgetary pacts that put a wall between the market economy and democratic politics. Public choice theorists have elaborated a rich critique of how democratically elected politicians compete to extract rents from productive activities that are then used to finance redistributive measures intended to solidify electoral support from the beneficiaries.

Parallel arguments have been developed by Marxists and other critics of capitalism. 'Bourgeois democracy' has been seen as unable to achieve the Enlightenment ideal of self-government precisely because of the institutional separation between politics and markets. In a 20th century version of this argument, capitalist states are constantly caught in the conflict between democratic legitimation and the logic of accumulation. Whenever the conflict is intense, it is the imperatives of accumulation that will prevail.

While Polanyi's analysis of the stalemate of the 1920s anticipated this latter formulation, his work also suggests an alternative and hidden history of modernity. In this argument, the advance of political modernity has actually sustained and supported economic modernity. The achievements of the protective counter-movement, usually facilitated by democratic or proto-democratic institutions, have actually created the conditions for further advances in society's productive capacities (Block and Evans 2005). Ironically, it is Karl Marx who provides us with the paradigmatic example of this usually hidden relationship. He shows that when the Factory Acts placed limits on the length of the working day in the 1840s, it forced employers to use technological means to increase the extraction of surplus value. Hence, the key measure that unlocked industrial capitalism's technological dynamism was imposed on industrialists by their political opponents.

Much of this hidden history remains to be written, but we know some of the critical highlights. The story begins with EP Thompson's (1975) argument that the 'rule of law' – so indispensable to market capitalism – did not spring full blown from an emergent *bourgeoisie*. On the contrary, its development depended on the victories of popular movements from below that were determined to participate in democratic self-government and use the law to restrain the power of elites. (See also Somers 1993.)

In the history of the United States, it is impossible to exaggerate the importance of popular democratic struggles in creating the conditions for a dynamic market economy. This history starts with the great popular movements to end the Atlantic slave trade, to abolish chattel slavery, and to extend full citizenship rights to both former slaves and women (Foner 1998). These struggles for the universalisation of citizen rights, while often opposed by economic elites, produced an ideal environment for market expansion. Similarly, movements for market protections by farmers and workers created a regulatory framework that has repeatedly saved capitalists from themselves.

The crowning moment of this alternative history occurred after the publication of *The Great Transformation*. The unprecedented global economic expansion between 1945 and 1973 testifies to the ability of market societies to combine economic dynamism with expanding social rights and protections for the citizenry. There can be little doubt that the compromises of 'embedded liberalism' contributed enormously to dynamic economic growth. To be sure, when the post-Second World War boom came to an end, resurgent market liberals insisted that these nearly 30 years of unprecedented growth were just an aberration. They argued that the success of the Keynesian welfare state could never be replicated and only a return to the ideal of limited government could recapture the forward march of economic modernity. However, the arguments and evidence amassed in support of this historical interpretation are, in fact, very thin and the uneven economic record of the last 20 years of ascendant market liberalism only reinforces the link between expanded democracy and economic growth (Howell 2002; Wilensky 2002; Huber and Stephens 2001).

Most importantly, this alternative narrative of modernity can be the foundation for new projects of social protection designed to deepen democracy and promote sustainable forms of economic development. The main obstacle to advancing such projects has not been the 'objective' logic of accumulation but rather a colossal failure of imagination. It is an urgent priority to foster a rebirth of social imagination that envisions new forms of political and economic co-ordination that would operate at different spatial levels (see the Chapters of Kandil, Joerges and Everson, and Stråth in this volume). Imagination, by itself, will not be sufficient to overcome the entrenched resistance of those committed to the global status quo. However, as at earlier moments in the trajectory of modernity, the exercise of imagination is the indispensable first step in the process of political transformation (Berman 1998).

References

Berman, S (1998) *The Social Democratic Moment: Ideas and Politics in the Making of Interwar Europe*, Cambridge, MA: Harvard University Press

Block, F (2001) 'Introduction', in Polanyi, K [1944] *The Great Transformation*, Boston, MA: Beacon Press

Block, F (2003) 'Karl Polanyi and the writing of *The Great Transformation*' 32 Theory and Society 275–306

Block, F and Evans, P (2005) 'The state and the economy', in Smelser, N and Swedberg, R (eds), *Handbook of Economic Sociology*, 2nd edn, Princeton, NJ: Russell Sage

Block, F and Somers, M (2003) 'In the shadow of Speenhamland: social policy and the old poor law' 31(2) Politics & Society 283–323

Blyth, M (2002) *Great Transformations: Economic Ideas and Institutional Change in the Twentieth Century*, Cambridge: Cambridge University Press

Burawoy, M (2003) 'For a sociological Marxism: the complementary convergence of Antonio Gransci and Karl Polanyi' 31 Politics & Society 193–261

Crouch, C and Streeck, W (eds), (1997) *Political Economy of Modern Capitalism: Mapping Convergence and Diversity*, Thousand Oaks, CA: Sage

Dobbin, F (1994) *Forging Industrial Policy: The US, Britain and France in the Railway Age*, New York: Cambridge University Press

Esping-Andersen, G (1990) *Three Worlds of Welfare Capitalism*, Princeton, NJ: Princeton University Press

Fligstein, N (1990) *The Transformation of Corporate Control*, Cambridge, MA: Harvard University Press

Foner, E (1998) *The Story of American Freedom*, New York: Norton

Friedman, T (1999) *The Lexus and the Olive Tree*, New York: Farrar, Straus and Giroux

Gray, J (1998) *False Dawn: The Delusions of Global Capitalism*, London: Granta

Hall, P and Soskice, D (eds) (2001) *Varieties of Capitalism: The Institutional Foundations of Comparative Advantage*, Oxford: Oxford University Press

Hicks, A (1999) *Social Democracy and Welfare Capitalism*, Ithaca, NY: Cornell University Press

Hollingsworth, R and Boyer, R (eds) (1997) *Contemporary Capitalism: The Embeddedness of Institutions*, Cambridge: Cambridge University Press

Howell, DR (2002) 'Increasing earnings inequality and unemployment in developed countries: markets, institutions, and the "Unified Theory"' 30(2) (June) Politics & Society 193–243

Huber, E and Stephens, JD (2001) *Development and Crisis of the Welfare State: Parties and Policies in Global Markets*, Chicago, IL: University of Chicago Press

Jessop, B (2001) 'The state and the contradictions of the knowledge-driven
    economy', in Bryson, JR *et al* (eds), *Knowledge, Space, Economy*, London:
    Brunner-Routledge
Kay, J (2003) *The Truth About Markets: Their Genius, Their Limits, Their Follies*,
    London: Penguin
Mosley, L (2003) *Global Capital and National Governments*, Cambridge: Cambridge
    University Press
Nestle, M (2002) *Food Politics*, Berkeley, CA: University of California Press
Polanyi, K (2001) [1944] *The Great Transformation*, Boston, MA: Beacon Press
Ruggie, J (1982) 'International regimes, transactions and change: embedded
    liberalism in the postwar economic order' 36(2) International Organization
    379–415
Scharpf, F (1991) [1987] *Crisis and Choice in European Social Democracy*, Crowley, R
    and Thompson, F (trans), Ithaca, NY: Cornell University Press
Somers, M (1993) 'Citizenship and the place of the public sphere: law, community,
    and political culture in the transition to democracy' 58(5) American
    Sociological Review 587–620
Stiglitz, J (2002) *Globalisation and Its Discontents*, New York: Norton
Streeck, W (1992) 'Productive constraints: on the institutional conditions of
    diversified quality production', in Streeck, W (ed), *Social Institutions and
    Economic Performance: Studies of Industrial Relations in Advanced Capitalist
    Economies*, London: Sage
Swank, D (2002) *Global Capital, Political Institutions, and Policy Change in Developed
    Welfare States*, Cambridge: Cambridge University Press
Swenson, P (2002) *Capitalist Against Markets: The Making of Labor Markets and
    Welfare States in the United States and Sweden*, Oxford: Oxford University Press
Thompson, EP (1975) *Whigs and Hunters*, New York: Pantheon
Vogel, SK (1996) *Freer Markets, More Rules: Regulatory Reforms in Advanced
    Industrial Countries*, Ithaca, NY: Cornell University Press
Wilensky, H (2002) *Rich Democracies: Political Economy, Public Policy, and
    Performance*, Berkeley, CA: University of California Press
Yamamura, K and Streeck, W (eds) (2003) *The End of Diversity?: Prospects for
    German and Japanese Capitalism*, Ithaca, NY: Cornell University Press

CHAPTER 2

THE VARIETIES OF ACCUMULATION: CIVILISATIONAL PERSPECTIVES ON CAPITALISM

Johann P Arnason

The following discussion will mostly be of the meta-theoretical kind: a reflection on ways of thinking about capitalism, and more specifically on ways of theorising capitalism as a civilisational phenomenon.[1] It may disappoint those who favour substantive analysis and expect a more adequate theory, cleansed of apriorism and ideological projections, to grow out of empirical studies. However, empirical inquiry is never separable from interpretive frameworks, and the present historical conjuncture must be seen as a compelling reason to reconsider the interpretive premises of established views, including the traditions of critical theory as well as the internal rationalisations of the capitalist order. A whole series of recent changes are unmistakably indicative of a new twist to capitalist development and – by the same token – of an urgent need for new analytical approaches. The trends in question can easily be read as signs of inventive and adaptive capacities, unrecognised by earlier observers; on closer examination, however, their implications seem ambiguous enough to raise basic questions about ways of defining and understanding capitalism as a social-historical phenomenon.

It is a commonplace that the capitalist form of economic life now faces no visible challenge from any alternative projects. The collapse of the only serious rival with global ambitions is an accomplished fact (notwithstanding the open questions about results and ramifications of the multiple exits from Communism); it may, however, be less obvious whether this victory justifies the triumphalist narratives that took off after 1990. If the Cold War was essentially a contest between two economic systems, one of which was found wanting after early or apparent successes, capitalism can claim to have passed a decisive test and to embody economic modernity, even though the fundamentalist vision of an 'end of history' may have to be abandoned. However, if the failed model was no more than a deviant and dependent alternative within the historical horizon of capitalism, centred on the ambitious but ultimately incoherent project of a politicised and mobilised economy, the lessons to be drawn are less straightforward. The Communist experience might be seen as a reminder of the broader historical contexts in which capitalist development unfolds and as an extreme example of the ideological and political factors (in this case fused in a

---

1   This essay was written during my term as a research fellow at the School of Languages, Cultures and Linguistics, Monash University. I am grateful for the support and hospitality of the School. I also wish to thank the participants in the Firenze seminar for helpful comments in earlier discussions.

combination of imperial and revolutionary traditions) that diversify its paths and give rise to more or less radical counter-projects. There is no easy way to settle this debate; for present purposes it is enough to note that it exists, and that the issue affects the very idea of an historical sociology of capitalism.

The *fin-de-siècle* transformations of capitalism pose problems which go far beyond short-term perspectives and link up with the most basic points at issue in debates on modernity. Theoretical responses have so far been less than adequate. It is widely agreed that the critique of capitalism has been disarmed and disoriented by developments during the last quarter of a century. Ambitious attempts to reformulate a critical frame of reference are in progress, but it would be premature to speak of a new paradigm. As for the affirmative approaches that might seem to have done better, there is no doubt that the claim to embody the logic of a triumphant system has strengthened the interdisciplinary appeal of economic models; however, when it comes to explaining the concrete workings of economic structures and processes, defenders of capitalism will often admit to insufficient knowledge.

A brief glance at more specific alternatives will highlight the shortcomings of both sides. World system theory, represented by the work of Immanuel Wallerstein and his associates (including some markedly heterodox variants), has been the most influential late 20th century version of the critical approach. There is no denying that it made some significant moves beyond the classical Marxist framework. The very idea of a capitalist world system, operating as such from the 16th century onwards, went much further than Marxian intimations of globality and pre-empted a challenge from the non-Marxist theories of globalisation. The classical Marxist vision of a revolutionary alternative, growing out of the internal dynamic of capitalism, was abandoned; on this level, world system theory brought contingency back in and rejected the belief in guaranteed progress. Last but not least (and with particular reference to the present theme), its effort to grasp capitalism as a total social-historical phenomenon led to interesting but in the end inconclusive reflections from a civilisational angle. The capitalist world system appeared as a specific civilisational formation, striving to impose its distinctive patterns and transfigure them into universal principles of civilisation as such. The civilising influence of capital, conditionally accepted by Marx, was thus subjected to a more critical scrutiny. However, these theoretical innovations did not add up to a sustainable paradigm. The model of an early modern world system has not withstood historical criticism: it turned out to be a vastly oversimplified picture of the complex interaction between European expansion and developments in other parts of the world. The idea of capitalism as a global system proved no less conducive to functionalist short-circuit explanations than the less explicitly transnational model had been. An unvarying emphasis on the primacy of economic factors (even if world system theory took their political expressions and intermediaries more seriously than classical Marxism had done), in line with the reductionistic basis-superstructure model, undermined the civilisational approach.

On the other side, the most significant intellectual manifestation of the new pro-capitalist *Zeitgeist* is a full and unreserved integration of *capitalist economic* institutions into the authoritative models of liberal order. Before the turn of the 1980s, theorists of political liberalism often tried to avoid unconditional alignment of that kind and insist on compatibility with a variety of economic regimes. It would be an overstatement to say that this position is no longer represented in theoretical debates, but the shift is massive and unmistakable. The enhanced self-legitimising capacity of capitalism, mentioned above, has thus been registered at the level of political philosophy. In this context, the decisive role of Hayek's work is well known. It is much less obvious that his ideas have had any major impact on the comparative study of capitalism as a social-historical phenomenon. The new fusion of political and economic liberalism has not found much of an echo in historical sociology. To the best of my knowledge, the only major exception is Jean Baechler's ambitious but idiosyncratic treatise on capitalism (Baechler 1995). For Baechler, capitalism is the economy of democracy and – as such – a defining feature of modernity. However, so far, his work has not attracted a large following.

To conclude this preliminary survey, let us note a last twist to the changing fortunes of pro- and anti-capitalist ideas. The apparent zero-sum game between them – the manifest decline of the latter and the somewhat insubstantial triumph of the former – should not obscure latent affinities. It has often been observed that latter-day defenders of capitalism are as committed to economic determinism as the Marxist critics were, but put it to very different ideological uses. The point can perhaps be made in more specific terms. Classical Marxism expected the systemic logic of capitalism to take a self-destructive turn and culminate in anti-capitalist revolution; this scenario has lost all credibility, but a similarly self-contained systemic logic – manifested in adaptive innovation and creative destruction – can be invoked to explain the survival and triumph of the capitalist economy. With appropriate modifications, classical Marxism can even be fitted into a genealogy leading to better understanding and unreserved acceptance of the capitalist order. If the tenuously grounded predictions of social polarisation and revolutionary mobilisation are subtracted from the *Communist Manifesto*, the remainder can easily be read as an early prophecy of global capitalism. Such exercises may be more effective on the level of popular imagery than in scholarly work. However, the affinity mentioned above is strong enough to suggest that a widespread and *prima facie* plausible way of thinking about capitalism – as an economic system with clear-cut defining features, intrinsic laws and inbuilt long-term trends – has been a common ground of advocates and critics. In view of the most recent ideological turn, it might be more apposite to speak of a slippery slope from critique to conformism.

It seems to be precisely this common ground that Fernand Braudel has in mind when he writes:

> The worst mistake is to assume that capitalism is an 'economic system', and nothing more; in fact, it depends on the social order, and exists from the outset on equal footing, adversarial or complicit, with the state – a particularly weighty player; it also benefits from the whole contribution of culture to the social edifice. For even if culture is unequally distributed and split between contrary currents, its main role is – in the last instance – to support the existing order. It is also inseparable from ruling classes that defend themselves by defending it. (Braudel 1977, 3: 540)

If we take the civilisational approach to begin with the rejection of the economistic illusion denounced by Braudel, it is critical in the elementary sense that it contests a distorted self-image which is rooted in the real history of capitalism but is not an adequate reflection of it. The positive side of the critique is, to put it briefly and broadly, a reconstruction of the cultural and political frameworks of capitalist development. There is no good reason to equate this civilisational perspective with critique in any more specific sense. It is compatible with widely divergent views on the capitalist economy, its impact on social life, and its implications for the human condition. Capitalism may be seen as an integral part of a more comprehensive civilising process, with no rationale for any critique going beyond the ongoing problems of adjustment within that framework. However, from a more critical point of view, the tensions and imbalances inherent in capitalist development represent a challenge to social order, and the response should be a long-term effort to civilise capitalism (this formulation has been used by advocates and historians of social democratic reformism). Finally, the most uncompromising kind of critique, that is, the search for a non-capitalist alternative, can take a direction which redefines the goal as an alternative civilisation. These positions – and other existing or conceivable ones – would have to confront each other within the civilisational frame of reference. The present paper will not go beyond prolegomena to that debate.

CLASSICAL LANDMARKS

Karl Marx

Having drawn on Braudel's work for a provisional outline of the civilisational approach, it seems appropriate to add some comments on older classics, and thus to align the present agenda of civilisational analysis with a longer intellectual history. As is well known, capitalism – perceived as a revolutionary force of the first order – was a key theme of classical sociology, whereas the idea of civilisation – inherited from the 18th century – remained under-theorised, and sustained interest in the problematic of civilisations in the plural was the exception rather than the rule. We may nevertheless note some significant points of contact between these two unequally developed fields of inquiry. Karl Marx, the most ambitious theorist and most influential critic of capitalism, had no doubt about its civilisational credentials. In the *Grundrisse*, concluding one of his most emphatic statements about the capitalist mode of production as an engine of progress, he refers to what he calls 'the great civilising influence of capital' (Marx 1973: 409). This is not simply a sign of general affinity with 19th century ideologies of industrialism. Marx's understanding of the main trends of his times was grounded in a specific vision of history and civilisation; its essentials were spelt out in earlier writings, perhaps – with regard to the points at issue here – most clearly in the *German Ideology*, where the distinction between 'civilised' and 'quasi-natural' (*naturwüchsig*) modes of production is more or less equated with the historical divide between capitalist and pre-capitalist forms (Marx and Engels 1976). For Marx, the unfolding and cultivation of human *abilities is the driving* force and defining *telos* of the civilising process; capitalist development takes this dynamic to a higher level and can therefore be seen as a civilising breakthrough. A strongly value-laden conception of civilisation in the singular is thus directly linked to anthropological assumptions and ideals in a way that leaves no space for significant variation between civilisations in the plural. As Marx's *obiter dicta* on the 'Asiatic mode of production' show, he could only interpret major civilisational divergences in terms of stagnation on one side and progress on the other. The slightly more differentiated treatment of pre-capitalist forms in his later writings did not break with the basic presupposition of unilinear progress.

This approach has far-reaching consequences for Marx's theory of capitalism. The dialectic of productive work and creative self-realisation is central to the civilising mainstream of history: it opens up the utopian perspective of a complete transformation of work into free activity, but it also reproduces – in changing forms – the tension between the two poles. Marx always envisaged a future enlargement of the realm of freedom, but the radical utopia outlined in the *Grundrisse* gave way to more moderate expectations in the last phase of his work. His analysis of capitalism was, however, consistently based on the idea that this form of social and economic life enhances both sides of the dialectic. Capitalist development increases and highlights the liberating potential of the productive forces, while at the same time imposing new constraints and reductive mechanisms in addition to those inherent in the basic structures of production. In the most elaborate version of Marx's model, the labour theory of value serves to clarify the latter aspect. The value-form of wealth, developed to the highest degree in the capitalist mode of production, is interpreted as an embodiment of labour, in its capacity as the most elementary and universally necessary social resource. The 'law of value' is thus ultimately rooted in the anthropological imperative of organised labour. This line of argument, with its strong emphasis on anthropological infrastructures, marginalises the question of institutional frameworks, beginning with those of monetary wealth. By the same token, the focus on elementary and universal patterns of meaning, inherent in the human condition (and never fully thematised as such), obscures the whole question of more specific cultural orientations as constitutive elements of capitalism.

Max Weber

Despite Marx's explicit concern with civilisational dimensions, his approach thus leads to a systematic minimisation and de-differentiation of the issues noted above as germane to a civilisational perspective. This shortcoming does not *ipso facto* devalue other aspects of his work: as we shall see, a more fully articulated civilisational frame of reference might allow us to reclaim some Marxian insights in a new context, and thus to strengthen the case for critical use of civilisational theory. However, a balanced assessment of Marx's strengths and weaknesses is impossible without reference to other classics, most obviously to Max Weber, and his more genuinely comparative historical sociology. Recent studies of Weber's work have gradually clarified his complex and evolving conception of capitalism; here I can only summarise the points most directly related to the present theme, beginning with the implications of a shift towards more emphatic and sustained use of the very term 'capitalism'. The affix 'ism' points to an orientation, and thus ultimately to a cultural meaning constitutive of the economic phenomena in question. In taking that aspect as a starting-point for further exploration, Weber followed Werner Sombart's lead (as for Marx, he is conventionally and – with the wisdom of hindsight – treated as an analyst of capitalism, but the fact that he was disinclined to use this word and preferred to speak of 'capital' in general and a 'capitalist mode of production' in particular is not insignificant). The effort to understand capitalism as a meaningful orientation of economic action led to a massive extension as well as an internal differentiation of the concept: Weber 'saw capitalism as being several thousand years old' and as having 'existed in several different forms' (Swedberg 1999: 9). It would not seem far-fetched to link the general defining feature of capitalism – the rational/methodical pursuit of monetary gain – to civilisation in the singular. Although Weber did not use the language of civilisational theory, his substantive work qualifies as the single most seminal contribution to civilisational analysis, and the problematic of rationalisation covers a large part of the ground that others have preferred to thematise in explicitly civilisational terms. If the basic concept of capitalism denotes a general trend towards the rationalisation of economic life (not the only trend of that kind), we can use it as a key to common directions or potentialities of civilising processes. 'Rational' modern capitalism, as Weber often described, then appears as a second-order rationalising shift; a pre-existing trend is intensified and systematised into a comprehensive form of economic life. From the civilisational point of view, the implications of this mutation are ambiguous. The radicalisation and universalisation of a much older trend suggests a triumph of civilisation in the singular (allowing for problematic aspects and paradoxical effects of this modern leap forward), whereas the specific logic of a distinctive pattern – modern capitalism as a 'historical individual' – lends support to the idea of a new and particular civilisation.

However, Weber's reflections on the different forms of capitalism do not begin with the basic distinction between traditional and modern types. The typological scheme outlined in *Economy and Society* distinguished six modes of capitalism, and four of them are presented as traditional types with a long history (Weber 1968: 63–221). For present purposes, and without going into details, they can be reduced to different relationships between the economic and political spheres. The forms of 'political capitalism' range from political foundations for regular economic monopolies to unconventional economic uses of political conjunctures; the traditional form of profit-making trade, listed as a separate mode, is in this context best understood as representing the highest level of autonomous economic action. The varying relationship to politics is reflected in different forms and degrees of economic rationality. As for the cultural component, it is – at the very least – present in and through the articulation of the nexus between economy and politics. For Weber, it is self-evident that cultural meaning enters into the making of institutional frameworks; if the comparison of macro-cultural units was – as he also saw it – essential to social-historical inquiry, it would have seemed appropriate to develop the typology of premodern capitalisms along such lines. Weber's studies of China and India went far enough to indicate the scope for comparative analysis of interconnections between the economic and political spheres (significant if one-sided pointers can also be found in the scattered comments on Islam), but they fall short of systematic approaches. The civilisational-analytical turn did not translate into corresponding perspectives on capitalism as a world-historical phenomenon.

When it comes to modern capitalism, Weber's most central topic, the problem can be posed in inverse terms: an overly self-contained and streamlined image of the new economic order (an ideal type that shades off into perceptions and prognoses of historical trends) blocks the road to better understanding of possible variations, notably those of a civilisational nature. Modern capitalism was, for Weber, a product of Western civilisation, and interpretations of his work have now convincingly refuted all attempts to condense a complex and unfinished genealogy into a single-factor explanation: a wide range of economic, political and cultural factors contributed – in different ways and at different moments – to the formation of an unprecedentedly rational and dynamic economic regime. The list includes religious transformations within Occidental Christendom as well as the tradition of political revolutions inaugurated by the Occidental city, but neither of these macro-historical currents can be singled out as an ultimate cause. On the other hand, the interaction of these multiple – and to a great extent extra-economic – factors culminates in an autonomous dynamic of the economic sphere. Weber's references to modern capitalism as a 'fateful force' and as a 'mechanical cosmos' leave no doubt about his views: in relation to other 'world orders', the economy had become a driving and dominant factor, and this amounted to an epoch-making transformation of the human condition. This did not mean an end to all dependence of economic institutions on cultural and political contexts. Weber's analysis of socio-cultural spheres and their changing interrelations (outlined most suggestively in his reflections on 'religious rejections of the world and their directions', Weber 1991: 323–59) is too unfinished for a clear picture to emerge. He obviously found it difficult to strike a balance between an empowered economy and an irreducibly multipolar image of society; his last writings show that both the genealogy of modern capitalism and the broader diagnosis of the modern condition were still open to further clarification and development. However, the points of contact with Marx's conception of capitalism should be noted. Weber's most emphatic definition of modern capitalism stresses the rational organisation of free labour, that is, the same core institution that had been central to Marx's analysis, albeit from a different angle. The rationality of capitalism also manifests itself in a permanent drive to expand and intensify human power over nature; in contrast to Marx, Weber seems to have been inclined to think that ultimate limits to this project might spell the end of capitalism. Finally, Weber's analysis of the economic order, seen as a distinctive socio-cultural sphere, implicitly posits the pursuit of general wealth – inconceivable without a thoroughgoing monetarisation of economic life – as an inbuilt goal.

Despite the open and inconclusive character of Weber's most advanced reflections on modernity, a more one-sided perspective prevails in the intercivilisational context. Modern capitalism appears as one of the most effectively universal inventions of the West, and obstacles to a comparable breakthrough loom large in the analyses of major non-Western civilisations. Varying ability to adopt Western-style capitalism as a ready-made model is noted in passing (the Japanese experience is singled out as a success story, and a more tentative case is made for a likely Chinese response), but no thought is given to the possibility of significant modifications to modern capitalist institutions in different civilisational settings. Reinvention at that level is clearly ruled out. Weber's idea of modern capitalism is too self-contained and monolithic to allow for a return to diversity; the well-established Western division between industrial and financial capital seems to be the only intra-modern distinction that he is willing to admit. He was, of course, well aware that really existing modern societies mixed modern forms of capitalism with enduring traditional ones, but this empirical fact did not cast any doubt on the ideal-typical construct of the modern element as such.

To sum up, Weber's work is doubly relevant to the present discussion: in virtue of its explicit programmatic orientation as well as the implicit perspectives which it failed to develop. More than any other sociological classic, Weber adumbrated the idea of multiple capitalisms, even if he found it easier to trace divergent patterns in past history than in the more decisive modern phase. He grasped the constitutive role of cultural and political factors in the formation of capitalist attitudes and institutions, but he also saw that cultural and political dynamics could – as in the course of long-term transformations within the Western civilisational complex – reinforce the economic factor. The Weberian version of the civilisational approach is, in other words, focused on the interrelations of cultural, political and economic spheres, and on historical variations to their relative weight. Weber's 'sociology of capitalisms' was thus inherently pluralistic, in the twofold sense that it assumed a plurality of mutually irreducible factors and mapped out a variety of capitalisms. But his comparative studies of civilisations, however innovative in other ways, did not make adequate use of this pluralistic potential.

Norbert Elias

Although Norbert Elias was much less interested in the problematic of capitalism than Marx and Weber had been, his magnum opus on the civilising process (Elias 1978–82) has some bearing on our questions. Elias's project was, among other things, an attempt to tackle Weber's unfinished agenda – or at least a part of it – in a more structured way. The civilisational frame of reference, with its strong emphasis on the multi-layered transformations of social power, was explicitly justified as an alternative to the more limited focus on rationalising processes. Here, the main points at issue concern the place and role of capitalist development in the civilising process. For Elias, this is a marginal theme and, to understand his views on it, we should first note a strong tendency to relativise modernist visions of European history. The idea of the 'long Middle Ages' – a period coming to an end around 1800 – underlines basic continuities of European history; Elias takes a further step and tries to show that core operative structures of social power took shape during the long medieval phase and continued to function in a fundamentally similar way – albeit in different forms on a different scale – under 'modern' conditions. This applies most obviously to interstate competition and its ramifications. However, the same can, *mutatis mutandis*, be said about forms of economic life: Elias stresses the long-term commercialising trend that accompanies other aspects of the civilising process and reinforces the all-round growth of interdependence. As he sees it, the multi-secular dynamic of a market economy, expanding at home and abroad, is more crucial to the overall European trajectory than any modern transformations. This economic component of the civilising process interacts with the political ones in multiple ways. The pacification of social life, due to the progress of state formation, is an essential precondition for commercial development; the growing fiscal demands of states and the growing wealth generated by monetarised economies led to closer contacts between the two spheres, but not along any uniform lines; at a more advanced stage, strategies of state intervention can have stimulating as well as adverse effects on economic life.

However, the most interesting aspect of Elias's argument goes beyond the analysis of complementarities within the civilising process. His account of power struggles and their unintended consequences relies on a generalised concept of accumulation, introduced in critical contrast to the view that limits the use of this term to capitalist economies or societies. For Elias, the transformative dynamics of social power can never be explained without reference to strategies, processes and structural logics of accumulation. The accumulation of power depends on the accumulation of specific resources; in the medieval European societies most extensively discussed in Elias's work, land was the resource *par excellence*, but ongoing civilising processes shifted the balance towards the accumulation of monetary wealth, which in the long run came to be perceived and pursued as the main aim.

To sum up, Elias introduces a generalised concept of accumulation, and allows for changing historical relationships between the dynamics of power and wealth. The implications of the conceptual shift will become clearer if we revisit the two classics mentioned above. For Marx, the revolutionary character of capitalism consists in two interrelated and self-perpetuating processes: the accumulation of abstract wealth and the permanent revolution of technological progress. By contrast, pre-capitalist modes of production are confined to a cycle of reproduction within limits set by a given pattern of needs, and therefore not open to a dynamic of accumulation. This strict dichotomy is, however, called into question by more nuanced reflections in other contexts. In his analysis of the labour process, Marx makes it clear that the capacity to produce a surplus, above and beyond the satisfaction of needs, is to be seen as a universal human ability; by implication, economies and societies could be distinguished on the basis of their ways to use and develop this potential. This would lead to a less simplistic typology than the distinction between capitalism and a whole quasi-natural pre-capitalist world. Comparative perspectives on specific ways of maximising and concentrating the surplus, with some allowance for cultural and political factors, could thus link up with undeveloped Marxian insights.

A broader concept of accumulation is explicitly used in Weber's introductory definition of modern capitalism. The drive to accumulate monetary wealth appears as an anthropological trait that can come to the fore in very different socio-cultural settings; capitalism begins when this 'primitive accumulation' (to use the term in a sense very different from the Marxian one) is subjected to rationalising discipline; and modern capitalism channels the rationalising trend into the organisation of production. However, this analysis of stages on the road to modern capitalism can also be read as an account of layers or components. The autonomy of the economic sphere in relation to other 'world orders' is, in the modern context, predicated on the generalised pursuit of wealth, which in turn presupposes the monetarisation of economic life. The dynamic of the economic order creates new openings for other kinds of capitalism, developing alongside the type which Weber saw as the most distinctively modern.

In recent and forthcoming writings on the 'rise of the West', seen from a revisionist perspective, Jack Goldstone questions the prevailing emphasis on accumulation as the motive force and formative principle of the modern economy. This view has, in his opinion, not only led to misunderstandings of the historical process that put the West ahead of the rest; it has also translated into misguided models of development and prescriptions for concrete developmental strategies. As he argues, the decisive Western achievement was the 'marriage of entrepreneurship and scientific engineering'; the result was an economy of permanent innovation. Neither the original breakthrough – the industrial revolution – nor the landmark innovations of later stages seem to have depended on significant prior accumulation of capital. This emphasis on innovation, in contrast to accumulation, raises questions that relate to our discussion of the classics. A key corrective is implicit in Goldstone's own analysis of the background to the industrial revolution. Drawing on the work of Joel Mokyr (2002), he stresses the crucial role of an 18th century 'industrial enlightenment'; this subculture, which brought together craftsmen and scientists, drew on early modern philosophical visions of knowledge as a guarantee of mastery over nature. The 'industrial enlightenment' gives a more concrete historical shape to the imaginary signification of rational mastery in infinite progress (Castoriadis). The accumulation of knowledge and – through knowledge – power over nature thus becomes an indispensable complement to the accumulation of wealth. This aspect of capitalist development was not unfamiliar to the classics; Marx's reference to the world becoming a 'system of general utility' sums up a widely shared understanding of changing relations between humanity and nature. Comparative perspectives may help to clarify the point at issue. Among premodern and non-Western economies, innovative capacities were clearly more pronounced in some cases than others, and the Chinese record is by common consent the most impressive. However, in the Chinese tradition, there was no parallel to the 'industrial enlightenment', no cultural reorientation towards the infinite expansion of rational mastery.

Fernand Braudel

To round off this part of the discussion, let us briefly return to Braudel's work. The above quotation from his concluding reflections on capitalism served to indicate the general direction of civilisational approaches to this field; a more detailed summary of his conceptual scheme will be useful when it comes to integrating ideas extracted from the classics with contemporary debates. He begins with a distinction between three levels of economic life. The most elementary one is the cycle of production, distribution and consumption; Braudel refers to it as 'material civilisation'. As the terminology indicates, we are dealing with basic components of civilisation in the singular, but there is also an opening to the plural: civilisations differ in regard to ecological contexts and the patterns of needs and activities that develop in response to environmental conditions. The second level is that of the economy in the more specific sense, that is, the networks of exchange. Here the pluralistic perspective becomes more important: although the market economy is part and parcel of the civilising process in the most general sense, its forms and levels of development vary greatly from one civilisation to another. Braudel never attempts a systematic study of such variations; he makes it clear that all aspects of civilisational patterns – from ecology to religion and from political power to kinship structures – affect the dynamics of markets. Finally, capitalism, as Braudel understands it, constitutes a third level which stands in a dependent as well as an antagonistic relationship to the second. Capitalism presupposes a market infrastructure, but it always entails efforts to break through or move beyond the routines and constraints of institutionalised exchange. It is, in other words, based on strategies of accumulation that easily shade into visions of windfall profits. In pre-industrial societies, long-distance trade is its privileged domain. Its breakthrough into the sphere of production marks the beginning of a great transformation which lies outside Braudel's field of inquiry (his work is explicitly focused on the period from the 15th to the 18th centuries).

Let us note two implications of Braudel's approach. First, capitalism is not a system, but an orientation of economic life and, as such, it is always linked to other orientations (those that prevail on the two other levels); its relative weight varies, but it never reaches the level of total takeover. Secondly, there is a threefold civilisational connection. The capitalist push beyond local or regional limits is inherent in the civilising process as such; although Braudel disagrees with Weber on many fundamental points, he seems to agree on the need for a genealogy that traces the metamorphoses of capitalism back to the beginnings of civilisation. On the other hand, a comparative analysis of capitalism must pay attention to different civilisational contexts; Braudel outlines a research programme that would deal with different configurations and destinies of capitalism within the major civilisational complexes. Finally, the crystallisation of cross-civilisational 'economic worlds' (this seems a better translation of 'économies-mondes' than 'world economies') is crucial to capitalist development, and no formation of that kind was more important than the one spearheaded (but not unilaterally dominated) by early European expansion.

The early modern economic world also exemplifies another important feature of capitalism. The international trading companies were state-protected monopolies; as such, they embody the convergent accumulation of wealth and power and, for Braudel, this is the rule rather than the exception. His emphasis on the early modern international trading companies might seem open to a standard objection from economic historians: they argue that the transfer of wealth through monopolistic trading practices was not of critical magnitude. However, this does not affect Braudel's main point: early modern capitalism evolved in a mutually reinforcing relationship to political (more particularly geopolitical) processes that for the first time created a global civilisational constellation and opened up possibilities for new economic developments, not least through the new division of labour established between Europe and the Americas.

CONTEMPORARY DEBATES

As will be seen from the above survey, the classics of historical sociology – whether they defined themselves as historians or sociologists – were keenly interested in capitalism as a civilisational phenomenon, and their insights as well as their unsolved problems and inconclusive explorations can still serve to guide further discussion. However, since the primary focus of this paper is not on the history of ideas, I will not pursue the question of unity, diversity and implicit convergence in that context; rather, the next task is to test the relevance of ideas drawn from classical sources to key themes of contemporary debates. The civilisational approach, as roughly defined by Braudel and reinforced through critical use of ideas inherited from the sociological tradition, will be confronted with issues that have more recently come to the fore. A successful combination of classical legacies on this level would be more convincing than purely analytical models of convergence (in the vein exemplified by Parsons's *Structure of Social Action*).

Three controversial themes – or sets of themes – are most pertinent to our purposes: the spirit of capitalism, the changing relationship between states and markets, and the varieties of capitalism. In all these cases, the cultural, social and political contexts of the capitalist order are brought into focus, but in divergent and contested ways. It remains to be seen whether civilisational perspectives can strengthen the separate strands of discussion further and bring them closer together. The following reflections on that question will centre on the basic concept of accumulation and its broader socio-cultural implications. This historical-sociological line of inquiry can also be seen as a step towards renewal of critical theory. It is now beyond dispute that an earlier version of critical theory based on internal contradictions or transformative dynamics attributed to capitalism – in other words: a self-destructive twist to its systemic logic – has been found wanting. The cunning of reason which it attempted to impose on capitalism seems to have been trumped by the cunning of capital. A less vulnerable alternative would have to begin with more sustained attention to the points highlighted by Braudel: the cultural premises, the social embeddedness and the historical variety of capitalist institutions. Critical perspectives must be grounded in closer analysis of these contextual aspects, rather than in constructs of intra-systemic transcendence.

As things now stand, however, each of the three problematics is marked by one-sided emphases and restrictive assumptions that obstruct the path to integration. This is reflected in mutual isolation of the main themes, as well as in fragmentation within the more specific fields. A brief overview of the difficulties will be useful. To begin with the spirit of capitalism, this topic of debate differs from the two others in that it is closely linked to a classical model. Max Weber's multi-faceted analysis of capitalism was discussed above; here I will only add a few words on his best-known contribution, the exceptionally influential account of the spirit of capitalism in the *Protestant Ethic*. In retrospect, four fundamental limitations to Weber's approach are apparent. Weber treated the spirit of capitalism as an extra-economic factor needed to overcome traditional resistance to the emerging capitalist order, not as a set of meaningful orientations permanently involved in the functioning of economic institutions. Within this historically limited frame of reference, he focused exclusively on religious sources of the spirit in question; as for its effects, he considered only the economic sphere and did not – at this stage – raise the question of the modern state and its dynamics. Finally, his emphasis on a mode of conduct and an attitude – innerworldly asceticism – obscured the significance of broader changes to interpretations of the world. No later formulations of the problem have led to systematic reconsideration of all these issues. More recent attempts to reintroduce or redefine the notion of a spirit of capitalism have often been made in response to new directions or problems of capitalist development: for example, analysts of East Asian economies and societies referred to the spirit of Chinese or Japanese capitalism, and the disconcerting results of capitalist transformations in post-Communist countries prompted speculation about an absent or defective spirit. The most important and original recent contribution to the debate, Luc Boltanski and Eve Chiapello's work on 'the new spirit of capitalism' (Boltanski and Chiapello 1999), centres on the new turn taken by Western capitalism since the 1970s. Boltanski and Chiapello do not take issue with Weber on all fronts. However, they stress three points that set their model clearly apart from arguments developed in – or inspired by – the *Protestant Ethic*: the spirit of capitalism is present and active throughout successive phases, it undergoes historical mutations, and it is capable of borrowing ideas and images from the critique of capitalism. Some further implications of their work will be discussed below.

The second controversy, on states and markets or 'states against markets' (Boyer and Drache 1996), is of more recent origin. It is directly related to the practical and ideological shifts of the last three decades, and more particularly to critical views on the much-proclaimed de-regulatory shift of Western economic policies. To regard the question of states and markets as an open and important one is to cast doubt on the finality of this transformation. However, at the same time, the question tends to be posed in limiting terms: the state and the market appear as complementary but also to some extent alternative co-ordinating mechanisms. Within this – broadly speaking – functionalist frame of reference, different views and strategies can be defended. It is still possible to distinguish between different combinations of state and market, with specific strengths and problems proper to each of them; from another point of view, recent advances of the market at the expense of the state represent a sea change of world-historical dimensions; but a case can also be made for projects of 'global governance' to match the global reach of market forces. The functionalist approach is less sensitive to the problematic of social power, and thus less adequate to the task of analysing the changes as transformations of economic and political power structures, and of their relations to each other. By the same token, it is not conducive to closer examination of the ideological currents at work, nor of their links to the constitutive imaginary significations of modernity. At that level of analysis, the debate on states and markets would link up with interpretations of the spirit of capitalism.

The third set of issues has mostly been treated separately from the first, but there is an obvious connection with the second: varieties of capitalism cannot be discussed without reference to varying relations between states and markets. This field has, however, been markedly more fragmented than the others. Four main schools of thought may be distinguished, all of recent origin (it was only after the disappearance of anti-capitalist challenges that the question of variations within the capitalist universe became acute). In the early 1990s, Michel Albert's *Capitalism against Capitalism* (1993, French original 1991) summed up a more widespread tendency to think in terms of polar alternatives. Against the Anglo-American model of liberal or neo-liberal capitalism, Albert defined and defended a model which he called 'Rhenan', although his account of it drew on Japanese and Swedish practices as well as German ones. The Rhenan version was supposed to allow for higher levels of state intervention and stronger social correctives to market principles. Albert later concluded that the Anglo-American model had won, and that the idea of a global alternative had proved as unviable within the capitalist world as outside it. As John Gray's polemic against global capitalism shows, this diagnosis could be given a negative turn: the Anglo-American triumph then seems to exemplify a kind of 'Gresham's law', whereby less civilised forms of capitalism prevail over the more civilised ones (Gray 1998).

Alongside this polarising paradigm, other analysts of contemporary capitalism have developed a more nuanced and research-oriented framework for comparative study. They stress the 'embeddedness of institutions', to quote the subtitle of a representative book (Hollingsworth and Boyer 1997), that is, the complex and historically conditioned social formations that give concrete shape to capitalist economies. It should be noted that, although this line of interpretation tends to begin with the institutional patterns of nation-states, some versions go beyond that point: for example, Hollingsworth and Boyer distinguish between national embeddedness and 'the present nestedness of major institutions which is a complex intertwining of institutions at all levels of the world' (*ibid*: 470). This macro-institutional perspective, with more or less pronounced internal variations, has perhaps been the most productive of the principal approaches to the field. However, it is contested by those who prefer to begin with a micro-economic analysis of the firm, seen as the most elementary unit of the capitalist economy; its internal workings as well as its relations with other economic actors raise problems that can be solved in different but functionally more or less comparable ways, and specific sets of solutions can then be equated with varieties of capitalism (Hall and Soskice 2001).

Finally, a fourth approach has developed at some distance from the others, and with a more specific thematic focus. Ivan Szelenyi and his associates have studied the rebuilding of capitalist economies after the collapse of Communist rule; they argue that the varieties emerging in this context are best explained as results of divergent exits from the general crisis of party-state regimes. Contrasting ideal types highlight the different relationships between institutions and cultural models on the one hand, economic actors and social factors on the other. A 'capitalism without capitalists', based on a project of institution-building and cultural reorientation, but not backed up by an indigenous entrepreneurial stratum, is characteristic of East Central Europe; conversely, 'capitalists without capitalism' – self-recycled members of the former ruling elite, successful privatisers but much less concerned with institutional restructuring – have shaped the course of events in the successor states of the Soviet Union and some parts of Southeast Europe (Eyal *et al* 2003). This comparative perspective does not extend to the Chinese path of transformation, which would obviously call for further conceptual distinctions. However, for present purposes, it is more important to note a general implication of the model: ideological and political patterns, rooted in historical constellations, are seen as sources of structural variations of capitalist development.

THE SPIRIT OF CAPITALISM: COMPONENTS, CONNECTIONS AND MUTATIONS

The following reflections will not aim at more than a rough sketch of ways to integrate the three lines of debate, and at the same time to concretise the civilisational perspective outlined above. It seems appropriate to begin with the spirit of capitalism and its historical contexts. Boltanski and Chiapello pose this question in innovative but ambiguous terms. They define their object of inquiry as an *ideology*, in a sense closer to Louis Dumont than to Karl Marx: a 'set of shared beliefs, inscribed in institutions, involved in actions and anchored in reality', and then go on to specify it as 'the ideology that justifies commitment to capitalism'; this commitment is needed because capitalism is 'an absurd system', where economic actors in general and capitalists in particular are chained to 'an endless and insatiable process, totally abstract and dissociated from the satisfaction of consumers' needs' (Boltanski and Chiapello 1999: 35, 42, 41). The spirit of capitalism is, in other words, explicitly linked to the operative goals of production (Weber's analyses, divided between religious traditions and elementary structures of economic rationality, were never clearly focused on this level). However, the next step is a narrowing down: the role of the internalised ideology is to sustain motivation. The one-sided emphasis on this point obscures the defining impact of cultural orientations on economic action. The question of capitalism as a cultural formation is never tackled in a systematic fashion.

The inbuilt goal of the capitalist economic order – the unlimited accumulation of abstract wealth – is inseparable from the cultural symbolism of money as the embodiment of wealth in general. However, literal interpretations of this symbolism (such as Marx's theory of value, at least in its most orthodox version) miss the main point. They treat money as an object of intrinsic value, rather than a meaning complex with an internal logic open to further rationalisation. It is not simply an institutionalised abstraction, but a framework for further development towards further levels of abstraction. The shift from gold to paper money, and then to the virtual money characteristic of contemporary capitalism, is the most obvious manifestation of this reflexive logic. More far-reaching ramifications are linked to reflexive dynamics in other domains. The global triumph of Western capitalism was made possible by a reflexive turn of technological progress, sometimes described as 'the invention of invention' but more precisely as the institutionalisation of innovation. This does not mean that the breakthrough to permanent innovation can be isolated from other aspects of the 'great transformation' and presented as the key to economic modernity. Economic historians have become increasingly aware of the 'industrial enlightenment' (Mokyr 2002) that preceded and prepared the industrial revolution. A vision of human mastery over nature was first articulated by early modern philosophers and then translated into more practical orientations and attitudes. However, the pursuit of power through accumulation of knowledge was not limited to the quest for mastery over nature. The rise and expansion of industrial capitalism was closely related to higher levels of reflexivity in the context of state formation, resulting in what has been called the 'knowledgeable state' (Pearton 1982). The intertwining of economic, technological and political innovations shifted the global balance of power in favour of the West.

In short, the reorientation of economic life towards the accumulation of abstract wealth is part and parcel of a broader shift which also involves new ways of accumulating power – political, military and administrative – as well as technologically applicable knowledge. Mutual connections are essential to all sides of this historical complex, even if the specific forms of interaction change from phase to phase. Consequently, the spirit of capitalism, its sources and its metamorphoses can only be understood in the context of cultural orientations that sustain and integrate the component parts of the whole constellation. The transformative dynamics of wealth, power and knowledge converge in an overarching and pervasive pattern of meaning: the collective mindset which Max Weber identified as a belief that all things can be mastered through calculation and Castoriadis as a phantasm of ever-expanding rational mastery. Rival ideologies can draw on this substratum in different ways. The Communist project was, to cut a long story very short, a failed attempt to outbid an existing model of accumulation: the three basic components – wealth, power and knowledge – were to be maximised and harmonised through a scientific world-view and its institutional applications. However, the ideological thrust of the alternatives that now capitalise on the Soviet collapse is also unmistakable. To single out innovation and entrepreneurship as the driving forces of capitalist development, to the exclusion of everything else, is to divert attention from the multiple and interconnected power structures involved in the process, and the same applies to generalised models of market rationality, supposedly applicable across the boundary between economy and politics.

To conclude, we must briefly reconsider the specific role and meaning acquired by the spirit of capitalism within the broader context outlined above. Christoph Deutschmann's insightful analysis of the 'religious nature of capitalism' is the most promising starting-point: it not only focuses on the operative spirit of economic institutions, but takes this fundamental correction to Weber's approach one step further by tracing the links to religious sources at the institutional level, instead of positing – as Weber did – connections between religious doctrines and the mentality of economic actors. For Deutschmann, the 'promise of absolute wealth', inherent in the economic logic of capitalism, is also an invitation to productive mobilisation of religious energies and visions, and thus to a 'reversal of the sacred cosmos into the secular world' (Deutschmann 1999: 122). If the religious constructions of transcendence can, in retrospect, be understood as projections of human creativity, the other side of this world-historical detour is the modern upgrading of human self-images and expectations through inputs from religious traditions. The capitalist contribution to this process is based on the symbolism of money, which goes beyond all utilitarian and functional perspectives (a brief glance at the sacral origins of money as an institution reinforces this thesis). However, the latent religious content manifests itself through more explicit secular utopias. The utopia of 'private power over the totality of human possibilities' (ibid: 104) is integral to the whole capitalist trajectory, but perhaps most powerfully present in the 'new individualism' diagnosed by several analysts of contemporary culture. In more specific contexts, utopian aspirations give rise to myths that crystallise around major technological breakthroughs; the imaginary projections of information technology are the most recent constructs of this kind.

STATES AND MARKETS IN HISTORICAL PERSPECTIVE

The above remarks on multiple forms and dimensions of accumulation also have some bearing on our second topic. The civilisational perspective shifts the debate on states and markets towards the long-term processes of state formation and capitalist development, with particular emphasis on their mutual irreducibility and changing interrelations. States in formation create or consolidate the most general preconditions for capitalist development: they include the pacification of social life (stressed by Elias), the overall rationalisation of social rules and norms (central to Weber's analyses of bureaucratisation), and the institutionalisation of controls needed to ensure the maintenance of legal order in general and property rights in particular (Epstein 2000). More specific infrastructural and technological inputs, at successive stages, often depend on state initiatives. Conversely, the expansion of commercial and later industrial capital created new opportunities and incentives for state-building strategies. Elias noted this aspect in connection with the development of taxation; Charles Tilly emphasised the role of credit in state formation and distinguished between capital-intensive and coercion-intensive patterns (Tilly 1990). The economic factors thus brought into play could also serve as bases for active state participation. A recent 'revisionist history' notes that 'the military-financial combinations of the early modern period ... preceded the military-industrial complexes of the nineteenth and twentieth centuries ...' (Black 2004: 14). In addition, as we have seen, Braudel stressed the fusion of capital and state power in the early modern trading monopolies.

These multiple interconnections of state formation and capitalist development are familiar to historians and historical sociologists. Taken together, they illustrate the range of historical variations as well as the importance of historical variation as well as the importance of autonomous dynamics on each side. However, the two processes can combine in more interpenetrative and mutually constitutive ways. To take a key example, the East Asian developmental state – crucial to recent debates on capitalism and its transformations – cannot be understood as a strategic response to problems posed by economic development as such. It was invented as an integral part of more comprehensive institutional restructuring, seen as essential to national survival and self-strengthening. There are good reasons to trace the Japanese construction of the developmental state back to the Meiji revolution of 1868. In this context, capitalist development was an indispensable corollary of modern state-building in a global arena, and the co-ordination of economic and political goals was from the outset conceived in flexible and adaptable terms. The more exclusively economy-centred strategy of the Japanese state after 1945 drew on the institutional legacy of the imperial phase in very ingenious and effective ways (Gao 1997). Less sustained patterns of co-ordination emerged in other historical settings. However, connections between the economic and the political spheres also involve the transfer of images and ideological constructs from one side to the other: visions of integral economic statism and projections of the market as a demythologised model of democracy grow out of historical experiences and conflicts.

State structures, state actors and state dynamics are still involved in – or at least relevant to – the recent changes that might seem to have strengthened the case for economic determinism. The political logic of neo-liberal projects may be less explicit and more conducive to ideological detours than its statist counterparts, but this does not mean that it is unimportant. Steven Vogel's analysis of the 'deregulation revolution' demolishes the ideological façade in a very convincing way: 'we should not be surprised that state actors have played a central part in the process. Deregulation would imply a retreat of the state, and we would hardly expect state actors to rally to the cause of retreat. However, reregulation merely implies a reorganisation of control, and state actors are deeply interested in the terms of this reorganisation' (Vogel 1996: 269). On another level, critics of the 'Washington consensus' and its blueprints for a neo-liberal world order have drawn attention to the role of American imperial (not just hegemonic) power, as a crucial but only half-acknowledged guarantor of the global economic regime; systematic analyses of this connection still have a long way to go and, in the public sphere, they are overshadowed by much less instructive discourses on empire.[2] Finally, the post-Communist experience has, in a more roundabout way, thrown new light on the political preconditions and underpinnings of capitalism. In the first stage of neo-liberal transformation, the ideological crusade against all real or suspected versions of statism and collectivism destroyed state structures and capacities to an extent that soon proved counter-productive; when the lesson was learnt, some of the erstwhile radical deregulators rediscovered their identity as state actors and redefined their agenda in that vein.

VARIETIES OF CAPITALISM

To conclude, let us briefly revisit the question of varieties within the historical boundaries of capitalist development. The separate lines of inquiry that share this

---

2   For the best discussion so far, see Mann (2003).

field call for conceptual integration. Some preliminary steps to that end may be suggested on the basis of the points made so far.

If the idea of capitalism as a self-contained system is rejected, the analysis of varieties cannot begin with the diversity of solutions to invariant problems. Rather, the very definition of the problems becomes a dependent variable, open to changing combinations of cultural and political factors; even the apparent turns to more exclusively economic terms of reference – exemplified by contemporary trends – are related to contextual preconditions. Interconnections with the dynamics of state formation, as well as with other aspects of the political sphere, affect the institutional make-up of capitalism. Shifting cultural currents and horizons lend specific meanings to the spirit of capitalism. As suggested above, an elementary layer of meaning relates to the accumulation of abstract wealth, but additional constructs and interpretations are involved at every historical juncture. A comparison of the cultural orientations that have fuelled and framed capitalist development, in successive phases and varying settings, would have to deal with different visions of progress, some of which are more easily turned against capitalism than others. Conversely, the spirit of capitalism is – as Boltanski and Chiapello have shown – capable of absorbing critical themes, and a more comparative approach might reveal a variety of such combinations.

All these considerations underline the need to place the problematic of capitalism in the broader context of modernity. The constitutive links to cultural and political patterns made it easier to equate capitalism with images of modernity as a whole. As 20th century changes to ideological conjunctures show, assumptions of that kind can serve very different purposes. For the Western socialist tradition and its global offshoots, capitalism became a common denominator of the problems of a really existing modernity, and a comprehensive solution to them was to centre on a new economic order. The most influential version of this view was based on assumptions which in retrospect seem more paradoxical than at the time: a self-destructive dynamic was imputed to capitalism but, at the same time, the forces expected to be released by this economic dynamic were to spearhead a project of collective autonomy, derived from cultural and political sources (the democratic imaginary). At the end of the century, ideological dominance had shifted to neo-liberal visions of capitalism as a defining, permanently indispensable and self-legitimising component of modernity.

Thus, more should be done to link the debate on varieties of capitalism to the more wide-ranging reflections on varieties of modernity, or 'multiple modernities', to use a more striking and widely accepted term. So far, contacts between the two lines of discussion have been very limited. Capitalism is a distinctly underdeveloped theme in S.N. Eisenstadt's writings on the different patterns of modernity. On the other side, the main contributors to the comparative study of capitalisms seem to have been even less interested in linking up with the pluralist turn in the theory of modernity. There is a vast field of historical and conceptual connections to be explored.

References

Albert, M (1993) *Capitalism vs Capitalism*, New York: Four Walls Eight Windows

Baechler, J (1995) *Le Capitalisme*, v 1–2, Paris: Gallimard

Black, J (2004) *Kings, Nobles and Commoners: States and Societies in Early Modern Europe, a Revisionist History*, London: IB Tauris

Boltanski, L and Chiapello, E (1999) *Le Nouvel Esprit du Capitalisme*, Paris: Gallimard

Boyer, R and Drache, D (1996) *States against Markets: The Limits of Globalisation*, London: Routledge

Braudel, F (1977) *Civilisation Matérielle, Economie et Capitalisme*, v 1–3, Paris: A Colin

Deutschmann, C (1999) *Die Verheissung des absoluten Reichtums: Zur religiösen Natur des Kapitalismus*, Frankfurt/New York: Campus Verlag

Elias, N (1978–82) *The Civilising Process*, vol 1, New York: Urisen Books; vol 2, Oxford: Blackwell

Epstein, SR (2000) *Freedom and Growth*, London: Routledge

Eyal, G, Szelenyi, I and Townsley, E (2003) 'On irony: an invitation to neo-classical sociology', Thesis Eleven no 73, 5–41

Gao, B (1997) *Economic Ideology and Japanese Industrial Policy. Developmentalism from 1931 to 1965*, Cambridge: Cambridge University Press

Goldstone, J (forthcoming) *The Happy Chance: The Rise of the West in Global Context*, Cambridge, MA: Harvard University Press

Gray, J (1998) *False Dawn: The Delusions of Global Capitalism*, London: Granta

Hall, PA and Soskice, D (2001) *Varieties of Capitalism: The Institutional Foundations of Comparative Advantage*, Oxford: Oxford University Press

Hollingsworth, JR and Boyer, R (1997) *Contemporary Capitalism: The Embeddedness of Institutions*, Cambridge: Cambridge University Press

Mann, M (2003) *Incoherent Empire*, London: Verso

Marx, K (1973) *Grundrisse*, Harmondsworth: Penguin Books

Marx, K and Engels, F (1976) *The German Ideology*, Moscow: Progress Publishers

Mokyr, J (2002) *The Gifts of Athena: Historical Origins of the Knowledge Economy*, Princeton, NJ: Princeton University Press

Pearton, M (1982) *The Knowledgeable State: Diplomacy, War and Technology since 1830*, London: Burnett Books

Swedberg, R (1999) *Max Weber's Sociology of Capitalisms*, Working Paper, Department of Sociology, University of Stockholm

Tilly, C (1990) *Coercion, Capital and European States AD 990–1990*, Oxford: Blackwell

Vogel, SK (1996) *Freer Markets, More Rules: Regulatory Reform in Advanced Industrial Countries*, Ithaca, NY: Cornell University Press

Weber, M (1968) *Economy and Society*, v 1–3, New York: Bedminster Press

Weber, M (1991) *From Max Weber: Essays in Sociology*, Gerth, HH and Wright Mills, C (eds), London: Routledge

THE *PROBLÉMATIQUE* OF ECONOMIC MODERNITY: CRITICAL THEORY, POLITICAL PHILOSOPHY AND THE ANALYSIS OF CAPITALISM

Peter Wagner

ENDGAME

CLOV Fini, c'est fini, ça va peut-être finir. […]

HAMM Et l'horizon? Rien à l'horizon?
CLOV Mais que veux-tu qu'il y ait à l'horizon? […]

HAMM Alors quoi?
CLOV Il fait gris. Gris! GRRIS!
HAMM Gris! Tu as dit gris?
CLOV Noir clair. Dans tout l'univers. […]

HAMM Qu'est-ce qui se passe?
CLOV Quelque chose suit son cours. […]

CLOV Ça veut dire il y a un foutu bout de misère. J'emploie les mots que tu m'as appris. S'ils ne veulent plus rien dire apprends-m'en d'autres. Ou laisse-moi taire. […]

HAMM La fin est dans le commencement et cependant on continue.

(Beckett 1957: 15, 47–49, 62, 91)

In the analysis of capitalism, critical theory constitutes a distinct intellectual tradition. Inaugurated by Karl Marx, it reaches from the Frankfurt School to the neo-Marxism of the 1970s to the recent debates about the inevitability of neo-liberal globalisation. While the conceptual weaknesses of this mode of thinking are well known, at least from Max Weber and Karl Polanyi onwards, critical theory nevertheless shows a remarkable persistence. The objective of this chapter is to analyse the tradition of critical theory in the light of its failure to grasp the inevitably political constitution of frameworks for economic action, but by doing so this chapter ultimately aims at understanding the strong reasons for the persistence of this intellectual tradition. Selecting Theodor W Adorno's work as a key example for both the neglect of the political and the persistence of the critical perspective, it will be shown how – despite a general insight into the possibility of discussing the economy politically – the place of political philosophy was evacuated in favour of a reasoning that emphasised epistemic obstacles towards analysing capitalism instead. From such an angle, then, any embedding of capitalism appeared impossible, and the well-known apocalyptic tendency of critical theory emerged forcefully – in the following to be captured by the notion of the endgame. In a second step, however, the chapter proceeds to demonstrate that the dimension of political philosophy in the critical analysis of capitalism can be restored. If Adorno and other critical theorists are read in this light, their observations on developmental tendencies of capitalism gain new meaning and provide insights that cannot be found in current debates about 'varieties of capitalism'.[1]

The idea of an endgame that is already being played is constitutive for critical theory. In Marx, it appears in the form of the self-overcoming tendencies of capitalism, as a combined result of competition and class struggle. In Lenin's view of imperialism as the highest stadium of capitalism, the idea of self-overcoming has been discarded and replaced by the emphasis on the voluntarism of a revolutionary *avantgarde* that will spell the end of capitalism. In Adorno, as will be shown in detail below, a totalising vision of a society in which everything is dominated by a single logic leads to profound pessimism. The debates of the 1970s and of the 1990s are less focused, but the idea of a terminal state of the social configuration is similarly central.

The persuasiveness of this idea of an endgame can – very broadly – be related to the respective historical state of capitalism itself. Marx himself was writing at a time of liberal ideology and rapid growth of world trade and was thus led to uncover the hidden dynamics of capitalism in terms of commodification, exploitation and alienation. He did not live to witness the nationalisation of European societies with the building of social-policy institutions from the late 19th century onwards, during which a revisionist Marxism emerged that indeed saw a prospect for social change due to reformist collective action in nation-states. The world-economic crisis of 1929 and the rise of Nazism provided the context for the renewed plausibility of a totalising view of the dynamics of capitalism, whereas the return to democracy after the Second World War shifted the emphasis again to significant varieties of political possibilities. This 'cycle' is reflected in Adorno's work, as will be discussed below. In the more recent past, the rise of 1970s neo-Marxism, after the student revolt and during the first post-war recession, was followed during the 1980s by a return of the political, this movement being usefully illustrated by the names of Louis Althusser and Elmar Altvater for the first period and the renewed interest in the works of Claude Lefort and Hannah Arendt for the second – the latter being authors who always were or became critical of the critical tradition precisely for reasons of neglect of the political. Finally, the rise of neo-liberalism was easily accepted by critical thinkers as a hegemonic *pensée unique* to which 'there is no alternative' in an era of globalisation, while there are currently signs that this intellectual fashion nears its end.

1   An earlier version of this chapter was presented at the Adorno conference held by the Institute for social research and University of Frankfurt, in September 2003. Thanks are due to Nathalie Karagiannis for detailed discussion of this chapter while in preparation.

From this ultra-brief contextual history of critical theory one may easily conclude that the central ideas of this tradition swing helplessly in and out of fashion with the economic and political tides. The main tenets of the theory are seen as refuted by the next historical transformation, only to be reinstituted a historical moment later. This, however, would be too simple a view of the mirroring of intellectual and socio-economic change. As shall be demonstrated in what follows, it is more fruitful to try to reconstruct the main argument of critical theory, to some extent inevitably against the intentions of its proponents, to see more clearly what is dead in this intellectual tradition and what is alive and can still serve us in our attempt at understanding the development of capitalism. Such a reconstruction will be attempted here focusing on a single but central contributor to critical theory, Theodor W Adorno.

As becomes immediately evident from the epigraph to this chapter, Samuel Beckett's *Fin de partie*, first performed in 1957, seems to have anticipated and joined together two diagnoses of our time that should emerge in their explicit forms only much later: on the one hand, the postmodernist notion that all meta-narratives of emancipation have been exhausted, and that words have lost all of their meaning; on the other hand, the conviction that global capitalism based on neo-liberal ideology effectively reigns the world. The two protagonists of the play, Clov and Hamm, are individuals of the kind presented in those diagnoses. Even though they still speak, they are highly alienated both from one another and from the world. Almost any social bond between them, and towards their parents, Nell and Nagg, the only other two persons on stage, seems to be severed. The references to the other address only needs that emerge from damaged lives, and those needs remain unsatisfied. The memory of an earlier, richer social bond is still on the mind, but it can no longer be retrieved in communication. What dominates, in contrast, is the wish to leave the other, a wish that remains unfulfilled because nobody is in fact able to leave. And this is a condition that is no longer going to change. The endgame does not lead to an end; it is going to last.

Theodor Adorno recognised the force of this representation immediately. A text from 1958, titled 'Attempt to understand the endgame', discusses *Fin de partie* as a representation of the human condition 'in the face of permanent catastrophe', of 'infinite catastrophe' and in light of the 'fact of damage' (Adorno 1974: 292, 319 and 289) as well as a further, and presumably highest, step in the history of modernism, the one in which modernism turns into 'that in modernity which has come of age' (Adorno 1974: 281). The exploration of these themes, in turn, is grounded on a broader reading of *Fin de partie*: 'The misery of the participants in the endgame is the misery of philosophy' (Adorno 1974: 295); and the misery of philosophy stems from its inability to grasp 'historical tendency' and 'social truth' (Adorno 1974: 287 and 289). Philosophy always has to be social theory at the same time, according to Adorno, and in our times such social theory will importantly have to draw on an analysis of capitalism.

INDIVIDUAL, RATIONALITY, CAPITALISM: RISE AND FALL OF THE AUTONOMOUS SUBJECT

Adorno reads *Fin de partie* as a diagnosis of the present. In its centre, he identifies the 'liquidation of the subject',[2] which leaves only 'a-social partners' in unintelligible interaction (Adorno 1974: 287, 290, 309). He tries to understand this condition first philosophically, namely in the light of the history of the subject as it was conceived across one and a half centuries of history of philosophy from idealism to existentialism (Adorno 1974: 290–91). The 'hypostasis of the individual' emerges in idealism, finding its full form in 'Fichte's free deed' (Adorno 1974: 293 and 310).[3] In existentialism, the relation between individual and context, recast as the person who experiences himself or herself aspiring towards harmony with the situation, is philosophised suprahistorically as the 'once and for all of Dasein' – at a moment, though, that turns out to be precisely the 'point of history, which breaks' (Adorno 1974: 288).[4] This 'historical moment' is the one in which 'the individual itself has revealed itself as a historical category, as a result of the capitalist process of alienation and as a stubborn protest against it, as something again perishable' (Adorno 1974: 285 and 290).

At this point, thus, Adorno connects the history of the philosophy of the subject to the history of capitalism, and he does so by suggesting an historical process that comes full circle. The positing of the all-powerful subject corresponds to the moment of the rise of capitalism, whereas at the advanced stage of mid-20th century capitalism, the transitory nature of this positing becomes evident when the subject turns out to be a historical phenomenon, at the point of withering away. For a fuller discussion of capitalism by Adorno, one would have to turn to the *Dialectics of Enlightenment*, but even in this text the main contours are clear. In terms of its material effects, capitalism is seen as objectifying the world and as annihilating everything natural, everything that precedes capitalism.

Capitalism produces these outcomes, because the radical positing of the subject eliminates constraints on human autonomy and enables the hubristic

---

2   When pointing out the 'reduction to the human being become animal', Adorno anticipates the idea of the reduction of human beings to their *'nuda vita'*, as recently discussed by Giorgio Agamben (1995). When he qualifies: 'The historical crisis of the individual has for the time being its limits in the biological singular being, its stage'(Adorno 1974: 300), the term 'for the time being' gains an uncanny connotation in our emerging age of human reproduction through genetic technology. (Unless specified, all translations are mine.) See Boltanski 2002 for a discussion of the shift of the idea of total revolution towards biotechnological transformation of the human being.

3   In the light of the task of this volume, the account seems in dire need of further specification. There are strong reasons not only to start this history earlier, with Descartes, for instance, but also to provide a linkage to the history of the individual in *political* philosophy, such as in Hobbes and Locke. Furthermore, Adorno also betrays here the totalising tendency in his own thought, when he namely voices the 'suspicion that it was never much different' (Adorno 1974: 310), in contrast to his attempt at historicising.

4   'The hybris of idealism, that is, putting the human being as its creator into the centre of Creation, has barricaded itself in the "interior without furniture" like a tyrant whose last days have come' (Adorno 1974: 316; 'Intérieurs sans meubles' is the first sentence of the stage description in *Fin de partie*).

thought of human omnipotence to emerge. This tension between the modern commitment to freedom and autonomy, on the one hand, and its outcome in the form of world objectification and destruction, on the other, leads to what Adorno calls the irrationality of rationalisation, in line with other 20th century social theorists such as Max Weber and Cornelius Castoriadis. In the context of his discussion of *Fin de partie*, Adorno links this insight to the concept of absurdity, seeing the latter as precisely the 'contradiction between the rational façade and the unalterably irrational' (Adorno 1974: 308). Thus, the emergence, or so it seems during the 1950s, of the absurd as a world-view does not mean the overcoming of the rational world-view, rather 'the latter comes to itself in the former' (Adorno 1974: 310). Mobilising the Hegelian motive of *Aufhebung* (sublation), but turning its meaning around, Adorno, again in affinity to Weber, proposes a concept of self-annihilation of capitalist modernity, and sees the endgame as the period in which the contradiction between the rational and the irrational moves towards resolution in accomplished self-annihilation.

At close reading, Adorno's position on the terminal nature of this endgame is unclear. In the phrase: 'ratio, having become completely instrumental, bare of any self-determination and of any determination of that which it disqualified, must ask for the meaning that was cancelled by itself' (Adorno 1974: 319), for instance, everything hinges on the meaning of 'must'. If it refers to a mere normative demand, then this demand can be seen as finally unrecognised after the cancellation of meaning, and the game is over. If there is something in the rational, though, that compels it to sustain the quest for meaning even under those conditions, then the contradiction stays alive. In the broader context of Adorno's writings, the former interpretation finds more support. In the analysis of Beckett's play, for instance, he links the analysis of objectification and alienation to core concerns of language and philosophy. The disintegration of language leads to illusions of communication (Adorno 1974: 306–07), and truth threatens to disappear from sight as the 'possibility of something true that cannot even be thought anymore' arises (Adorno 1974: 319).[5] In conclusion of such a line of thought, Adorno states the inescapability of 'negative ontology' (Adorno 1974: 319) and notes that the contemporary world is in such a state of regression that it disposes of 'no counter-concept anymore' that could be held against that regression (Adorno 1974: 289).

Extracting from these notes Adorno's perspective on capitalist society, we can see that he links a very basic conceptualisation of *capitalism*, which focuses on alienation and reification and was readily available for him through the Marxist tradition, with a social *epistemology* that draws on the Enlightenment quest for truth and freedom but is employed here to assess the intelligibility of capitalism

---

5   His few remarks about the knowledge forms of late-capitalist society, behaviourism, psychology and rational choice theory (Adorno 1974: 293 and 307), themes that are more developed in other writings, are meant to support this observation of a loss of language and truth. In a more unusual remark, Adorno notes that functionalist sociology sees 'the zoon politikon as role' (Adorno 1974: 312) – a remark that opens the way for linking social theory to political philosophy, but is never followed up on (see below).

from within a given capitalist society, and combines both with a long-term view on history – or rather with a rudimentary *philosophy of history* – that links the advance of capitalism with the decreasing persuasiveness of the concept of the autonomous individual and the decline in the intelligibility of the world.

This combination of an analysis of capitalism with epistemology and philosophy of history shaped Adorno's approach to a theory of society. Already in a lengthy discussion of Karl Mannheim's *Mensch und Gesellschaft im Zeitalter des Umbaus*, written in 1937,[6] Adorno appreciates Mannheim's attempt at providing a diagnosis of the contemporary social transformations, but identifies as its major problem the claim to provide a 'value free' analysis of society, that is, its specific epistemic claim. In his critical review, Adorno diagnoses an 'overestimation of appearances' as the consequence of that stand, and this overestimation in turn entails the neglect of the more important underlying reality of capitalism. In such light, most significantly, major political changes, such as what Mannheim calls 'fundamental democratisation', are seen as a 'phenomenon of mere façade' (Adorno 1986a: 17, see again 43ff) that can only be properly understood on the basis of a fuller theory of capitalist society that does not depend for its conceptualisations on the observation of appearances.

Such a view, though, places a gigantic burden on the 'genuine theory of society' into whose context the findings of social research have to be placed, according to Adorno (1986a: 44). To see in how far his own social theory lived up to this exigency, a look at his writings about those same phenomena, related to 'mass democracy', of which he claimed that mainstream sociology was unable to grasp them properly, is necessary. Adorno, namely, even though these aspects of his work are largely forgotten, was interested in political institutions, in the actual running of public affairs, and was able to make distinctions within the same totality of 'capitalist society'.

DEMOCRACY UNDER CONDITIONS OF CAPITALISM: ADORNO AS A POLITICAL SCIENTIST

Rather than insisting to consider 'fundamental democratisation' as a mere 'phenomenon of façade', as he did in 1937, Adorno acknowledged in 1949 that the 'idea[s] of democracy' can be given 'a more concrete meaning' if and when democratic leadership takes the place of the prevailing forms of mass manipulation: 'Today perhaps more than ever, it is the function of democratic leadership to make the subjects of democracy, the people conscious of their own wants and needs as against the ideologies which are hammered into their heads by the innumerable communications of vested interests' (Adorno 1986b: 268). In the position Adorno takes here, significant differences between empirically existing varieties of democracy exist; no theoretical insight imposes the

6   Mannheim 1980 – this is the revised English version that appeared while Mannheim was in British exile.

conclusion that under conditions of capitalism the idea of democracy will always only be applied 'in a merely formalistic way' (Adorno 1986b: 268).

This observation is confirmed when Adorno in 1951 explicitly addresses the 'difference in political climate between America and Germany': 'The American state, namely, is well recognised by its citizens as a societal form of organisation, but nowhere as one that flows above the lives of the individuals, that commends them or forms even an absolute authority.' In the US, according to the returned exile, large parts of the population do not have 'the feeling that the state is something other than they themselves', and Adorno goes as far as claiming that this nuance of difference between McCarthyist US and post-Nazi Germany entails 'a more happy relation between the supreme form of societal organisation and its citizens' in the former (Adorno 1986c: 290–91).

A year later, Adorno continues his reflections about the state of democracy by addressing a theme that should gain much more prominence in the work of Jürgen Habermas rather shortly afterwards, the formation of public opinion. His observations on opinion research contain elements of the critique of a merely aggregative mode of empirical social research that were in the centre of his articles on sociology and empirical research. However, he not only insisted that richer forms of opinion research – 'in closest context with the most advanced knowledge about society as a whole' – are possible (and indeed experimented with in Frankfurt), but he also praises the 'democratic potential' of opinion research that 'in consciousness of the contradictoriness of our societal state' can develop towards the fulfilment of its 'genuine democratic function' (Adorno 1986d: 300–01).

One can again recognise here Adorno's concern for varieties of democracy, some of which are normatively more desirable than others, and the attainability of which needs to be assessed with the help of a social theory that does not preclude by theoretical *fiat* any of those possibilities but that is interested in the analysis of the state of the 'societal play of forces': 'In a society in which democracy is meant to be neither an empty slogan nor a merely formal principle, it will at least be necessary to assess, ever again, from below, all institutional claims to represent public opinion' (Adorno 1986d: 295).

One may want to question the value of these of Adorno's writings. The comparison of political organisation in the US and Germany may today resonate with those strands in the revival of republican political thought that claim continued existence of that political tradition in the history of the US, but it will sound at least crass and surprisingly one-sided from the pen of this very European intellectual (Adorno 1986e: 394), and is rather devoid of any more sophisticated insight from historical political sociology. In addition, in the light of Jürgen Habermas's analysis of the structural transformation of the public sphere, Adorno's hope for a democracy-sustaining version of opinion research appears unfoundedly optimistic.[7]

---

7 Of current significance is certainly the following warning: 'One should be aware, though, not to demand of governments that they orient themselves exclusively, at all times and with regard to decisions about all issues at the vote of public opinion as it is presented in the poll results' (Adorno 1986d: 300).

As weak as the analyses are in substance, however, these political writings demonstrate that there were elements in Adorno's thought that lent themselves towards the elaboration of a social theory in which political organisation gains significance on its own and accounts for important varieties of societal configurations. These elements, however, appear as a rather minor thread in Adorno's work; they do not add up to any sustained component of his theorising, and accordingly they have never altered the underlying social ontology of his social theory.

THEORISING THE PRESENT: THE TASK OF SOCIAL THEORY

Adorno's social theory remained firmly anchored in the totalising 'critique of bourgeois society' (Adorno 1974: 284). Overall, the elements of a more subtle nature, some of which were retrieved above, can hardly be seen as providing the 'concrete mediation' (Adorno 1986a: 25) between the basic theory and the appearances that Adorno himself had called for. The reason for this lack, however, should not be searched primarily in Adorno's difficulty to relate the theoretical to the empirical. If these aspects and elements of his work have remained rather undeveloped, substantive reasons for such neglect must be taken into account.

Returning to Adorno's interpretation of *Fin de partie*, the suspicion arises that he himself, while being able to formulate the key criterion for a necessary philosophy and social theory, was aware of the fact that such philosophy and social theory remained still on the horizon and were far from being accomplished. Shortly after having stated that 'the irrationality of bourgeois society in its late phase is resistant towards attempts to be grasped; those were good times still, when a critique of bourgeois society could be written that took that society by its own ratio', he adds, slightly hesitatingly, the call: 'One could almost turn that into a criterion for a necessary philosophy: that it shows itself at the height of this' (Adorno 1974: 284).

The precise meaning of this call depends on the referent for the final 'this', which remains unclear – not a rare occurrence in Adorno's writings. It could be that Adorno demands of philosophy to analyse bourgeois society critically by demonstrating that its irrationality has taken on such a form that it can no longer be grasped. This would be in line with his reference to a 'negative ontology' in the same text and with the gist of the later *Negative dialectics*. However, it would also mean abandoning philosophy altogether, which thus would not show itself 'at the height' of this situation at all but would declare itself defeated by the hegemony of the irrational. Furthermore, it would mean accepting the performative contradiction that arises when a quite ordinarily intelligible analysis of capitalism is mobilised as the foundation for identifying the utter unintelligibility of society. Another interpretation seems much more fruitful. The necessary philosophy would show itself 'at the height' of the situation in as far as it places into the centre of its attention not the irrationality of contemporary bourgeois society – for which 'late phase', by the way, has not proven to be a useful term – as such, but its resistance to being grasped, and to do this by analysing the specific nature of the contradiction between the rational and the irrational under contemporary conditions.

If Adorno did not entirely make up his mind about this choice, this indecisiveness seems to stem from a dilemma that critical social theory faces up to the present day. On the one hand, the longing of critical theory since Marx has been the identification of a dynamics that could be denounced as driving societal development towards normatively ever more undesirable states. To fulfil this longing, a theoretical argument had to be deployed that was applicable with a considerable degree of generality: such dynamics would need to exist across all capitalist societies and it would need to unfold over time.[8] Critique would gain its power in proportion to the generalisability of its denunciation. On the other hand, such an approach, if taken to extremes, disarms itself in as far as it tends to present insurmountable dynamics, in the face of which all human action is futile. And it risks losing plausibility whenever and wherever societal developments are too varied and too complex to sit easily with any sweeping generalisation. Adorno's early attempt to declare 'fundamental democratisation' of European societies after the First World War as rather insignificant succumbs to such a verdict, but his later writings on democracy try to remedy the earlier misjudgment, even though never in a fully convinced way. The interpretation of *Fin de partie* consciously combines the radical version of the argument about an underlying dynamics of capitalist society with an historical diagnosis that situates the present at 'the nadir' of the history of the subject and, we may say, of modernity. This, precisely, is Adorno's Hegelianism in reverse.

This theoretical attitude, however, can much more easily be criticised than it can be entirely discarded. The strong alternative, which would emphasise the contingency of historical developments and, thus, the plurality and diversity of existing varieties of capitalist societies, both across time and across space, risks replacing the problematic overconfidence in theoretical presupposition and teleological reasoning with mere observational detail and/or flat presentism.[9] Adorno's way of theorising, in contrast, preserves a sense of long-term transformations, and of some direction of such transformations that, indeed, can be experienced – even though during some periods more than others. The critical rendering of such an experience is the one of loss; in Adorno's version this loss is not conceptualised in a conservative way, as the loss of a more harmonious past, but as a modernist critique of modernity, a critique of modernity's tendency towards self-cancellation. At this point, the distinction between the two ways of interpreting Adorno, as introduced above, becomes crucial.

---

8   *Dialektik der Aufklärung*, it may be recalled, is dated 'Los Angeles 1944'. In the absence of any specification in the text itself, this combination of date and time may be taken to suggest that emerging consumerist US and Nazi Germany are both included into the scope of the analysis. This can be seen as an intellectual misconception of highest proportions, denying a variety that was life-saving for these authors themselves, but it can also be seen as precisely reflecting the aporia of critical social theory here discussed.
9   Minimising further referencing, I just point to Johann Arnason's contribution for a constructively critical discussion of this debate.

If Adorno needs to be read as seeing modernity's self-cancellation as accomplished, then no rise from the nadir of critical theory is thinkable. History has unfolded in such a way that it entirely confirms the critical theoretical presuppositions. If Adorno – maybe against himself – can, however, also be read as offering a diagnosis of a specific present, marked by a particular – historically prepared, but not determined – articulation of the tension between the rational and the irrational, then his theorising can offer elements upon which an appropriate recasting of the relation between an historical-empirical analysis of societal developments in the recent past and present and a social and political theory of capitalist modernity can be built – elements that exist neither in standard versions of Marxism nor in the presentist expressions of the debate on the varieties of capitalism. To see how Adorno's work can be put to such use, I need to redescribe it first in terms of a social theory of modernity.

CRITICAL THEORY, POLITICAL PHILOSOPHY AND THE THEORISING OF MODERNITY

Even though it can be conceptualised in highly variable ways, any theory of modernity, arguably, needs to be centrally based on an idea of autonomy, of human self-determination, or freedom. This insight was common to key thinkers of modernity such as Kant, Hegel, Marx and Weber. For a long time, a common way of discussing theories of modernity was to distinguish affirmative from critical approaches, with the former taking autonomy as the goal towards which modernity was effectively directed and the latter emphasising the delusionary, even deceitful character of modernity's commitment to autonomy. During the 20th century, but drawing on Kant's distinction in the three critiques, sub-spheres of society – such as economy, politics and science – were systematically distinguished in many strands of social theory. The normative diagnosis of a society then depended on the realisation of autonomy in all sub-spheres in which it seemed viable and on the harmonious or contradictory relation between the sub-spheres.

The assumption of sub-spheres is highly problematic, not least because it tends to mislead – all declarations of some authors to the contrary notwithstanding – the empirical analysis of social configurations of modernity to identify those spheres with institutional-organisational arrangements, such as markets, enterprises and unions, or parties and state institutions. Instead, without being able to go into detail of reasoning here, I propose to look at the aspects of modernity rather as *problématiques* that any society has to address, and that societies under the imaginary signification of modernity address by recurring to a notion of autonomy (for more detail see Wagner 2001). *Political* modernity refers then to the commitment to *collective self-determination*; *economic* modernity refers to the autonomous determination of the ways in which *human needs* are satisfied; and *epistemic* modernity refers to the unconstrained search for *knowledge and truth*. In all cases, the commitment to autonomy could be – and was – justified both on normative grounds, containing its own reason within itself, and by the increase in mastery of the world that it would bring about. The commitment to autonomy was thus allied to a commitment to rationality and mastery.

Recasting it in such terminology, Adorno's theoretical position entailed a view of modernity as focused on a certain conception of the economic, that is, capitalism as economic modernity, in alliance with a certain view of the epistemic, that is, the world to be known in as far as it is measurable and carved up into quantifiable elements. The particular nature of Adorno's approach stems from three features that we have already noted above, but that can now be discussed in different terms. First, he takes the analysis of economic modernity for granted, namely as the critical analysis of the outcome of the liberation of economic action, basically accomplished since Marx, and recognises the inescapable tendency of such economic modernity towards alienation and reification. Secondly, epistemic modernity, that is, the Enlightenment tradition, while inaugurating the theme of the free subject, was misconstruing the human being as an abstract individual and thus failed to develop an adequate notion of autonomy. Thirdly, the historical trajectory of economic and political modernity was conjoined in such a way that the rise of capitalism accompanied the 'zenith' of the philosophy of the autonomous subject, now identifiable as a misconception and an illusion, while the full development of capitalism marks the 'nadir', the 'endgame' of any such conception.

In more general, say, for want of a better expression, meta-theoretical terms, this thinking is characterised by a very strong social ontology, and this in two major respects. First, it deploys its concepts in such a way that they, and the conceptual edifices they contribute to, are 'stretched' to cover a large variety of societal situations, basically the history of the Northwestern quarter of the world since the Enlightenment and the industrial and market revolution. Secondly, the basic concepts are arranged in such a way that the same, static conceptual constellation determines the 'spatio-temporal envelope' (Latour 2000: 259) that the theory postulated. To speak very crudely, this constellation meant some *economic-epistemic* determinism in the light of which all other aspects of human social life fade into insignificance. Most importantly for my purposes here, such conceptual arrangement implies that it is impossible for any expression of *political* modernity, of collective self-determination to acquire significance for the understanding of modernity overall, or of certain historical forms of it.

By describing Adorno's social theory in such a way, a first step is made to advance the claim, to be detailed in what follows, that an alternative social theory and political philosophy is possible that retains the critical capacity of Adorno's approach, but that is able to address varieties of configurations of modernity, again both across space and over time, in a more differentiated and, thus, more adequate way. The social ontology of such an approach needs to be 'weaker' than Adorno's in two precise ways, each one leading to an opening towards a mode of inquiry that was underused in the theorising of the classical Frankfurt School. First, it needs to accept the possibility that configurations of modernity are of such a variety that a move from one to another requires conceptual change – change in the language of interpretation. This insight requires an opening towards comparative-historical sociology, and in particular towards those – mostly more recent – strands of historical sociology that are conscious of social change being accompanied as well as brought about by reinterpretations of the human condition (Wagner 2003). This latter aspect leads over to the second ontological move. The required social ontology needs to be weak also in the sense of accepting that, even for a precisely delineated given social configuration, its concepts do not exhaustively determine the social world. Rather, it would recognise that its concepts, drawn as they always are from the social world to which they refer, are also elements of justification either of a given social arrangement or of activities to create a different social arrangement (Wagner 2005). In the history of social theory, this insight was of course not unknown, but it was translated into the opposition between affirmative and critical social theory, a dispute that was meant to be decided by epistemic means alone. Instead, the observation would need to be led to the more general insight that normative justifications, and disputes over them, are empirical components of a social configuration. This insight leads the theory then to an opening towards normative politico-philosophical reasoning, not in the sense of a separate discipline, however, but as an integral part of both the societal analysis and of the positioning of the theoretical endeavour itself.

Taking both of these elements together, an image of the 'necessary philosophy' emerges as a comprehensive, politico-philosophically sensitive historical sociology of social configurations of modernity, at the core of which the relation between social theory and political philosophy is kept open and in which the elaboration of a critical diagnosis of the time is an objective that is to be accomplished by means of situating the present within an historical horizon that is not determined by any logic of development but the interpretation of which itself is a persistent task in the present. The meaning and effect of the integration of either of these two elements will be discussed in some more substantive detail in the following paragraphs, starting with the opening towards political philosophy and moving subsequently to the question of historicisation.

CRITICAL THEORY AND THE PLACE OF THE POLITICAL: THE PURPOSES AND THE COMMON

The duo of approaches to social theory that dominated much of the post-Second World War period, critical theory and (neo-)Marxism on the one hand, and the evolutionary social science of modern societies on the other, shared the assumption that social configurations were shaped and held together by social processes and structures of social relations. It was, thus, jointly opposed to all thought that considered societies to be (always) politically constituted in the first place, a thinking that was for a long time confined to political philosophy and even lived there rather at the margins. In the light of the above, however, the question of the justification of collective action within a polity as well as the one of the self-understanding of a polity in its boundaries needs to be an integral part of a comprehensive social theory.

For the sake of clarity of reasoning, it is useful to pursue this issue by starting out from the perspective that takes the political, and in particular the constitution of the polity, as the primary question of social and political theory, as it is the case with the approaches proposed by Hannah Arendt and Claude Lefort and, to a considerable extent, also by Cornelius Castoriadis. The political is here understood as all action that is concerned with determining which matters are common to members of a collectivity and with handling them in common. The question of the political can be seen as being approached in a modern way if and when a collectivity deliberates about these issues autonomously, in collective self-determination. Significantly, political action, on the one hand, presupposes a collectivity, to determine both the reach of the 'common' and, under modern conditions, the right to participation in self-determination. On the other hand, the determination of the boundaries of a polity is itself a political act, a constitutive one and, thus, possibly the most important one. Political thinking that does not, or at least not fully, accept the 'imaginary signification of modernity' can either ignore the latter question entirely, because it sees polities as always already pre-constituted, or draw on non-political resources to find an answer to the question of the constitution of the polity, such as the assumption of a need for a common language did in nationalist political thought. In contrast, modern political thought needs to take the question of the founding of the polity as the most fundamental political question of all. Accordingly, it has, from social contract theory onwards, included a hypothesis about the founding moment in its reasoning, even though often only to keep the issue at bay and move on to consider the workings of an already constituted polity.

This latter move has contributed to obscure the impact that founding assumptions can have on the very understanding of the political. The tradition of contract theory postulates that human beings, who are ontologically separate individuals, enter into association for a common *purpose*. This understanding paved the way for a later social science that lost the sense of the political. Sociology drew on the term 'society', which originally referred to an association for a purpose, for the conceptualisation of its basic unit of analysis. Accordingly, functionalism aims to explain societal development as needs-driven, thereby obscuring the fact that such explanation resides on nothing but a prior assumption. The conceptual alternative within the framework of social science becomes clear when one compares Ernest Gellner's insistence that the functional needs of industrialism were the driving force behind nation-building in Europe, on the one hand, with, on the other, the assumption that some common world, here conceptualised as residing in the common hermeneutic engagement with the world through language, must pre-exist collective action, because common purposes can only be developed or identified on such a basis.

The question whether polities are constituted over common *purpose* or by virtue of the fact of togetherness and *sharing a world* and common problems can to some degree be opened to historical investigation, including importantly comparative investigation of highly differently constituted polities, but it will not be answered by those means. Even if one takes a cautious stand, though, and accepts the existence of common needs and purposes, to be dealt with by a division of social labour, for instance, the decision to deal with such needs and purposes in common will always remain a political act. Therefore, a conceptual move that makes the political derivative of the economic is in no way justified, or, in other words, the *problématique* of political modernity cannot be subordinated to the *problématique* of economic modernity, as happened in critical theory.

At the same time, however, the gliding from a socio-economically driven social theory to a mode of political philosophy that detaches the political from the socio-economic, as a response to the above, also needs to be avoided. Such gliding has occurred both in mainstream individualist liberalism and in some more radical thinkers such as, notably, Hannah Arendt and, to a lesser degree, Claude Lefort; it is part of the general intellectual devaluation of sociology and critical theory compared to the renewed interest in individualist political theorising and the rise of cultural studies. A more appropriate response would have conceptually to articulate the political with the economic.[10]

Such articulation could start out from a double assumption. First, rather than being asocial or apolitical, the modes of dealing with needs, in as far as they *relate* human beings to each other, create a common. The term 'relation' refers to a variety of highly different phenomena, which also have found different degrees of attention in social theory. The very *creation of community by exchange* is a theme known from at least the idea of 'doux commerce', as discussed by Albert Hirschman (1977), for instance. In such light, extension of exchange relations thus potentially also *extends community*, historically diagnosed – in sometimes overdrawn ways – as extension from the local to the national, and as extension from the national to the global today. Such extension of exchange, though, may also *disrupt existing community organisation* by breaking out of existing confinements – a strong theme in Marx – and then, in turn, support arguments and, eventually, action towards *recreation of community*, such as the conscious building of inclusive national arrangements in response to the threat of the 'dissolution of society', as analysed by Karl Polanyi. In this latter case, the *relation* in question takes on the particular nature of *regulation* and becomes a conscious collective act, a society acting upon itself by political means, with varying degrees of participation – in Europe moving historically towards the internally all-inclusive, externally closed form of modern democracy – and of deliberation.[11]

THE HISTORICAL HORIZON OF CONTEMPORARY CAPITALISM: THE PLAUSIBILITY OF MODERNITY'S SELF-CANCELLATION

Even though the last remarks have resorted to the means of historical illustration, thus far only a general conceptual scheme has been offered. It is much richer than Adorno's way of integrating the analysis of capitalism into a comprehensive

---

10 For the sake of brevity, the discussion of epistemic modernity will be briefly suspended here, to be taken up again later.

11 Deliberation may here usefully be understood as the communication about handling things in common and distinguished from regulation as the (self-) acting upon society by means of rules and policies – thus avoiding the barren opposition between a substanceless conception of the political, on the one hand, and an overly economically determined one, on the other. (As regards regulation, it is important to add that it may also occur through non-intentionally created social phenomena, such as habits, customs, trust.)

social theory and thus begs the question whether there are any strong reasons why Adorno's thought did not move into a similar direction. An answer to that question was already hinted at above: his observations of society led Adorno to the suspicion that long-term historical transformations had occurred that could not be grasped by considering the relations between political, economic and epistemic modernity as an open constellation containing a variety of possible interpretations, but that, instead, a particular articulation reigned in a rather durable way over European and North American societies. We have described this articulation as an economic-epistemic determinism that erases the political, or, in terms of the imaginary signification of modernity, as a configuration in which the commitment to autonomy under the conditions of capitalism as the prevailing form of economic modernity produces reification and alienation that, in turn, undermine the search for certain knowledge and the attempts at collective self-determination, that is the expression of autonomy in epistemic and political terms.

In the conceptual terminology proposed here, this diagnosis describes an *historical possibility*, which is formulated in somewhat extreme form, but which cannot be ruled out as a possibility, indeed needs to be taken seriously as a possibility that finds at least partial confirmation in observations of social life. Given the structure of the argument, it will never be possible fully to assert such diagnosis as an empirical given at a certain moment in history. Its force as a critical diagnosis of the present resides more in the *identification of normatively problematic tendencies* in modernity. To sustain it in a credible way, however, one would need an *historically plausible* account of a major change in the ways in which the various *problématiques* of modernity are addressed, a change that makes the self-cancellation of modernity likely. In the following, the basic elements of construction of such an account shall be sketched, even though in a very crude way. Despite this crudeness, though, the account aims to perform the two openings that were above presented as necessary for a revived critical social theory, the opening to political philosophy and to historical sociology.

The threefold commitment to autonomy and mastery that was discussed above is often seen as finding historical expression in the scientific and philosophical revolution, in the market and industrial revolution and in the liberal and democratic revolution. Any detailed analysis will show that justifications were given in and for those great transformations that at least partly resonated with the modern commitment to – individual and collective – autonomy and mastery. However, even while neglecting all historical qualification and comparison, we can state that none of the three events determined the others and, more particularly, that none of them can be regarded as having been brought about by the consolidated interest of a rising capitalist class, the *bourgeoisie*. How then, one needs to ask, assuming that Adorno's view has some validity, is it possible that a certain interpretation of economic modernity cannot only prevail, but also dominate over the others in such a way that self-cancellation threatens to occur?

The reasoning proceeds in three steps. First, a tendency towards self-cancellation can be diagnosed already with regard to individual aspects of the *problématique* of modernity. We may just take Marx's analysis of economic modernity as an example.[12] Marx accepted the commitment to autonomy as a background for the rise of capitalism, expressed in the liberation of economic action both as freedom of commerce and as freedom to buy and sell labour-power. However, he asserted that 'behind the backs' of the actors this freedom was undermined by the transformation of human relations into relations between things, between commodities. Reification of the world and alienation of the human beings from their own selves, from others and from the world are the result.

This diagnosis, however, secondly, does not offer any reason why such problematic development could not be halted or reversed within the context of a societal configuration, or in Polanyi's words, by virtue of the embeddedness of economic action. A belief in the balancing between the various *problématiques* of modernity was indeed held by the Enlightenment conviction of a harmonious unfolding of freedom and reason, and it was revived in Talcott Parsons's functionalist account of modernity in which the separate workings of the subsystems of society will provide an overall beneficial outcome. Despite his insistence that under capitalist conditions false consciousness held human beings in its grip and that institutionalised political action was reduced to the workings of the executive committee of the *bourgeoisie*, Marx himself saw a reversal of such epistemic and political condition as possible in principle, unlike Adorno, at least according to the predominant interpretation of the latter's writings. Between Enlightenment optimism and Frankfurt School pessimism, a conceptually more open perspective would hold that the various *problématiques* of modernity, even though all based on an assumption of autonomy, are likely to express themselves in different 'rationalities', to use Adorno's terms, and that there is no *a priori* reason to assume that those rationalities would be balanced by the working of some higher principle. Thus, the tension between the individual rationalities may give rise to an overall irrationality, as Weber and, following him, Adorno assumed.

However, thirdly, such lack of reconciliation does not necessarily entail the dominance of one rationality – in the case of these analyses, an individualist-instrumental one – over all the others. Conceptually speaking, the reasoning should keep pursuing the issue as one of an articulation between the various *problématiques* of modernity. In particular, any argument about the dominance of one aspect over the others would also need to give reasons for the weakness of those others. After all, it has been maintained until the 1970s, and not without practical results, that a political embedding of economic action is possible in the context of the European nation-state, on the assumption that the direction of regulatory action could be determined on the basis of rather certain knowledge about the common world to which one is referring.

The forms of knowledge in question were, in particular, a political philosophy that translated its conception of justice into ideas about a political community of

---

12 Similar critical analyses of epistemic modernity and of political modernity have been offered, by Nietzsche and Weber, for instance, but for the sake of brevity, we limit ourselves to this one example, which is most significant in the context of our discussion here.

responsibility, and a socio-economic theory that could balance apparently opposed interests in the framework of a broader theory of society and its development. The former was a compromise between a liberal and cultural-linguistic theory of the polity, and the latter the conjoining of Keynesianism with the sociology of modernisation. Such knowledge forms underpinned the democratic Keynesian welfare-state of the post-Second World War period. They were never beyond critique, and a detailed analysis of their operation is still needed at the time of their demise. However, their persistence and efficacy over a relatively long period demonstrates that action in common with reference to a world in common is possible even under conditions of advanced capitalism, or, in other words, that the commitments to epistemic and political modernity do not necessarily become completely subordinated to the capitalist interpretation of economic modernity.

This observation provides the key for rephrasing the question. If, and in as far as, there is nevertheless validity in Adorno's perspective, one would need to show how action in common with reference to a common world becomes more difficult under conditions of capitalism. A reasoning of plausibility for such difficulty to arise can indeed now be provided. The difficulties arise from the conjoined effect of two historical transformations in the development of European capitalism and democracy.

For the sake of simplicity, we assume that pre-capitalist, pre-democratic Europe was a rather stable world in which autocratic rulers defined the common and acted upon it as a master does in his household. The scientific and philosophical revolution, our historical shorthand for epistemic modernity, cast doubt on the stability of the world, partly in thought, but more significantly in experimental action. The market and industrial revolution, our historical shorthand for economic modernity, introduced a hitherto unknown idea of infinity into the way of dealing with needs. This idea, now mostly known as the profit motive, suggested the liberation of economic forces through formally free exchange of commodities on markets and, thus, inaugurated an accumulation-driven economy, which, in turn, found support in the means provided by science-enabled technology. In this combination of effects, persistent and rapid processes of world-transformation were inaugurated.

The liberal and democratic revolution, in turn, our historical shorthand for political modernity, gradually widened the free participation of inhabitants of a territory in the deliberation about the common matters to be dealt with in common. One can assume, *ceteris paribus*, that the widening of political involvement entails an increasing diversity of views about the common and about the rules to regulate it. The attempts at organising modernity from the late 19th century onwards can precisely be interpreted as a means to counteract such rising diversity while accepting the inescapable commitment to inclusive democracy (see Wagner 1994). The more individual human beings see themselves as 'unit citizens' with a stake of their own in the determination of the common; that is, the less they see themselves as tied into pre-existing networks of social relations held together by common values and beliefs (with those networks defining the boundaries of the polity itself or at least an identifiable sector of the polity), the more difficult will the deliberation about common matters become.

Considering these two processes together, the transformation of the world and the transformation of the political relations between human beings, and accepting them as by and large valid descriptions of the history of the past two or three centuries, the idea that an epistemic-economic determinism *de facto* reigns the world becomes plausible. The more problematic the creation of a relation to a common world and to particular others becomes, the more compelling becomes a relation to the world that focuses on the measurable and a relation to others that starts out from the individual atom, both relations joined together by an instrumental attitude. This view of human relations is not convincing as such, and theoretically it is flawed as many discussions in social and political philosophy have demonstrated; it is compelling, however, as a default view in the absence of attainable alternative views.

In addition, it becomes particularly difficult to avoid in historical moments in which the attainability of other views is extremely low. This was the case during the 1950s after life- and world-destroying deeds and events of unprecedented nature, and it may be so again at the beginning of the 21st century, after an era of rapid technological change and the extension of relations of exchange in terms of trade and of communication. The paradox of so-called globalisation resides in the fact that, on the one hand, the world was never as common as nowadays, the extension of relations having created potential community while, on the other hand, existing structures of communication about the common world – most importantly in the national polities, but also in the social sciences and philosophy – have been opened up, and uncertainty about the world in common has been increased as a consequence. Structures of collective self-determination at the global level, such as the United Nations, may then easily, even though erroneously, appear as a 'phenomenon of mere facade'. However, globalisation will need to be understood as world-making, as a dispute over varieties of possible modernities, now for the first time acted out on the global level. Such world-making takes the existing extended relations as a background, and it needs to institute a frame of reference for it, as a common world, with a view to creating possibilities to act in common.

In conclusion, then, it is important to retain Adorno's insight into the increasing difficulties to develop a valid view of the world in common, that is, an answer to the epistemic *problématique*, and the increasing risk that collective self-determination, the answer to the political *problématique*, will have only superficial effects on the common matters. However, while these difficulties indicate a strong possibility for the answer given to the economic *problématique* to dominate over the other two, there is no necessity for this to occur.

Despite the reasoning of plausibility provided above, a reasoning loosely rooted in historical observation over the past two centuries, the articulation of the relation between the *problématiques* of modernity remains a matter of historical contingency. Such contingency is ultimately inscribed into the modern commitment to autonomy itself. Thus, there is no endgame in the history of modernity. The 'endgame' is a known hypothesis of social theory, as a combination of rational choice theory and individualist liberalism, but also in the postmodern liberalism of Richard Rorty's kind in its affirmative version, and in Marxism and critical theory in its critical version. However, even if in the latter version the motive of alerting of an 'infinite catastrophe' that could be is understandable, such motive is ultimately nothing but the mirror image of the complacency of affirmative social theory.

In the light of the above recasting of Adorno's position, the possibility of 'infinite catastrophe' needs to be counteracted by an analysis of the possibilities to act in common with a view to reconstituting a common reference to the world terms under contemporary condition. Such analysis will require a social theory that is based on an historical sociology of changing configurations of modernity and that analyses the justifications for those varieties in terms of a political philosophy that is contextually sensitive in the sense of being aware of the empirically available justifications for each of those varieties. Adorno's position contains insights needed for such social theory that can be found neither in the rationalist-individualist and behaviourist-neo-positivist views of mainstream social science nor in the cultural studies that have taken much of the intellectual space held by critical theory at Adorno's times. However, on its own, it does not yet provide an easy access way to such a 'necessary philosophy'.

References

Adorno, TW (1974 [1958]) 'Versuch, das Endspiel zu verstehen', *Gesammelte Schriften 11: Noten zur Literatur*, Frankfurt/M: Suhrkamp, 281–321

Adorno, TW (1986a [1937]) 'Neue wertfreie SoziologieAus Anlaß von Karl Mannheims "Mensch und Gesellschaft im Zeitalter des Umbaus"', *Gesammelte Schriften 20/1: Vermischte Schriften I*, Frankfurt/M: Suhrkamp, 13–45

Adorno, TW (1986b [1949]) 'Democratic leadership and mass manipulation', *Gesammelte Schriften 20/1: Vermischte Schriften I*, Frankfurt/M: Suhrkamp, 267–86

Adorno, TW (1986c [1951]) 'Individuum und Staat', *Gesammelte Schriften 20/1: Vermischte Schriften I*, Frankfurt/M: Suhrkamp, 287–92

Adorno, TW (1986d [1952]) 'Öffentliche Meinung und Meinungsforschung', *Gesammelte Schriften 20/1: Vermischte Schriften I*, Frankfurt/M: Suhrkamp, 293–301

Adorno, TW (1986e [1962]) 'Auf die Frage: Warum sind Sie zurückgekehrt', *Gesammelte Schriften 20/1: Vermischte Schriften I*, Frankfurt/M: Suhrkamp, 394–95

Agamben, G (1995) *Homo sacer: Il potere sovrano e la nuda vita*, Turin: Einaudi

Beckett, S (1957) *Fin de partie*, Paris: Minuit

Boltanski, L (2002) 'The left after May 1968 and the longing for total revolution', May 2002 (69) *Thesis Eleven* 1–20

Hirschman, A (1977) *The Passions and the Interests*, Princeton, NJ: Princeton University Press

Latour, B (2000) 'On the partial existence of existing and non-existing objects', in Daston, L (ed), *Biographies of Scientific Objects*, Chicago, IL: University of Chicago Press, 247–69

Mannheim, K (1980) *Man and Society in an Age of Reconstruction*, London: Routledge and Kegan Paul

Wagner, P (1994) *A Sociology of Modernity*, London: Routledge

Wagner, P (2001) *Theorising Modernity*, London: Sage

Wagner, P (2003) 'As intellectual history meets historical sociology: historical sociology after the linguistic turn', in Delanty, G and Isin, E (eds), *Handbook of Historical Sociology*, London: Sage, 168–79

Wagner, P (2005) 'Social theory and political philosophy', in Delanty, G (ed), *Handbook of Contemporary European Social Theory*, London: Routledge

PART II

MONEY, WORK, PUBLIC POLICY AND ADMINISTRATION: CONTEMPORARY CAPITALISM AND ITS HISTORICAL TRANSFORMATIONS

PART II.

CHAPTER 4

THE MONETARY ISSUE AND EUROPEAN ECONOMIC POLICY IN HISTORICAL PERSPECTIVE

Bo Stråth

Politics is the process of prioritising values. Moreover, the market is not a non-value-based isolated sphere composed of rational maximisers. It is a social institution building on an intricate set of formal and informal rules, norms and values, and an entire set of scientific presuppositions about the nature of money, the market and the relationship between fiscal and monetary policy. Emerging as an historical result of both political and economic forces, the 'market' is not necessarily counterpart to politics (Magnusson and Ottosson 1997). Hence, the most certain division is not between politics and economy but found on the level of values: the neo-liberal idea maintains that initiatives and responsibility should be located within the individual. The thrust of the new emphasis on the market since the 1980s was a shift from the state to the individual as vessels of social responsibility (Stråth and Wagner 2000). Monetary regulation as the reflection of political implementation of values is the main argument in this chapter.[1]

Monetary regulation is, like social regulation, historically inscribed in states and in their international co-ordination and competition. The first major attempt to transgress national regulation was the gold standard. In the wake of growing free trade from the mid-19th century, the interest in stable exchange rates and predictability expanded. Many states attempted to emulate the example of Britain, the world's leading commercial and industrial power. Regional multinational currency unions and agreements based on gold were designed in the 1860s and a global scheme was considered. The Latin currency union (France, Belgium, Italy, Switzerland established in 1865; Greece joined in 1869) was based on gold and silver and the extent to which it functioned according to design is unclear. The Scandinavian currency union (Sweden and Denmark 1873, Norway joining in 1875) was based on gold. The dramatic, not to say tectonic, shift of the power balance that the Prussian victory over France in 1870–71 represented created the preconditions for the emergence of the gold standard more generally. The French indemnity payments to the new German Empire were calculated in gold. The French payments in gold made it possible for Bismarck to unify Germany also in monetary terms and to introduce the gold standard. Correspondingly, France was forced to leave bimetallism because of the changed value relationships between gold and silver. The French measures triggered a wave of transitions from silver to gold and the Scandinavian currency unions

---

1   I am most grateful to David Andrews, Lars Jonung, James Kaye and Peter Wagner for critical comments to earlier versions of this chapter.

should be seen in this framework. Gold became the universal gauge and value transposition for money. This was an order that emerged after a series of political decisions with the aim to regulate the monetary side of the free trade framework. The order emerged politically at a series of international conferences. At these conferences the principles were discussed rather than negotiated. There was no negotiated scheme but each country decided on the internal value of gold in terms of its currency. Through this definition in each participating country, a fixed exchange rate emerged to all other currencies that were defined in gold. Libertarians and ultra liberals regard the gold standard as a consequence of an order which emerged spontaneously without any signs of political guidance. However, as a matter of fact, not only the politically regulated free trade framework but also the changed power-political context, after the establishment of the German Empire, were factors that hardly can be seen as spontaneous.

As Karl Polanyi argued in his *The Great Transformation*, the 19th century order was based on the fiction of self-regulating markets with economic man as its master, rationally calculating individuals operating as utilitarian optimisers disentangled from social ties and responsibilities. On that point, capitalists and socialists were miraculously united. Ricardo and Marx, Bismarck and Lassalle, John Stuart Mill and Henry George and after them von Mises and Trotzky equally shared the faith (Polanyi 2001 [1944]: Chapter 2). Gold was the transubstantiate value representation of labour and capital – transubstantiate in the Eucharist sense of blood becoming wine.

It was a considerable achievement that the gold standard was established in the 1870s, despite the long-term economic depression that began in that decade, and triggered nationalistic rhetoric and protectionist politics with the gradual breakdown of the free trade order. Protectionism underpinned Karl Polanyi's theory of the social embedding of the economic forces analysed by Fred Block in the first chapter of this volume. The depression lasted until the 1890s when the armaments race in the wake of the nationalistic politics promoted protectionism and vice versa.[2] The impact of that race on economic recovery is not easy to estimate in quantitative terms, but it seems reasonable to assume a connection from the standard explanation of the recovery to protectionism, nationalism and the armaments race. The standard explanation refers to the discovery of gold in Alaska and the introduction of the cyanide process in gold production. More gold brought inflation and contributed considerably to the economic recovery. The question was where the expanding gold stock was placed. The never-realised alternative to arms production was social investments. The social issue was discussed since the 1830s with increasing intensity and conflict, but from the 1890s until 1914 it was in most countries ever more subordinated to the question of national strength through arms.

The gold standard had a clear and fixed regulation of the exchange rates. It was in a time which did not know financial politics in the contemporary sense and

---

2   Although the general trend was upwards there were cyclical fluctuations during the period from 1895 to 1914. However, the gold standard was maintained through the whole economic cycle until 1914.

state expenditures were small. As long as this situation lasted, the fact that the order did not contain any control of capital flows did not mean very much. However, it became a big problem when the First World War provoked a dramatic increase of state expenditures. The financing of the War with rapid monetary expansion dissolved the connection between national currencies and gold. Free trade politics created the monetary gold order. The order survived protectionism but War politics broke it down.

Nostalgic attempts to recreate stability and order after the War led to the reintroduction of the gold standard in the 1920s. The architects hardly realised the consequences of the expansive monetary politics and manipulation of state budgets during the War. The degree of state intervention in the economy was established at a level unforeseen before the War. The demands on the state and the capacity of the state to respond to growing demands imploded a second time in the 1930s when social protests required financial expansion in response to the Great Depression. The marching masses and the perception of them as a revolutionary threat 15 years after the Russian revolution was more than the rigidity of the gold and international agreements around it could resist (Eichengreen 1992 and 1996). This time the shift was definite. This was a second confirmation, after the protectionism of the 1880s, of Polanyi's embedding thesis (see Block, Chapter 1 in this volume). A counter-movement emerged to protect society from the expansion of markets. The developments from the 1870s to the 1930s demonstrate that the dynamics of the market fiction, despite their profound opposition to state intervention, consistently relied on the systematic and continuous use of the power inherent in the fiction of the state. The idea of a self-regulating market economy was, as Fred Block (*ibid*) emphasises, utopian in the sense of utterly unrealisable. The stabilisation politics based on the gold standard was in a certain sense an automatically working order but governed by state institutions.

The collapse of the world economy in the 1930s and the political responses to it as well as the imperatives that Second World War put on governments created new insights in the possibilities of economic regulation. An understanding of a clear connection between monetary and fiscal policies emerged. The crucial issue was the regulation of capital flows between and within states. The gold standard before 1914 was based on free capital movements and expectations about a stable gold and currency value that stabilised the order. The gold standard between 1925 and 1936 was based on currency controls.

So too was Bretton Woods when, after 1945, a new standard to create international stability and predictability was negotiated. The negotiations reflected the new power situation. The dollar replaced gold and the scheme agreed upon in Bretton Woods mirrored the strength of the USA. The experiences with gold resulted in a scheme with more flexibility to respond to monetary crises than was the case with the rigid gold standard. The dollar order was equipped with rules that allowed for adjustments of the exchange rates. However, as Dave Andrews has demonstrated, there was no compulsory control, and several questions must be raised concerning the extent to which Bretton Woods really was as cohesive a system as has been argued. From the very beginning, the order contained many contradictions reflecting the bargaining situation in 1945 with its power structure and the search for compromises that occurred under that dictate. The contradictions dealt in particular with tensions between the goals of capital mobility, exchange rate stability and national policy autonomy. These contradictions were not solved in Bretton Woods but built into the order (Andrews *et al* 2002). This is a retrospective view in the analysis of why the order collapsed. At the beginning some confidence, yes, even belief in the new monetary order emerged and lasted as long as did economic expansion in the wake of the reconstruction boom. This belief obscured the contradictions.

With the dollar as a gauge, although with limited commitments for its trustee, the West European countries established an order of mutual convertibility (1950–58), the European Payment Union, which was succeeded by the European Monetary Agreement. The dollar standard functioned reasonably well as long as the USA was a lender on global financial markets. In the 1960s the USA's status shifted to that of a debtor. Lyndon Johnson's Great Society programme and the Vietnam engagement dramatically changed the preconditions of the dollar-based regulation. De Gaulle exploited this situation with zeal. The peak of his campaign against the USA was probably when he threatened the Federal Reserve to change his dollar reserves for gold. The Bretton Woods order implied that the dollar ultimately, as a back up, was supported by a fixed exchange rate to gold, and the order functioned as long as nobody questioned this commitment in the same way a bank functions: as long as the depositors do not question its capacity to give them their money back.

Tensions emerged between the EEC and the USA in the 1960s in the area of monetary regulation. These tensions were parallel to the tensions in the security political field. There the questions emerged as to whether the USA was really prepared to redeem its promise to protect Western Europe with its nuclear umbrella. Didn't the intercontinental missiles make such a commitment dangerous for the USA? The 1960s were in many respects a turning point, not only for the Bretton Woods system, but for the whole international order established after 1945.

Against this backdrop, various plans for autonomous European monetary regulation emerged in the 1960s. These plans culminated at the EEC summit in The Hague in December 1969. It is an irony of history that when this happened De Gaulle, the most vehement adversary of the USA and the dollar, had left the scene, and the steps in The Hague were a massive rejection of his politics in other respects. In the strategy decided upon to enlarge the Community, and at the same time deepen integration, the summit initiated a process ultimately leading to the Werner Plan (October 1970) for a European economic and monetary union and the Davignon Plan for a European security political union.

Since its inception, the question of European monetary regulation has been contested and has undergone several important ideological shifts, from ideas of political management of the economy (somewhat improperly called Keynesianism), expressed in the formulation *economic and* monetary union, ideas which were about to develop into *dirigisme* when the Werner Plan was launched

(Skidelsky 1977; cf Stråth 1987), to more market-oriented views in the 1980s, and then to something more complex and ambiguous at the beginning of the 21st century. This shift was expressed through the reduction of the Maastricht union to just a *monetary* union without an economic political/finance political design.

The establishment of the European inner market and the European integration as a market project can at the first glance be seen as a disembedding project in the sense of Polanyi (see Block, Chapter 1 in this volume). However, the European market is, on closer inspection, more re-embedded than disembedded. The new market language in the 1980s was combined with the emergence of new institutions of social protection or the shift of the protectionist measures from the national to the European scale of governance. The Single European Act (SEA), which established the Internal Market in 1987, was a document imposing 279 new EEC rules and measures. It was an act of political standardisation and regulation, rather than some form of passive surrender to the market forces.

The Werner Plan for a European economic and monetary union drafted in less than six months after the summit in The Hague and agreed upon in 1970 by the EEC heads of state and government had a clear social element with its emphasis on employment guarantee and social politics. This 'EMU of 1970' was not only a monetary union but also an economic union including ideas of harmonised budget politics. What happened to this idea between the Werner Plan and the Maastricht Treaty, where the Union was seen much more in strictly monetary terms than in the Werner Plan?

The language of the Werner Plan seems in crucial respects to belong to another time. The fiscal policy and the political commitment to full employment were pronounced in the plan of 1970, as was the philosophy of political management of the economy. Today the emphasis is much more on monetary stability, stable currency rates, fiscal discipline and – eventually – a low rate of inflation. At the end of the 1960s, the welfare model was based on the state, seen as a national community of destiny, Fordist production methods and a certain basic belief in political governance of economies through fiscal and monetary politics, with many variations among countries, a belief which cannot be deduced from a cohesive 'Keynesian' theory, as already noted. The conflict level grew in the labour markets and the political language became radical and militant. Revolutionary language evoked memories of the 1930s. The European integration process had stagnated due to the effects of de Gaulle's policies. He resigned in 1969 as a consequence of political radicalisation. The tension with the US was obvious throughout the 1960s, although it was dampened by the rhetoric of the Cold War. This tension can be connected to the processes of de-colonisation and, later, to the Vietnam War. The tension reflected concern about the control of the economy nationally and globally.

National welfare arrangements and full employment guarantees were dependent on the functioning of the international economic order, and this was not least a matter of political power and control. This order was very much built on beliefs and these beliefs became weaker at the end of the 1960s before vanishing entirely during the first half of the 1970s. Around 1970, political leaders in Western Europe were on the retreat. They looked desperately for instruments with which they could regain the initiative. In this scenario, the EEC summit in The Hague in December 1969 was crucial.

The Werner Plan should not only be understood in terms of the economic rationality behind it, but also in its context of political power and prestige. The plan was an expression of the political effort to promote the old European dream of unification and fill it with new content adjusted to a new historical situation where the transatlantic tensions grew in the wake of the Vietnam War and the waning trust in the dollar and in American security commitments. On this latter point, the Werner Plan should be seen in relation to the simultaneous Davignon Plan for a European security political union.

The first EMU collapsed in the economic crisis of the 1970s. The oil price shock and the return of mass unemployment changed the framework and the preconditions. The 1970s saw the disintegration of an economic model based on mass consumption and mass production in a mutually reinforcing relationship, a model in which organised interests in most nations took part in some form of tripartite bargaining – with varying power relationships – that negotiated about the achievement of high economic performance and the distribution of the fruits of growth in productivity. While the patterns of interests and identities were much more complex than any that can be described by a purely tripartite (the state, the employers and the trade unions) scheme, the broad basis of social bargaining was ideas of trade union or employee interests and a solidarity of workers against employers and capital. The promoter of compromise formulae between conflicting interests was the state and the idea of national interests. When many firms in industries such as coal, steel and shipbuilding faced bankruptcy in the 1970s, these established solidarity and interest patterns changed.

In 1977, the MacDougall Report to the European Commission suggested a 'neo-Keynesian' strategy to bridge the economic crisis and the collapse of key industries. A serious attempt was made in 1977–78 to translate national tripartite bargaining structures, which had functioned so well during the era of economic growth in the 1950s and 1960s, to a European level alongside a politics of de-industrialisation in industries such as shipbuilding and steel. However, in the European bargaining about capacity reduction and layoffs, ties of solidarity between employers, trade unions and governments followed national lines rather than those of transnational sectoral and group interests (Stråth 1987 and 1996). The proposals in the MacDougall Report were never realised. In a certain sense, national interest and solidarity ties that eroded when local task forces for plant survival emerged were re-established around the negotiation tables in Brussels and a European pattern of interest and solidarity ties never emerged.

In 1977, the OECD published the McCracken Report with a different recommendation of action to confront the crisis than EEC's MacDougall Report. While the prescription of MacDougall was 'neo-Keynesian', McCracken was neo-liberal. McCracken's recommendations invested solutions and hopes in the market. The OECD's suggestion won the support of the governments, which meant a general breakthrough for market liberal government approaches, and the MacDougall Report was forgotten. The Werner Plan was stone dead long before all its stages were due to be implemented. The 'snake', later the European Monetary System and its Exchange Rate Mechanism, and other responses to the dollar's collapse absorbed the political energy.

The gradual abandonment of the convertibility principle (fixed exchange rates), and its gradual replacement by the goal of full employment in many countries was part of the framework conditions when in the wake of two oil price shocks high inflation undermined economic stability. There was a large increase in public debt in the 1970s and even more so in the 1980s. In the 1990s there was, against the backdrop of the budget deficits, an apparent shift back to policy preferences and behaviour reminiscent of the pre-1914 period. The concept of a 'nominal anchor' returned to prominence in the form of the inflation targeting adopted in several OECD countries (Bordo and Jonung 2001: 265).

The welfare state and mixed economy language was transformed into the market rhetoric when the new budget rigidity was politically legitimised. This transformation was a new oscillation in a centenary debate about the state or the market as the location of social security. The state and the markets can be seen as historical points of refuge in the social production of trust and confidence. Economic-political instruments are monetary and fiscal policies. The monetary and fiscal regimes jointly determine the stabilisation policy regime. The monetary and fiscal regimes are linked. The monetary regime is influenced by the rules governing the fiscal regime, and vice versa. Bordo and Jonung (2001) have studied the development of this interaction since the beginning of the 20th century, when fiscal policies in a modern sense emerged. They discuss responses to expansive monetary and fiscal policies, in two alternative scenarios, on the one side when the monetary and fiscal process was constrained by adherence to the rule of a fixed price of gold or some other standard such as the dollar, and on the other side when the price expectations were based on guessing the monetary and fiscal authorities' actions in a discretionary regime aiming at, for instance, stabilising the rate of unemployment. Their historical framework identifies two types of monetary regimes, one based on convertibility into *specie*, that is, on an ultimate source of liquidity and – one might add – transsubstantial value not under the discretionary control of the monetary authorities, such as gold or dollar, and the other based on *fiat*. The former prevailed in various guises until US President Richard Nixon closed the gold window in August 1971, thereby terminating the gold convertibility feature of the Bretton Woods order. Under a *fiat* money regime, or a paper standard, where the supply of money is under the control of the monetary authorities, which is the norm today, governments can choose either fixed or floating rates. Macroeconomic politics under *fiat* monetary standards is closely related to the conduct of fiscal policies as, for instance, in the case of war time inflationary finance, or, one might add (although not mentioned by Bordo and Jonung) combating unemployment (Bordo and Jonung 2001: 226–27; for Europe, Maes 2002; Gros and Thygesen 1998).

EMU deviates in several respects from the historical scenario analysed by Bordo and Jonung. The most important difference is that the Maastricht EMU does not have any fiscal policy at the same legal level as the monetary policy. The Growth and Stability Pact (GSP) has been added on to the EMU Treaty. On the other hand, the emphasis on monetary stability has a clear feature of convertibility, that is, fixed exchange rates.

Under still largely uninvestigated circumstances, the European Economic Community in the 1980s initiated the process of construction of a new confidence. This occurred through an adjustment to the new market language with the Single European Act (SEA); simultaneously, the internal market was seen as a new regulative level to control economic forces. Politics, which had been played down as powerless and become de-legitimised at the Member State level, returned through the backdoor at the European level. In this development, it was not easy to discern whether politics was seen as governing the economy or subjugated to it. There were contradictory views in this respect. However, the intensified European market integration in the 1980s can, as already emphasised, hardly be understood in terms of deregulation, but rather as a great reregulation project, and there was much more continuity to the project for a European political economy that collapsed in the 1970s than is assumed in the frequent arguments for a clear break between the 1970s and the 1980s. It could be argued that Jacques Delors infused new confidence in the old European project.

The SEA, and the process initiated by Jacques Delors, continuing with the Maastricht and the Amsterdam Treaties, can at first glance be seen both as a confirmation of the neo-liberal market language, with its emphasis on untied market transactions and, at the same time, as an attempt to regulate and control the unfettered Prometheus. However, the confirmation of the neo-liberal market language was tantamount to the confirmation of a very particular meaning of neo-liberal. Less than following the market language of American economic experts, it was the matter of an emphasis on monetary stability through budget rigidity, in particular inspired by the German government, an emphasis that had an affinity with neo-liberal theory but should not be mistaken for being identical with it (see below).

Europe has been moving towards a monetary union with perfectly fixed exchange rates. On the road to that end the Exchange Rate Mechanism (ERM) within the European Monetary System (EMS), established in 1979, was modelled after Bretton Woods, although not based on gold, but with more flexibility and better financial resources. It appeared successful in the late 1980s when Member States followed policies similar to Germany, the central currency country. However, the ERM broke down in 1992–93 in a manner similar to the collapse of Bretton Woods in 1968–71. It too collapsed for similar reasons, the combination of pegged exchanged rates, capital mobility and policy autonomy was overstretched. ERM collapsed in the face of massive speculative attacks on countries following policies inconsistent with their pegs to Germany as well as on countries that seemingly were following the peg rules, but whose ultimate commitment to the peg in the face of rising unemployment was doubted by agents in financial markets. The policy responses to the reunification of Germany were instrumental in initiating the breakdown of the ERM (Bordo and Jonung 2001: 258–59).

A major problem in the history of European economic and monetary integration has been the co-ordination of fiscal and debt policies. The stability pact within the EU is designed to bring about the fiscal discipline deemed necessary for EMU. The pact can be seen as a political attempt to establish a link between rigid fiscal politics and monetary rigidity.

The issue of budget rigidity should be related to the issue of a social policy as a mitigating dimension to disintegration in the wake of market integration. The social dimension returned in the 1990s, certainly diluted in comparison to the Werner Plan, but nevertheless coming back. Attempts by national governments to restore lost legitimacy activated the social dimension, although there was less co-ordination at the European level than that, for instance, the Werner Plan had envisaged. National pressures in the 1990s were transmitted to European regulation through benchmarking, and negotiation and co-ordination of standards.

An historical reading of the establishment of EMU seriously challenges the idea that there are two separate and well demarcated rationalities, one political and one economic, with simple hierarchical relationships in terms of dominance and subordination. Politics and the economy are integrated and entangled. Nothing demonstrates this better than the way in which the criteria for the GSP were determined. They most certainly were not deduced from any economic theory but emerged at the negotiation table under political definition of what is reasonable where the aim was to reduce the risk of inflation and where no interest in political redistribution was at hand in the context of the dominating market language. The breakthrough of the idea of a European Monetary Union a second time after the collapse of the Werner Plan must be seen in the political rather than economic context of the German reunification. The price for Mitterrand's approval of the *Wiedervereinigung* was that the deutschemark was changed for the euro.

The Werner Plan highlighted the non-monetary dimension of economic redistribution of resources through finance politics. There was the same terminology of the relation between the economic and the monetary in Delors's report on a European Monetary Union in 1988, which was implemented through the Maastricht Treaty in 1991, but the economic-political dimension occurred in a much more diluted language. However, the real monetary straightjacket came with the growth and stability pact, which was part neither of the Delors Report nor of the Maastricht Treaty. The GSP was negotiated later when it became clear that Italy might fulfil the criteria and join the club of the monetary union. Before the Maastricht Treaty, Italy was hardly perceived to be an original member of EMU. In particular, the German Minister of Finance (CDU) Theo Waigel was worried about lax budget politics and inflation, and was keen to establish rules to prevent such developments. The German monetary conservatism, based on historical experiences, aiming at monetary stability, imposed budget rigidity which, although having some affinity with neo-liberal theory, as has been emphasised, should not be mistaken for it. Against the backdrop of this German imposition it might be seen as an irony of history that some 10 years later it was the German (SPD-Green) government that together with the French conservative government began to undermine the GSP.

David Andrews has emphasised continuities in the Maastricht EMU from a specific viewpoint. Long before the negotiations of the Maastricht Treaty, the central banks of the Community's Member States had developed numerous informal practices regarding their mutual relations. In 1964 the Council of Ministers established the Committee of Governors of Central Banks of the Member States of the EEC. The work in – and influence of – the Committee of Governors demonstrates that, rather than being a neo-liberal project, EMU is based on monetary conservatism, supported in particular by Germany, and on the idea of institutionalised monetary autonomy and the fiction of the economy and the polity as two separate spheres (Andrews 2003).

The contours or, better, the potential of a social Europe emerged in the Maastricht EMU not as in the Werner Plan by redistributing financial politics, but in much vaguer terms through a set of social commitments. 'Social Europe' is by no means clearly defined but a concept full of various and contested meanings. The social protocol added to the Maastricht agreement (at this point not included in the actual agreement due to the refusal of the conservative British government to ratify any agreement which included general social obligations levied on the Member States) implied in one sense a breakthrough for a new European agenda, when a social dimension was added to the market language. However, in relation to the Werner Plan it was rather a matter of degrading. The social commitments increased in the Amsterdam Treaty of 1997, which included social priorities and obligations and, for the first time, a commitment to employment as a main political objective of European politics, although – it must be said – at 'as high a level as possible' instead of as earlier in the Member States 'full employment', indicating a lowered ambition (we note that the Lisbon summit in 2000 once again introduced 'full employment' as a prioritised political task). In Luxembourg in 1997, a fully developed European employment strategy was established.

Certainly, the new EMU drafted in Maastricht did not contain the economic political redistributive dimension with fiscal implications that the Werner Plan did. Or, better put, the fiscal implications were different; not welfare allocation but monetary stability was the dictate. It would be wrong to see the powerful position of the European Central Bank as the simple expression of neo-liberal politics. The situation was – and is – more complex than assumed. The territory of the bank continues to be contested.

Most certainly, the relationship between the social agenda introduced in the Amsterdam Treaty and the EMU is a complicated matter. However, from the Delors White Paper in 1993, which was developed at the EU summits in Essen in 1994, Dublin in 1996, Amsterdam and Luxembourg in 1997, and Cologne in 1999, as well as in the development of social dialogue between the partners, there was a slow emergence of a view which emphasises increased economic integration (SEA and EMU) as a precondition for economic growth, as well as for rising employment and a social Europe. This means that it is no longer possible to argue for monetary stability without looking at the social consequences of unemployment and social exclusion. This is certainly the most important effect of Amsterdam, which without doubt sets a new operational framework for the European Central Bank (ECB) and Monetary Union. Nevertheless, it also seems clear that politics must be translated into power. When Ireland and Portugal had difficulty complying with the stability criteria, they were immediately warned. Germany and France ignored every warning in this respect under invocation of political necessity. The conclusion is clear: regarding the European policy agenda today, European integration is a contested turf where different voices and different interests put different emphasis on either macroeconomic stability or employment and social issues. Legal rules are one thing; perceptions of and reactions to political pressures are another.

Hence, rather than a sharp and frontal confrontation between two conflicting views, and sharp discontinuities in development since the 1970s, a pattern of co-existing and competing tendencies emerges. Their mutual challenge to one another entangles them in a bundle of continuities rather than separating them into distinct phases, where only one tendency exists. There was a continuous tussle under social bargaining and redefinition of interests rather than sharp confrontation. In retrospect, we can see how the mutual strength of the competing tendencies changed. In the 1980s, the market language dominated in the framework of the political regulation and standardisation of the internal market, and in the 1990s the approach emphasising the social dimension and some form of collective responsibility and solidarity became increasingly vociferous. One indication of this shift in the 1990s was Social Democratic governments in a number of West European countries. Nevertheless, the point is that the two approaches perpetually presupposed and constituted one another. The other point is that the transformation in the 1990s in a more social direction was never a return to the situation around 1970. Such a return was impossible through the experiences of the market language in the 1980s, which in the 1990s were integrated in the response to new social challenges. On a more general level, it can be said that we can never walk backwards in history, but only retrieve and translate earlier experiences, under value deployment, into new contexts, where experiences are stratified on experiences, histories on histories.

The interaction between the two views, the market-oriented and the state-oriented, and the shift in their mutual strength occur under value transformation. In the 1980s, ideas of social discipline and punishment in the sense of Foucault emerged to the effect of a shift in their mutual strength. Budgetary discipline required new norms. State budget rigidity went hand in hand with individual market flexibility. This view no doubt represented other values than the welfare-capitalist solidarity. Both state discipline and individual flexibility were described in a Darwinian metaphoric language of competitive fight for survival. This was a different language from the ideas of general affluence in welfare capitalism (Stråth 2000). These norms of discipline and punishment continued to exert influence, even after the new shift in strength between the two approaches in the 1990s.

Since the 1980s, there have been two trends mutually constitutive and oppositional, the one towards a monetary unification through financial rigidity without distributive ambitions and with the GSP as the most distinct expression, the other towards a 'social Europe' (Maastricht 1992, Essen 1994, Luxembourg and Amsterdam 1997, Köln 1999, Lisbon 2000), emphasising redistributive ambitions, however, less in financial terms than in terms of equal standards and political co-ordination. The second trend is based on 'soft law', that is, it is less legalised than the first one. The single market and the Delors Report can be seen as attempts to bridge the two trends. Both deal with political regulation of the market. It is not that the first trend deals with an economic rationality and the second with a political.

The historical experiences provoke expectations and plural constructions of future horizons, but they by no means determine the future. Basically, there are three principal directions in which EMU can move:

(1) erosion of the growth and stability pact where each country employs expansive budget politics and the Maastricht criteria lose credibility. This would be a scenario with a certain similarity to the gold standard collapse in the 1930s although perhaps less dramatic and less violent;

(2) budget rigidity is maintained and triggers national competition with social standards, even social dumping *within* Europe; and

(3) accommodation of EMU and GSP and the role of ECB and the draft of new rules with a clear redistributive political dimension to respond to situations similar to those the German and French governments have experienced over the last few years.

I do not attempt to evaluate the probability of these scenarios, or a combination of them, but I want to emphasise them. The three alternatives illustrate the distinction Peter Wagner makes in this volume between disruption of existing and recreation of new community. Scenarios 1 and 2 are clear cases of disruption while scenario 3 can be seen as a conscious collective act of regulation by political means. Taken together they describe historical possibilities and options, and underline the openness towards the future and the variety of rationalities and kinds of entanglements of the political, the economic and the social. This is to say that what was maintained from the 1930s until the 1970s, that a political embedding of economic action is possible, in the context of the Member States is feasible and at the EU level at least as an option. The most recent trend seems to point towards a settlement through the open method of co-ordination, which is a very fragile institutional arrangement for these types of decisions. On the other hand, the experiences not only of the gold standard but also of the GSP demonstrate that legally binding agreements are not always final.

Regarding available options today, Europeanisation as well as globalisation should be seen as varieties of possible world-making and as dispute over 'varieties of the possible' to use Wagner's distinction in Chapter 3 of this volume. Openness means that history does not repeat itself in the insertion of the political since the experiences are interpreted in a new situation where the autonomous potential of the Member States (although not necessarily nationalism as ideology and rhetoric) has declined, that is, the preconditions have changed. Modernity is an issue of historical contingency rather than path dependency.

The verdict of the European Court of Justice concerning the GSP in July 2004 demonstrates the weakness of the pact, which on central points is vague and ambiguous and partly politically unrealistic. The attempt to fetter Prometheus through the pact has not been very successful to say the least. The whole construction was from the outset very fragile. The Ministers of Finance have failed to develop a shared view and neither do the Council and the Commission co-operate as the pact assumes. Neither has the dialogue between Brussels and the European Central Bank developed as expected.

It is difficult *not* to connect somehow the slow economic growth in Euroland as compared with other economic regions in the industrialised world, the failure to create new jobs, and the persisting mass unemployment to the lack of a European co-ordination between fiscal and monetary politics. In any case, the number of critical voices increases who consider an erroneously constructed monetary union to be part of the answer to the weak economic performance in Euroland. What initially was thought of as an instrument to prevent the Member State governments, in particular Italy, from operating with budget deficits, where the Commission was thought of as the guardian of the new economic thrift, and the ECB as the guardian of low interest rates, a mix which would guarantee growth and wealth, simply does not work. The German monetary traditionalists imposed their price when Mitterand deprived them of the Mark. The price was a lack of fiscal flexibility, which, in turn, is being imposed through political pressures through the backdoor, at the price of the erosion of the rules of the GSP.

The options for the future of the EMU and the GSP concerning the links between economy and polity have, as Feriel Kandil emphasises in her chapter in this volume, a clearly normative dimension. The normative question is what rules of action should be chosen for public policies to decrease the tension among principles of social justice and of economic efficiency. The answer to that question means giving values to concepts such as liberty, equality and efficiency (see Kandil, Chapter 11 of this volume).

What we possibly discern today is a pattern of a less cohesive EU under a less clear direction and government. The migration of power since the end of the Cold War from the Commission to the Council has lead to growing emphasis of the EU as an incremental bargaining process with the open method of co-ordination and bench-marking as tools. The EU has become less teleological and at the same time more complex. The EU seems to be more than just market integration, but what more and how much more is an open issue. The openness, in terms of future developments between extremes as collapse and tightening into a federation, has grown. Karl Deutsch and (neo-)functionalist perspectives of the gradual emergence of higher degrees of intensity through spill-over from the market integration also into social and redistributive politics is one possibility, but such theories function in principle only when looking back to past developments and do not say anything about prospects and future developments. What seems clear, however, is that whatever direction developments will take, politics and economics are interwoven. Moreover, as Kandil emphasises in this volume, the question goes beyond the embedding of the economy and involves normative issues. The question deals with the *good* public action which combines social justice and efficiency.

In the framework of this European development, the question is how social imagination could be created to enable new forms of political and economic co-ordination that would operate at different spatial levels, among them the European. The question is how to give the European economic integration a robust social embedding (cf Block, Chapter 1 in this volume). Is it probable that the governments with their open method of co-ordination and benchmarking will provide such a social framing of the market? How solid is that approach in the case of market failure?

What hope is there then for a new constitution of the EU with a social dimension? The first problem with that question concerns the realisation of an EU constitution at all. If so, it will not have much in common with a constitution in the proper sense of the term, namely those that emerged out of the French and American Revolutions as a model. The EU regulative and normative arrangements will, in crucial respects, remain at the intergovernmental level. There is little in the proposal which can be interpreted as a step in a federal direction and towards a European kind of stateness. The term 'constitution' has been the historical connotation of a constitutional moment of high condensation where all political forces unify in a decisive step and the helm is determinedly shifted in a new direction. The use of the term constitution in the EU debate today is far from that historical model. The social dimension of the new 'constitution' does not go beyond the achievements through the method of open co-ordination and it is not a guarantee of these achievements. It is difficult to see the references to the social dimension in the proposal for a European constitution as the social embedding to which Polanyi refers (Liebert 2004; Millns 2004; Joerges and Rödl 2004).

In Polanyi's view, corrections of social disintegration in the wake of economic integration came from social protest. The case in point is the assault of the masses on the gold standard in the 1930s. The necessity to integrate the protest provided new rules of protection and a new embedding. Polanyi's perspective is the history of the working class and their role in the construction of the national welfare states, but today there is no working class and the framework is not the nation state. The relevant question must be what protest potential there is today at a European and global level (for this question, see Bronzini, Chapter 10 in this volume).

In the shadow of the fall of the 'real socialism' in the 1990s, a new, young and extra-parliamentarian political left emerged. As opposed to the established left, the new movement is extremely anti-capitalistic and anti-liberal. They are vehement adversaries of globalisation as well as of both the EU and the USA. The utopian imagination goes in the direction of a society without power, market and classes. Widely different associations and movements are part of this protest, for instance the anti-globalists with Attac as the most prominent representative, anarchists, antifascists, antiracists, reclaim the street, pacifists, revolutionary socialists, radical feminists, Islamic fundamentalists, house occupiers, animal rights activists, Palestinian groups, and militant ecologists in the Friends of the Earth and Greenpeace. This protest certainly has much in common, but quite often these groups disagree. They lack a shared programme and most of them are also without central leadership and a stable organisational structure. What unifies is a deep aversion to the dominating economic and political system of the West, which is seen as the root of the global penury and the ruthless exploitation of the environment, of racism and oppression of women, of armament and war. The attack of 11 September 2001 was not an external attack but an internal system collapse, an implosion. The protest is radical in the sense that it rejects internal reforms of the system and requires something radically new. The rhetoric of the movement no doubt operates against the backdrop of a socialistic and communistic model, but at the same time the language is untheoretical and eclectic and it has nothing in common with the severe conceptual paradigm of Marxism. The movement is loose-living and receives considerable motivation from conspiracy theories, which describe a world governed by hidden power groups, for instance the multinationals, in particular the American oil companies, the neo-liberals in the World Bank and the International Monetary Fund, internationally operating media magnates, Jewish finance elites, neo-conservative fundamentalists and the EU bureaucracy in Brussels.

It is not immediately easy to see the moulding and formative force of these disparate movements, moulding and formative in the sense of Polanyi as creators of new social embedding. The common denominator can be described more in terms of anti than pro and the utopian imagination is without operative goals. It is, of course, feasible to think that such operative goals can come from the established order in imaginative attempts to integrate the protest, that is, the power of the protest would be indirect. Thus far we have, however, seen little of such imaginative attempts. Police protection – and, if necessary, police violence – has been the response. Political summits mediate the image of entrenched leaders taking shelter behind walls of steel and cement protected in paramilitary battles in the streets. The image is destructive much more than constructive. At the same time, the protest is widely seen as a rather marginal phenomenon. At the level of the EU and EMU, apathy and listlessness among citizens are much stronger expressions of the existing state of legitimacy deficit rather than vociferous protest.

The conclusions are clear: it is difficult to discern the imaginative re-embedding power in the sense of Polanyi because of lack of operative goals and canalisation of the movement's energy in clear directions against clear targets. On the level of specific parts of the protest, concrete goals might exist, but for the movement as a whole there is nothing similar to the class performance of the 1930s. The movement has had little avalanche effect which could broaden it to a mass movement. Using an historical analogy we could relate the protest to the 1830s rather than the 1930s. The 1830s was the time when the social issue emerged on the political agenda everywhere in Europe. Poverty was for the first time seen not in terms of individual blame and responsibility but as a societal and political question in the framework of the perceived systemic shortcomings of the emerging capitalist order. The protest that provoked growing attention to the social issue was multifold and in many respects well developed and well argued, although there was a lack of political organisation and theoretically elaborated counter positions. The connection of the contemporary protest movement to the EU and the euro is widely de-legitimising. From this point of departure, a strong theoretical and political position might emerge without the mistakes of the tight and rigid organisation that the Marxist protest ended in. The authors of *Europa, costituzione, movimenti sociali* clearly discern such a potential in the contemporary protest (Bronzini *et al* 2003; cf Bronzini 2003; see also María Gómez Garrido, Chapter 6 in this volume).

Through the Europeanisation of the jurisdiction, the money, the regional and agricultural policies, and the markets for commodities, services, capital and labour, social inequalities are increasingly generated and regulated at the European level. Perceptions of social inequality are no longer limited to the national arena. An important question is whether the emergence, interpretations and regulations of social inequalities is transformed by new centre-periphery structures in the EU of the 25. Thus far, there has been an obvious tension in the fact that the EU is an economy but not a polity, a market but not a state. The social disintegration in the wake of market integration cannot be matched by redistributive politics to adjust for inequalities however they are defined. This tension is in particular discernable in the EMU. Martin Heidenreich talks about a trilemma of enlargement, increased political co-operation and budgetary neutrality which might lead to either convergence of Eastern and Western performance levels or to differentiation of the regional income and employment situation in Central and Eastern Europe. The capital regions and the Western border regions in Central Europe are developing dynamically. The prospective consequences are a long-lasting prosperity gap between Eastern and Western Europe and increased regional differentiation within Central Eastern Europe. Such social differentiation has been obvious since the 1970s also at the core of Western Europe. Without redistributive political measures, the reproduction of long-established disparities might emerge. The fact that they are long-established is no guarantee against social protests and claims for a more equal distribution of welfare within the EU (Heidenreich 2003).

The social re-embedding impulses might come from the euro which, ironically enough, was invested with symbolic value to describe a unified Europe. The currency could easily become the symbolic target of a social protest as did gold. EMU and the euro remain for many an elite project which, however, in a situation when the ordinary man experiences harder economic living conditions and growing insecurity and uncertainty about the future, can easily take on symbolic value and express lack of legitimacy and polarising images of people against the elite. We talk here about popular, or populist, *perceptions* of the EU as ruled by an elite, whether financial, bureaucratic, technocratic or political. The debate about a democratic deficit in the EU feeds such perceptions where the contradictory popular reaction is less political power and responsibility to the EU level, that is, less redistributive capacity. There are other frequent popular perceptions: the EU as a peace project, as a market project, as a male-dominated project, as Fortress Europe, etc. Such perceptions both compete and overlap, and their mutual strength changes over time. They are decisive for the degree of allegiance and legitimacy invested in the EU.

In the situation of obvious social tensions, the euro has the potential of receiving symbolic power of quite a different kind than what was intended at its introduction. It is worth emphasising that in technical monetary terms the euro has probably more similarities with gold than with the dollar. Without a distinct redistributive financial power, the difference to national currencies is considerable and that point is probably the weakest of the whole construction and the potential trigger of de-legitimising protest.

Having said this, it should also be underlined, however, that this conclusion is no prediction or prognosis. Nothing is said about the probability of such developments. However, it would be politically unwise to underestimate the potential for such developments.

References

Andrews, DM (2003) 'The Committee of Central Bank Governors as a source of rules' 10(6) Journal of European Public Policy 956–73

Andrews, DM, Henning, C, Randall, C and Pauly, LW (eds), (2002) *Governing the World's Money*, Ithaca, NY: Cornell University Press

Bordo, MD and Jonung, L (2001) 'A return to the convertibility principle? Monetary and fiscal regimes in historical perspective: the international evidence', in Leijonhufvud, A (ed), *Monetary Theory and Policy Experience*, International Economic Association Conference Vol 132, Basingstoke and New York: Palgrave

Bronzini, G (2003) *I diritti del opopolo mondo*, Rome: Manifestolibri

Bronzini, G, Friese, H, Negri, A and Wagner, P (2003) *Europa. Costituzione e movimenti sociali*, Rome: Manifestolibri

Eichengreen, B (1992) *Golden Fetters: The Gold Standard and the Great Depression, 1919–1939*, Oxford: Oxford University Press

Eichengreen, B (1996) *Globalizing Capital: A History of the International Monetary System*, Princeton, NJ: Princeton University Press

Gros, D and Thygesen, N (1998) *European Monetary Integration*, Harlow: Longman

Heidenreich, M (2003) 'Regional inequalities in the Enlarged Europe' 13(4) Journal of European Social Policy

Joerges, C and Rödl, F (2004) 'Social market economy as Europe's social model', in Magnusson, Lars and Stråth, B (eds), *A European Social Citizenship? Conditions for Future Policies from a Historical Perspective*, Brussels: PIE-Peter Lang

Liebert, U (2004) 'European social citizenship: preconditions for promoting inclusion', in Magnusson, L and Stråth, B (eds), *A European Social Citizenship? Conditions for Future Policies from a Historical Perspective*, Brussels: PIE-Peter Lang

Maes, I (2002) *Economic Thought and the Making of European Monetary Union: Selected Essays*, Cheltenham and Northampton, MA: Edward Elgar

Magnusson, L and Ottosson, J (eds) (1997) *Evolutionary Economics and Path Dependence*, Cheltenham: Edgar Elgar

Millns, S (2004) 'Between hard choices and soft options: the gender dynamics of a European social citizenship', in Magnusson, L and Stråth, B (eds), *A European Social Citizenship? Conditions for Future Policies from a Historical Perspective*, Brussels: PIE-Peter Lang

Polanyi, K (2001) [1994] *The Great Transformation*, Boston, MA: Beacon Press

Skidelsky, R (1977) *The End of the Keynesian Era: Essays on the Disintegration pf the Keynesian Political Economy*, New York: Holmes and Meyer

Stråth, B (1987) *The Politics of De-Industrialisation: The Contraction of the West European Shipbuilding Industry*, London: Croom Helm

Stråth, B (1996) *The Organisation of Labour Markets: Modernity, Culture and Governance in Germany, Sweden, Britain and Japan*, London: Routledge

Stråth, B (2000) 'The concept of work in the construction of community', in Stråth, B (ed), *After Full Employment: European Discourses on Work and Flexibility*, Brussels: PIE-Peter Lang

Stråth, B and Wagner, P (2000) 'After full employment: theoretical and political implications', in Stråth, B (ed), *After Full Employment: European Discourses on Work and Flexibility*, Brussels: PIE-Peter Lang

CHAPTER 5

THE BRETTON WOODS AGREEMENT AS AN INVITATION TO STRUGGLE

David M Andrews

Monetary arrangements play a key role in regulating the political economy; so do financial arrangements. The first, broadly speaking, concerns the supply of money; the second its allocation. In this chapter I focus on the part played by international monetary and financial arrangements in restricting or facilitating political authorities' discretion over domestic economic policy.[1]

My focus is the Bretton Woods agreement, or more formally the Articles of Agreement of the International Monetary Fund (IMF) – the legal framework of the contemporary international monetary system – as negotiated towards the end of the Second World War. The significance of this agreement is probably evident to most readers, but it nevertheless bears underlining. The past half century has witnessed the greatest expansion of global trade and prosperity in human history. However, there have also been numerous and often sharp clashes, both within and across countries, about the division of these remarkable spoils, and more generally about the control of national and global economic forces. The practices of global money and finance sometimes referred to as the Bretton Woods system have been at the centre of many of these clashes.

Bold generalisations about 'the Bretton Woods system' are difficult to sustain for at least two important reasons. The first such reason, and the subject of this paper, is that the Bretton Woods agreement was, in important respects, internally inconsistent; this meant that some deviation from its initial premises was inevitable, although the form that those deviations would assume remained unclear. These internal inconsistencies were rooted in the plan's failure to come to grips with the long-term incompatibility of national policy autonomy, exchange rate stability, and international capital mobility – an incompatibility that had been at the centre of Karl Polanyi's analysis of *The Great Transformation* (1944). However, Polanyi was not alone in his views, many of which echoed mainstream economic thinking of that era. The chief negotiators of the Bretton Woods accord – Harry Dexter White of the United States and John Maynard Keynes of Britain – shared this same general perspective, and were largely in agreement about how the post-war international monetary order should resolve the associated policy trilemma. Their respective proposals, although differing on other matters, reflected this

1   I am grateful for comments on earlier versions of this chapter from Jeffrey Chwieroth, Benjamin J Cohen, Scott Cooper, Orfeo Fioretes, Eric Helleiner, and Andrew Walter, as well as the members of this project. Remaining errors of fact and interpretation are entirely my own.

underlying agreement. Nevertheless, the formal compact that resulted from their labours was considerably less coherent than either of their original plans, as this chapter demonstrates.

A second reason why generalising about the Bretton Woods system is difficult derives from the first: the inconsistencies within the original Bretton Woods architecture prompted different solutions at different times. The result has been a hodge-podge of practices reflecting an evolving framework for multilateral monetary co-operation more than they do any uniform 'system'; hence the difficulty in determining when, if ever, the Bretton Woods system 'ended'. Note that such leading scholars as Alan Milward, Robert Gilpin, Benjamin Cohen and Barry Eichengreen give different dates for its termination, underscoring the lack of agreement about what constituted the essence of 'Bretton Woods'.[2]

To help avert this confusion, I suggest that students of the period might fruitfully distinguish among three aspects of the post-war international monetary system conventionally referred to as 'Bretton Woods'. These are, first, the joint plans of Keynes and White; secondly, the actual text of the agreement signed in 1944; and, thirdly, subsequent practice. In this chapter, I address the first two of these aspects, leaving the third for another occasion.

The chapter examines the failure of the Bretton Woods agreement to provide a definitive resolution to the inherent conflict between the aims of exchange-rate stabilisation, national monetary policy autonomy, and capital account liberalisation. White and Keynes developed plans for the international monetary system that were largely convergent in terms of core principles regarding these matters; the text of the Articles of Agreement negotiated at Bretton Woods endorses most of their shared vision, but also diverges from it in important respects. The present study focuses on the differences between the formal agreement and the designers' original plans for it.

The Articles are complex and ambiguous; they embody rival principles subject to no easy resolution. They therefore constitute, as Edward Corwin once said of the foreign policy provisions of the US constitution, 'an invitation to struggle'.[3] As we shall see, the role of capital controls has been at the centre of this struggle. However, before turning to the text of the agreement and an exposition of this struggle, it is important to understand the historical and intellectual setting in which the Articles were negotiated.

THE HISTORICAL SETTING

There is a certain irony that the resort town of Bretton Woods has come to represent international co-operation in monetary affairs and in the management of the international financial system. It was not the woody isolation afforded by the Mount Washington Hotel but the parochial politics of national coalition

---

2   Milward (1984: 44); Gilpin (1986: 134); Cohen (1977: 90); Eichengreen (1996: 136).
3   Corwin (1957: 171).

building that determined the conference location. The timing of the conference was designed to finalise agreement before the November 1944 congressional elections, in which the Republicans were expected to make major gains; the location was intended to help woo New Hampshire's incumbent Republican senator.[4]

The very notion was audacious: convening an international conference to chart the institutional configuration of the post-war world while the outcome of the largest military conflict in human history still remained in doubt. The stated objective of this conference was to create a system that would permit national economic policy autonomy to co-exist with a great expansion in international trade.[5] Washington and London had publicly embraced these objectives as early as the signing of the Atlantic Charter; the two points were later married in the first article of the IMF charter. There a statement of 'the purposes of the International Monetary Fund' included the following:

> ... to facilitate the expansion and balanced growth of international trade, and to contribute thereby to the promotion and maintenance of high levels of employment and real income and to the development of the productive resources of all members as primary objectives of economic policy.[6]

Similar domestic objectives – especially full or near-full employment and income growth – had become the mantra of national economic policy in numerous countries, and in many cases either had been or soon would be adopted into the legislative framework of government.[7] Broad commitments for later trade liberalisation were undertaken during the war as well, often at American insistence, but these were more controversial. Concrete negotiations on post-war trade relations were considered too sensitive and potentially too divisive to be undertaken by allies in a desperate military campaign.

This calculation was probably correct; trade negotiations did begin immediately after the war's end, first between the US and Britain and later on a multilateral basis, and ended in the acrimonious collapse of efforts to establish an international body with authority to govern trade relations. The allies embraced trade expansion as a principle, but only at a high level of abstraction. This obfuscation helped mask divisions not only between the wartime allies but also within them.[8]

---

4   See Eichengreen (1996: 97, fn 7).

5   On the primacy of national stability, see Nurkse (1944: 10) as well as both the Keynes and White Plans. As for the trade component, the White Plan opens with the following statement by US Treasury Secretary Henry Morgenthau: 'It is generally recognized that monetary stability and protection against discriminatory currency practices are essential bases for the revival of international commerce and finance' (Horsefield 1969: 83).

6   The original IMF Articles of Agreement are reproduced in Horsefield (1969: 185–214); all further citations to them refer to this source.

7   For a discussion, see Gourevitch (1986).

8   On the post-war negotiations, see Miller (2000). The Havana Charter, which outlined the juridical framework for an International Trade Organisation, was signed but not ratified by the United States, where the Senate had become hostile to the concept; in its place the provisional Generalised Agreement on Tariffs and Trade (GATT) became the basis of post-war trade liberalisation.

On the other hand, it was believed that a monetary framework accommodating both trade growth and economic policy autonomy could be agreed upon during the war. Such a framework would lay the groundwork for the difficult trade negotiations to follow while at the same time serving an important public diplomacy function. On the latter point, the April 1942 draft of the White Plan argued that 'specific proposals' on the subject of a future monetary order 'will help win the war' by providing 'assurance that a victory by the United Nations [that is, the war-time anti-Nazi coalition] will not mean in the economic sphere, a mere return to the pre-war pattern of every-country-for-itself, or inevitable depression, [and] of possible widespread economic chaos ...'.[9]

In fact, both the British and American plans were aimed at least in part at undermining German propaganda efforts concerning the 'New Order' (the Nazi economic program for conquered Europe), which had a substantial monetary dimension of its own.[10] In the lengthy preliminary negotiations that eventually culminated in the Bretton Woods agreement, Washington and London were looking to cement the commitment of their own publics to the war, and to inspire their partners as well, by devising a mutually agreeable framework for the world's economic future – a framework that would compare favourably with the Nazi programme.

Preparations towards this end had begun as early as the summer of 1941, following the decision of the US government to demand an end to the discriminatory practices of the British empire; this was 'the consideration' received by Washington as part of the terms of the Lend-Lease Agreement. The British government immediately enlisted the services of John Maynard Keynes to draw up a proposal for postwar currency arrangements that would render this development on the trade front less threatening to the UK's fragile economic interests.

THE DESIGNERS' VISION

Washington and London thus began an extended bilateral negotiation on postwar monetary arrangements long before convening an international conference on the same. To summarise the two governments' positions, British negotiators hoped to avoid a return to the inter-war monetary system with its substantial biases against net debtors (a position that the UK seemed destined to occupy for the foreseeable future). US negotiators were sympathetic to this concern but equally determined not to permit profligate governments unlimited access to the resources of creditor states (as American negotiators imagined the United States would remain after the war). Discussions on the issue of international liquidity therefore remained divisive.

---

9   Horsefield (1969: 38). A somewhat cleaner version of this rationale was reproduced in the final, official version of the White Plan (Horsefield 1969: 84).
10 See the discussion and notes in James (1996: 34).

Nevertheless, on broad issues regarding exchange rate arrangements, currency convertibility, and the control of capital movements, the Anglo-American negotiations reflected a substantial degree of intellectual consensus, rooted in the shared experiences of the inter-war period, as the following passages reveal.

Beliefs about exchange rate stability

Unsurprisingly, there was a substantial consensus among economic experts on the deficiencies of the inter-war monetary order.[11] Exchange rates had been used during the inter-war years as instruments of discriminatory trade policy, particularly within Europe; there was therefore a strong bias against any framework that would permit this to recur. At the same time, fixed rates were suspect as the partial restoration of the gold standard was believed to have contributed to the Great Depression, and subsequently to the rise of fascism in Europe and Japan, in three related but distinct fashions.

First, the gold-exchange standard of the 1920s and 1930s had transmitted local economic shocks throughout the international system due to the system's core principle of absolutely fixed exchange rates.[12] Without any degree of exchange rate flexibility, adjustment to deficit-producing shocks could not take the form of raising the relative prices of tradable versus non-tradable goods.[13] Instead, deficit adjustment had to occur through reductions in national income through some other macroeconomic channel.[14]

Secondly, the monetary system had suffered from a general deflationary bias resulting from the asymmetry of adjustment obligations in the system. Deficit states had either to contract their economies or to leave the gold standard, but surplus states were under no offsetting obligation to expand their economies. The resulting bias towards deflation, like the transmission of shocks, was politically sustainable when national politics remained an elite-driven process and when public expectations regarding governments' economic responsibilities were relatively low. However, in the context of mass political parties and heightened economic expectations that had generally prevailed among developed states at least since the end of the First World War, and in some countries even earlier, neither of these system characteristics was politically viable.[15] The result was a growing instability within the system and susceptibility both to price shocks (as

---

11   On the war-time academic consensus regarding exchange rates and its subsequent breakdown, see Bordo and James (2001).

12   As explained later in this chapter, under the gold standard only gold holdings counted as international reserves; under the gold-exchange standard negotiated in 1922, foreign-exchange holdings could be counted as reserves as well.

13   So-called 'expenditure-switching policies'.

14   So-called 'expenditure-changing policies'.

15   Changes in the willingness of mass publics to tolerate deflation is a major feature of the analysis in Milward (1984), Eichengreen (1996) and James (1996). Rodrik (2000) incorporates it into a generalised schema or 'trilemma'. However, the concept figured in earlier analyses of international monetary relations as well (eg, Cohen 1977: 86–87).

was the case with commodities beginning after 1925) and financial shocks (beginning with the collapse of Vienna Creditanstalt in 1931).

This susceptibility to crisis related to the third perceived deficiency of the gold-exchange standard: its tendency to break down periodically, leading to trade protectionism. On the other hand, and regardless of the deficiencies of fixed rates, there was little stomach in either official or academic circles for an international monetary system based on genuine exchange-rate flexibility.[16] Flexibility meant discretion, and discretion was closely associated with discrimination – a lasting impression left by the Nazi experience.[17] The problem, then, was to establish a golden mean between excessive exchange rate fluidity and rigidity.

This certainly was the academic consensus, as reflected in an influential study of the inter-war currency experience commissioned by the League of Nations. Ragnar Nurkse was the primary author, but the League study very nearly represented a collective work – especially given the substantial efforts Nurkse made to consult with the leading lights of the economics profession.[18] Nurkse's main duty while at Princeton University was preparation of this report, to be based on lessons from the monetary experience of the 1920s and 1930s. The report was then circulated to the delegations at the Atlantic City meeting that prepared the formal agenda for the Bretton Woods conference.[19]

Thus, Nurkse's work represented the official consensus view of the economics profession regarding the relationship among national economic policy, international trade and exchange rates. In it he argued that the supposed benefits of both competitive devaluations and floating exchange rates were illusory.[20] The League study therefore rejected small and frequent changes in currency's parities, even if these could be internationally negotiated.[21] The objective should instead be a system in which parities would initially 'be made by mutual consultation and agreement' and subsequent changes would be rare. Importantly, exchange rates

---

16 This statement requires qualification; certainly the British team was more anxious to permit a limited degree of exchange rate flexibility than was its American counterpart. For example, see the discussion by Keynes in Horsefield (1969: 17).

17 The classic study remains Hirschman (1945).

18 Nurkse was certainly familiar with the views of the profession. He studied in Edinburgh and then Vienna, where he worked with Gottfried Haberler, Friedrich von Hayek, Fritz Machlup, Ludwig von Mises and Oskar Morgenstern. He then took a position with the League of Nations Financial Section in Geneva. With the advent of the war, that unit was moved to Princeton, where he worked with JB Condliffe, Marcus Fleming, Folke Hilgerdt, Jacques Polak and Louis Rasminsky. Note also that Chapter VI of the League study, concerning exchange stabilisation funds, was not written by Nurkse; on this point see Bordo and James (2001: 8).

19 Officially the United Nations Monetary and Financial Conference. In this context the United Nations referred to the wartime allies, not to the as yet uncreated institution headquartered in New York City.

20 Nurkse (1944: 115).

21 'Changes in exchange rates are likely to be more effective the less frequently they occur. Exchange stability should be the norm and exchange adjustment the exception' (Nurkse (1944: 225); see also (1944: 141)). It would not be until the 1950s, with the publication of Friedman (1953) and Haberler (1954) that sustained intellectual arguments in favour of exchange rate flexibility would be advanced.

'should not be altered by arbitrary unilateral action'.[22] Indeed, Nurkse argued that one of the failings of the inter-war system was the absence of a permanent forum for multilateral consultation. Consultations were an essential means to promote policy co-ordination and, in Nurkse's view, 'it was partly because of the lack of proper co-ordination during the stabilisation period of the 1920s that the system broke down in the 1930s'.[23]

White and Keynes did not depart from this orthodoxy, at least not in their official capacities as representatives of their countries. The proposals they put forward at Bretton Woods reflected the near unanimity amongst professional economists on the desirability of exchange rate stability.[24]

Consensus on capital controls

Controls on capital movements were central to the Anglo-American discussions, especially given the strong association drawn by most analysts between speculative capital movements and the exchange rate instability of the 1930s. As with exchange rates, the views of contemporary professional economists regarding the desirability of capital controls were relatively straightforward. Speculative capital movements – 'hot money' – played a central and wholly negative role in the League of Nations report. Nurkse argued that flexible currencies typically overshot their equilibrium values due to movements of speculative capital; furthermore, once stabilised at the wrong level there was no international mechanism for national authorities to undertake appropriate changes in a co-ordinated fashion.[25] The absence of adequate restrictions on capital movements had meant that when 'official controls stepped in to steady the exchange by one means or another' during the 1930s, the level at which they did so 'was often reached in quite abnormal conditions'.[26] In other words, the competitive devaluations of the 1930s were believed to have been driven largely by speculation.

In support of this contention, Nurkse quoted approvingly from Gottfried Haberler's 1937 warning that:

> When ... national policies cease to regard the maintenance of exchange stability as something which must take precedence over all other considerations ... speculation regarding the probable movement of the exchanges, and capital movements in connection with such speculation, are normal and inevitable.[27]

---

22 Nurkse (1944: 141).
23 Nurkse (1944: 117). In addition, Nurkse commented negatively on inter-war competition between financial centres, presaging Charles Kindleberger's (1973) and later Stephen Krasner's (1976) views on the desirability of a monetary and financial hegemon by some 30 years.
24 See again the qualification in fn 16.
25 Nurkse (1944: 116–17).
26 Nurkse (1944: 123).
27 Nurkse (1944: 131), quoting Haberler (1937: 431).

Of course, this passage admits of other interpretations, and Haberler himself famously revisited the subject some 10 years later.[28] However, Nurkse regarded the statement as supportive of his basic thesis that control of capital movements was necessary in order to reconcile exchange rate stability with national policy autonomy.

On this point, Keynes and White were in complete agreement.[29] As Keynes put it in 1942, 'control of capital movements, both inward and outward, should be a permanent feature of the postwar system'.[30] Elsewhere, he made the more general case: 'In my view the whole management of the domestic economy depends upon being free to have the appropriate rate of interest without reference to the rates prevailing elsewhere in the world. Capital control is a corollary to this.'[31] White enthusiastically agreed: 'A good case could be made for the thesis that a government should have the power to control the influx and efflux of capital, just as it has the authority to control the inflow and outflow of goods and of gold.'[32]

Based on this fundamental consensus, Keynes envisioned a system of controls that would be capable of distinguishing 'long-term loans by creditor countries, which help to maintain equilibrium and develop the world's resources, from movements of funds out of debtor countries which lack the means to finance them'. Controls would provide means 'of controlling short-term speculative movements or flights of currency whether out of debtor countries or from one creditor country to another'.[33] To this end, the British White Paper of April 1943 strongly advocated a system of capital controls that would mandate international co-operation. 'Control, if it is to be effective, probably requires the machinery of exchange control for *all* transactions, even though a general permission is given to all remittances in respect of current trade.' Continuing:

> ... such control will be more difficult to work by unilateral action on the part of those countries which cannot afford to dispense with it, especially in the absence of a postal censorship, if movements of capital cannot be controlled *at both ends*. It would, therefore, be of great advantage if the United States, as well as the other members of the Clearing Union, would adopt machinery similar to that which the British Exchange Control has now gone a long way towards perfecting.[34]

Keynes was not alone in this belief; White went even further. In his Preliminary Draft Proposal of April 1942, he argued that, as a condition of membership in his proposed Stabilisation Fund:

---

28 Haberler later became a leading voice in favour of exchange-rate flexibility; see footnote 21. On the evolution of his thinking, see the discussion in Bordo and James (2001: 12, 21–24).

29 Eichengreen (1996: 96, 97–98) argues that 'the White Plan ... foresaw a world free of [capital] controls', but this is not at all correct.

30 In Horsefield (1969: 13). This text was reproduced verbatim in the British White Paper of April 1943 (see Horsefield 1969: 31).

31 In Moggridge (1980a: 149).

32 In Horsefield (1969: 67).

33 In Horsefield (1969: 32), from the official April 1943 White Paper.

34 In Horsefield (1969: 31).

Each country agrees (a) not to accept or permit deposits or investments from any member country except with the permission of that country, and (b) to make available to the government of any member country at its request all property in form of deposits, investments, securities, of the nationals of member countries, under such terms and conditions as will not impose an unreasonable burden on the country of whom such a request is made.[35]

In other words, White recommended that capital movements be made subject to the approval of the sending state, that such approval be revocable by the state, and that if permission was revoked the sending state (not the individual or firm) would be entitled to both demand and receive the transferred capital assets.

Such draconian measures, White admitted, were 'far-reaching and important'. However, their 'acceptance would go a long way toward solving one of the very troublesome problems in international economic relations, and would remove one of the most potent disturbing factors of monetary stability,' namely speculative capital movements and capital flight. 'The search for speculative exchange gains or desire to evade the impact of new taxes or burdens of social legislation have been one of the chief causes of foreign exchange disturbances,' he argued. Thus, 'it would seem to be an important step in the direction of world stability if a member government could obtain the full co-operation of other member governments in the control of capital flows'. Such mandated co-operation 'does not mean that capital flows between foreign countries would disappear or even greatly subside; it means only that they would not be permitted to operate against what the government deemed to be in the interests of any country'.[36]

This proposal evoked immediate objections, principally from international financiers and elements of the central banking community. However, it was not until very late in the day that these objections gained traction within the Roosevelt administration, and hence I do not address them here. The central point is that Keynes and White saw largely eye-to-eye on the basic issue, as also did the vast majority of professional economists. Full freedom of capital movements was almost universally regarded by governments and their academic advisers as an expendable virtue at best and, at worst, an actual vice.

The tension between convertibility and liquidity

In both the United States and Britain, discretionary power over national monetary policy had become located in national finance ministries. This concentration created a potential for abuse, as even representatives of those institutions recognised. Finance ministry officials wished to maintain the autonomy they viewed as necessary to pursue demand-stimulus policies, but they did not want to destabilise the monetary and trading systems they were so carefully constructing; this would have been counter-productive. In addition, stable

---

35 In Horsefield (1969: 66). This text is from the April 1942 draft. The July 1943 publication adopts substantively the same position, but with somewhat clearer language; see Horsefield (1969: 96).

36 In Horsefield (1969: 66–67).

policies were believed necessary to ensure the minimal conditions for successful international policy co-ordination, hence the attractiveness of some form of external discipline on policy.

Convertibility of national currencies into gold and foreign exchange represented just such a form of external discipline. Convertibility meant that private individuals and firms could exit (together with their wealth) if national economic authorities proved incompetent or if the system proved injurious. Since there were no generally accepted alternative models for achieving discipline – as, for example, with more recent notions of targeting either inflation or the growth of bank reserves – governments were prepared to tolerate convertibility. There nevertheless remained a strong bias against any arrangement that would subordinate the national economy to international market forces, as had been the case under the gold standard.

Hence there was a corresponding debate about the forms that international liquidity (or official reserves) would assume. Convertibility and liquidity are indeed best thought of in tandem. The willingness of governments (especially of governments likely to run payments deficits) to convert *fiat* money into valuable reserves at fixed rates and upon popular demand was suspect at best. The credibility of these commitments hinged on whether and how these governments believed that they could acquire additional reserves (official liquidity) in a crisis. Put differently, convertibility is a less bitter pill to swallow when liquidity is abundant.

The same concerns had preoccupied negotiators at the international monetary conference of 1922 in Genoa, Italy. The solution adopted there had been to 'economise' on the use of gold reserves by permitting central banks to include foreign-exchange holdings in their reserve accounts; hence the term 'gold-exchange system' for the resulting monetary arrangements.[37] This decision resulted in a one-off expansion in official liquidity. However, as discussed previously, the system retained a general deflationary bias since net creditors could hoard their payments surpluses while net debtors had to choose between reducing demand in their economies or going 'off gold'. Some new arrangement was needed.

These concerns were central to Keynes's thinking. Keynes's general vision called for a plan that 'must operate not only to the general advantage but also to the individual advantage of each of the participants, and must not require a special economic or financial sacrifice from certain countries'.[38] 'Our British problem' of perpetual payments deficits status weighed heavily on his mind.[39]

In his formal proposal, Keynes argued for the Genoa formula of counting gold-plus-foreign-exchange earnings as international reserves, in order to avoid reliance on 'the technical progress of the gold industry' to determine overall

---

37 On the gold-exchange system, see James (1996: 18–19); and Cohen (1977: 84–89).
38 In Horsefield (1969: 20).
39 See fn 16.

reserve levels. To this the Americans readily agreed.[40] However, Keynes's next proposal was far more controversial. He advocated the creation of an international money, the 'bancor', as 'an instrument of international currency having general acceptability between nations'. In his view, this was the key to establishing a multilateral payments system, wherein 'blocked balances and bilateral clearings are unnecessary' as each state would balance its books against the system rather than against individual trading partners. The overall volume of reserves would be 'governed by the actual current requirements of world commerce, and is also capable of deliberate expansion and contraction to offset deflationary and inflationary tendencies in effective world demand'.[41]

Keynes thus envisioned a system of extensive balance-of-payments financing based on use of the bancor and the obligation of creditor governments to invest their surplus reserves abroad. To achieve this end, each member government would have a certain maximum limit, based on its overall volume of international trade, which neither its total 'credit' nor 'debit' position with the new institution ought to exceed. 'In the case of debit balances this maximum has been made a rigid one, and, indeed, counter-measures are called for long before the maximum is reached.'[42] However, 'in the case of credit balances no rigid maximum has been proposed'. Instead, creditors could limit their exposure only by limiting their payments surpluses – for example, by 'voluntarily curtailing their exports'.[43] Unsurprisingly, this suggestion did not satisfy the Americans.

The two governments also had divergent views for the new institution proposed to anchor these arrangements, as suggested by the rival names they proposed for it – Keynes's 'Clearing Union' and White's 'Stabilisation Fund'. Keynes had in mind 'to generalise the essential principle of banking as it is exhibited within any closed system':

> If no credits can be removed outside the clearing system, but only transferred within it, the Union can never be in any difficulty as regards the honouring of cheques drawn upon it ... Its sole task is to see to it that its members keep the rules and that the advances made to them are prudent and advisable for the Union as a whole. [Horsefield 1969: 22]

However, it was precisely the capacity to draw funds out of the system – that is, convertibility – that had obliged the members to 'keep the rules' in the past, and the Americans were unwilling to abandon this safeguard. The related questions of convertibility and liquidity were thus the greatest source of tension between the British and American teams in the pre-Bretton Woods negotiations, and remained a contentious subject at the conference itself.

---

40 Although this apparent agreement was misleading, as I describe later in this text.
41 In Horsefield (1969: 20–21).
42 Keynes's 'counter-measures' were the forerunners of what is now called conditionality.
43 In Horsefield (1969: 26).

BRETTON WOODS: THE NEGOTIATED AGREEMENT

The preceding passages outlined the largely shared views of the British and American negotiators with respect to most key policy issues. The agreements finally reached at Bretton Woods wove these elements into a more or less coherent whole – or at least they appeared to do so. The delegates endorsed policies aimed at exchange rate stability and currency convertibility in the context of a new system for the provision of official liquidity; they also endorsed individual states' use of capital controls. To insure compliance with these rules, to regulate the provision of official liquidity, and to provide a forum for the exchange of views and the promotion of policy co-ordination, they invented the International Monetary Fund and, as a partner institution, the International Bank for Reconstruction and Development (or World Bank). Finally, to eliminate rival forums that might be hostile to these objectives, they advocated the destruction of the Bank for International Settlements (BIS), the central bankers' club established in the inter-war period to facilitate repayment of German war debts.[44]

However, this description of the core agreements, although broadly accurate, is also somewhat facile. In fact, each element of this mosaic depended on every other element, and there was never clear agreement about the concrete meaning of certain key provisions. As a result, every element of the Articles was subject to challenge. Looking ahead, at one time or another every key feature of the agreement was to be either suspended temporarily or abandoned altogether.

In fact, the reliance on capital controls was challenged even before the conclusion of the conference, as was an apparent understanding between the British and Americans on the definition of official reserve currencies. Within a few years, the key tenets of the agreement on currency convertibility, the sources of official liquidity, and even exchange rate stability were effectively suspended. The IMF survived, but was never really able to perform its central statutory functions. The BIS survived as well, and central bank co-operation eventually re-emerged as a primary mechanism for international collaboration in managing the international monetary system – entirely in opposition to the designers' wishes. This, however, is to get ahead of the story of the negotiations, to which I now return.

Exchange rates: national discretion

The approach to international exchange rates agreed at Bretton Woods followed a logic similar to that of the proposals of Keynes and White. Exchange rates would

---

44 Resolution V at the Bretton Woods conference called for the liquidation of the BIS 'at the earliest possible moment'. This qualifying language may have represented British hesitancy to insist upon dismantling the BIS as a necessary precondition of the Fund's creation (as James 1996: 49–50 argues), or it may simply have been an implicit acknowledgment that the institution was at least temporarily out of reach in neutral Switzerland, surrounded by German-controlled territory (for this argument see Helleiner 1994: 53–54).

be both fixed (in the medium term) and flexible (in the long term). Thus, Article IV of the IMF Articles of Agreement held that 'the par value of the currency of each member shall be expressed in terms of gold as a common denominator' (section 1a). Furthermore, 'each member undertakes to collaborate with the Fund to promote exchange stability, to maintain orderly exchange rate arrangements with other members, and to avoid competitive exchange rate alterations' (section 4a). However, changes in the par value would be permissible, subject to the Fund's approval. Such changes 'may be made only on the proposal of the member', and only in order 'to correct a fundamental disequilibrium'. Finally, they could be undertaken 'only after consultation with the Fund' (sections 5a and 5b).

Thus, the Articles of Agreement established both the sanctity of a par value fixed to gold and an institutional mechanism for the alteration of that value when necessary. The key qualifying conditions were 'fundamental disequilibrium', which was left undefined, and 'consultation with the Fund'. The Fund was left with the task of making its determination without much further guidance from the text of the Articles – merely the admonition that 'the Fund shall concur in a proposed change ... if it is satisfied that the change is necessary to correct a fundamental disequilibrium'. However, the fund was expressly forbidden to 'object to a proposed change because of the domestic social or political policies of the member proposing the change' (section 5f). As for a proposed change in the external value of the national currency, the Fund's determination was to hinge on whether the disequilibrium occasioned by the existing exchange rate was likely to be self-correcting over the course of a normal economic cycle.

This formulation was consistent with the overarching commitment to national policy autonomy discussed previously. The national state had emerged from the First World War with a greatly expanded range of activities, and a correspondingly expanded set of expectations on the part of citizens regarding the delivery of safety and prosperity. In his early proposals for a reconstruction of the monetary order, Keynes had noted that these expectations – a 'craving for social and personal *security*' – would only be multiplied after the conclusion of the Second World War, and this analysis was widely shared.[45] Thus the verdict of the representatives of the mostly democratic governments assembled at Bretton Woods was unsurprising: to the extent that any trade-off existed, or was perceived to exist, between national prosperity and international market efficiency, national prosperity was to prevail. It was, after all, the government of Franklin D Roosevelt that convened the conference, a man who in April 1933 had ended the gold convertibility of dollars held by domestic residents and later proclaimed, during the proceedings of a World Economic Conference meeting, that 'the sound internal economic system of a Nation is a greater factor in its well-being than the price of its currency in changing terms of the currencies of other nations'.[46]

45 In Moggridge (1992: 654, original emphasis).
46 Cited in James (1996: 24).

The formula was clear: the welfare of individual states was not to be subjugated to the dictates of the international monetary system.[47] While exchange rate stability was the aim, individual governments retained substantial discretion about when a change in their currency's official parity was required. However, the negotiations about the exchange rate regime were also influenced by decisions regarding liquidity and convertibility.

Liquidity and convertibility: continued tension

As noted above, this subject had been the chief sticking point between Keynes and White during the years preceding the Bretton Woods conference. In the end, White's team rejected the bancor scheme and turned their attention instead to limiting US obligations for stabilising other countries' payments imbalances. Keynes eventually abandoned his call for essentially unlimited creditor exposure to net debtors and instead argued that the maximum liability of a creditor state should be the sum of all the other members' quotas.[48] Under the terms of the quota scheme he was proposing, this would have capped American liability at $23 billion; White's team instead offered $2 billion. The resulting compromise reflected the relative negotiating power of the two sides: the US obligation was fixed at $2.75 billion, and the total of all quotas at $8.8 billion (as opposed to Keynes's proposal of $26 billion). It was a bitter disappointment for the British and, ironically, a decision that would come back to haunt the United States during the 1960s, when suddenly the dollar came under market pressure. However, White insisted that this was all that could be extracted from a sceptical Congress on the verge of switching from Democratic to Republican (and isolationist) control.

On the other hand, the paucity of official financing on offer probably helped tilt the exchange rate negotiations in the British direction. I have already noted the 'fixed but adjustable' formula for parities; in addition, the Articles included a 'Scarce Currencies' clause[49] and provided for periodic reviews of quota assignments (Article III, section 2). Finally, the Article XIV ('Transition Period') permitted members an extended derogation of their general obligations under Article VIII during the postwar period. That period was left undefined except in

---

47 Note, however, that the April 1942 draft version of the White Plan held that supermajorities of the fund should be able to overturn any 'monetary or banking or price measure or policy ... the effect of which ... would be to bring about sooner or later a serious disequilibrium in the balance of payments' (Horsefield 1969: 68). In short, White contemplated a degree of 'multilateral sovereignty' (Horsefield 1969: 40) that the rest of the US government was not prepared to endorse. This suggestion disappeared from the final, official text of his proposals.

48 The Articles outlined a system of quotas, or the required contributions of member states to the IMF. Quotas could be filled partly in national currency but had to be held at least partly in gold or other member country currencies. A member's quota was determined based on its GDP; its voting power in IMF deliberations was proportional to its quota.

49 Under the terms of Article VII (Scarce Currencies), the fund could declare a currency to be scarce if it lacked sufficient holdings thereof, in which case it could authorise various measures aimed at increasing its holdings and permitting members to restrict payments in the scarce currency.

the form of admonitions that, 'as soon as conditions permit', members 'shall take all possible measures to develop such commercial and financial arrangements with other members as will facilitate international payments and the maintenance of exchange stability' (section 2). As it turned out, most European states would not find that conditions permitted undertaking this obligation for more than 10 years.

The dollar as an official reserve currency

The special reserve currency status conferred upon the dollar appears to have been the result of some deft parliamentary manoeuvring by White in his role as conference chair.[50] Keynes had understood that the formula from the Genoa conference of 1922 would be replicated: namely, that central banks could count their foreign-exchange holdings – *all* their foreign-exchange holdings – together with their gold assets in computing their foreign reserves. He does not appear to have become aware until the conference was nearly at an end that Article IV of the Fund's charter had granted the dollar a distinct status apart from all other national currencies.[51]

Thus, Article IV, section 1a holds that 'the par value of the currency of each member shall be expressed in terms of gold as a common denominator or in terms of the United States dollar of the weight and fineness in effect on 1 July 1944'. This special status for the dollar was the rhetorical basis for Charles de Gaulle's later charge that the dollar enjoyed an 'exorbitant privilege' in the Bretton Woods system. The truth is rather more complex; the role that the dollar eventually assumed in international monetary affairs had less to do with this formality than with the breadth and depth of the US financial system, as demonstrated by the continued leading role of the dollar long after the par system mandated by the Bretton Woods agreement had broken down. Indeed, in retrospect the dollar's special status contributed to the difficulties that US authorities later had in negotiating desired reforms of the Bretton Woods system, including a devaluation of the American currency relative to its major trading partners.[52] However, at the time of the New Hampshire meetings, no such difficulties were known or even contemplated. The episode did, however, exacerbate tensions between the British and American delegations.

Capital controls: weakening of the Keynes-White proposals

The key difference between the convergent elements of the Keynes and White Plans and the agreement actually endorsed at Bretton Woods concerned capital controls. Certainly the final Bretton Woods agreement retained elements of the anti-liberal consensus between White and Keynes on this subject; for example,

---

50 White's efforts to confer a special status on the dollar may have been intended to offset the US concession to the British on the Scarce Currency clause; see Eichengreen (1996: 98).

51 For a discussion of how this phrase was inserted into the Articles, see James (1996: 50).

52 See Gavin (2004).

Article VI provides that 'members may exercise such controls as are necessary to regulate international capital movements'. Such provisions led Keynes, shortly after the conference, to declare triumphantly that 'not merely as a feature of the transition, but as a permanent arrangement, the plan accords to every member government the explicit right to control all capital movements. What used to be heresy is now endorsed as orthodox'.[53]

However, Keynes's public remarks reflected a healthy measure of wishful thinking. As noted above, private finance (especially in the major international banking centres, New York and London) had strenuously objected to the plans of Keynes and White to impose a system of strict and potentially mandatory controls on the international flow of capital. These objections were eventually taken seriously by the White House.

The financiers' objections were generally of two kinds: principled and practical. The principled objections were vehement. It was one thing to suggest that the policies of the state should not be hostage to international markets; it was another thing to suggest that the financial interests of individuals and firms should be hostage to the state (or even to foreign states). This argument had considerable traction in the United States, and even within the Roosevelt administration – particularly following Republican gains in the 1942 congressional elections.[54]

So did the banking community's practical objections. Here the argument was that it would be difficult, if not impossible, to distinguish between 'productive' and 'speculative' capital movements, or for that matter even to separate out those transactions aimed at financing trade (which both Keynes and White regarded as the central purpose for reconstructing a genuinely international monetary system). The original proposals in both the US and UK plans were, on this view, unworkable. The provisions of Article VI noted above were therefore subject to an important qualification: the right to control capital movements could not be exercised in a fashion that restricted payment on current transaction (for example, trade). As the financiers argued that there would be no factual way to distinguish financial movements that were intended to facilitate trade from those with other purposes, this qualification was potentially far-reaching.[55]

Meanwhile, the British team was re-evaluating a key passage in the White Plan in light of precisely these sorts of practical concerns. The passage in question decried the use of 'such foreign exchange restrictions, bilateral clearing arrangements, multiple currency devices, and discriminatory foreign exchange practices *as hamper world trade and the international flow of productive capital*'.[56]

53 In Moggridge (1980b: 17).
54 For a summary of the objections of the New York banking community to White's proposals and the Roosevelt administration's response, see Helleiner (1994: 39–49).
55 Along similar lines, economists continue to distinguish between 'autonomous' and 'accommodating' transactions, but this is a theoretical distinction with no counterpart in any actual national accounting system. See the discussion in Cohen (1977: 20–24).
56 In Horsefield (1969: 86, emphasis added). This text is from the official, July 1943 version of the White Plan; but promoting 'flow of productive capital' had also been featured as a central purpose of the Stabilisation Fund in the original, April 1942 White Plan (see Horsefield: 46). Compare in this regard Helleiner's discussion of the topic (1994: 44–45).

Keynes had of course originally argued that the system for post-war capital controls should be able to make distinctions of precisely this sort – that is, between 'productive' and 'speculative' capital movements. However, the British government, backed by the Bank of England, had since come to fear – probably on the basis of arguments such as those being advanced by American banking interests – that maintaining such distinctions would become virtually impossible. As a consequence, the 'productive capital' clause might invalidate provisions elsewhere in the agreement authorising capital controls of any kind.[57]

What was the end result of this collision of rival concerns and understandings? In the end, the Bretton Woods agreement represented a compromise – a fudge, if you will – on the whole issue of capital controls. In deference to British objections, the Articles made no reference to 'productive capital' or to its promotion as an objective of the fund. However, in exchange, the passages concerning capital controls were very weak compared with those of either the Keynes or White Plans.

For example, Article VI (Capital Transfers) states that 'members may exercise such controls as are necessary to regulate international capital movements, but no member may exercise these controls in a manner which will restrict payments for current transactions or which will unduly delay transfers of funds in settlement of commitments' (section 3).[58] Any suggestion that co-operative controls would be mandatory was deleted. Indeed, Article VI makes no reference whatsoever to co-operative controls, and the only hint of mandated controls concerned the 'net use of the fund's resources to meet a large or sustained outflow of capital'.[59] Article VIII (General Obligations of Members) does make reference to co-operative controls, but purely in a permissive sense; such co-operation is neither mandated nor even encouraged. Instead, 'members may, by mutual accord, co-operate in measures for the purpose of making the exchange control regulations of either member more effective'. However, even this weak authorisation is subject to the proviso that 'such measures [must be] consistent with this Agreement' and explicit reiteration of the prohibition of 'restrictions on the making of payments and transfers for current international transactions' (sections 2a and 2b).[60] This hardly amounted to the sort of heresy Keynes later claimed the Bretton Woods compact represented.

---

57 Evidently the British did not come to this conclusion until early 1944, some two years after the phrase had been mooted in White's draft proposal.
58 The section includes exceptions relating to the Scarce Currencies clause of Article VII.
59 'The Fund may request a member to exercise controls to prevent' such usage of its resources; see Article VI, section 1a. This too represented a diminution of the Fund's right, in previous drafts, to 'require' rather than merely request such measures.
60 The only power provided to the fund in Article VIII to mandate action regarding capital movements concerned the provision of information, not the imposition of controls. Thus: 'the fund may require members to furnish it with such information as it deems necessary for its operations, including ... national data on ... known capital transfers.' However, even this provision was limited by the proviso that 'members shall be under no obligation to furnish information in such detail that the affairs of individuals or corporations are disclosed' (sections 5a and 5b).

CONCLUSIONS

That the IMF's Articles of Agreement failed to reflect the full vision of their chief negotiators should come as no great surprise. Accords of this nature are subject to multilateral negotiation and domestic ratification; both these forms of interaction are difficult, and compromises are to be expected.[61] Without concessions to the concerns raised by the financial community, the Bretton Woods agreement risked failure in the US Senate. Such concessions are a recurrent pattern of international life; the foregoing analysis has simply demonstrated how this pattern influenced the monetary regime formally agreed at the end of the Second World War.

To summarise those findings, the international financial regime envisioned by White and Keynes would have been enormously restrictive, with controls on capital flows that were to be biting, mandatory, and internationally controlled. This was a key element to complete their integrated vision of an international monetary system based on limited exchange rate flexibility, maximum national autonomy, full currency convertibility and limited multilateral financing. Instead, the Articles of Agreement reflected a much more ambiguous commitment to capital controls, and rendered the matter subject to national discretion rather than international mandate. This was a stark departure from the strong system of capital controls that the British had consistently sought, and that the US Treasury team had initially endorsed. However, it was the shape of things to come. Indeed, at a press conference held during the conference, White was obliged to declare that while other countries were at liberty to impose capital controls, 'the United States does not wish to have them'.[62]

The failure to endorse a comprehensive scheme for controlling capital movements, in conjunction with the limited resources of the IMF, combined to make the Fund almost irrelevant in the immediate post-war period.[63] European recovery required offsetting capital inflows to balance the continent's demand for everything from industrial equipment to consumer goods. However, in an environment of fixed rates, limited official liquidity, and ineffective capital controls, private capital flowed in the opposite direction – away from war-torn Europe and towards the safe haven of New York.[64] European states therefore refused to take on their Article VIII convertibility responsibilities. Even so, absent Marshall aid, the commitment to fixed rates would likely not have survived the 1940s. Indeed, it required a combination of the Marshall Plan, continued inconvertibility, a tightening of capital controls in Europe, a massive exchange rate realignment in September 1949 and, beginning in 1950, the multilateral

---

61 Putnam (1988); Milner (1997), including Chapter 5 on Bretton Woods and the International Trade Organisation.
62 In van Dormael (1978: 185).
63 This the League report had clearly foreseen: 'If, in addition to trade and other normal transactions, such a fund had to cover all kinds of capital flight, it might have to be endowed with enormous resources. In fact, no fund of any practicable size might be sufficient to offset mass movements of nervous flight capital' (Nurkse (1944: 188)).
64 See Milward (1984).

payments scheme of the European Payments Union before the continent's currencies were stabilised. Small wonder, then, that so many scholars choose to regard the post-1958 shift to European currency convertibility as marking the start of the 'classical' Bretton Woods system, since almost every aspect of the Articles had been violated at one point or another in the preceding decade.[65]

However, the international monetary practice during the 1960s also failed to correspond with the terms either of the Keynes and White plans, or the formal IMF agreement, and during the 1970s even the accord's central provisions about fixed-but-adjustable exchange rate parities were abandoned. For most scholars, this meant the end of 'Bretton Woods'.[66]

However, John Ruggie (1982), in an analysis heavily influenced by Polanyi, argues that the shift to floating rates in the 1970s, despite its violation of the procedural norms of the Bretton Woods pact, was in keeping with the agreement's substantive principles.[67] The argument here echoes his conclusions. The IMF was created to facilitate a massive growth of international trade while preserving the maximum degree of national autonomy. The rules outlined in the fund's Articles of Agreement have been regularly violated almost since they came into existence; those rules have nonetheless continued to frame international monetary collaboration efforts that have been quite successful, at least with respect to these overriding goals. Instrumentalities have changed, but the underlying objectives have not; indeed, many of the world's monetary crises have resulted from an unwillingness to distinguish between principles and instruments.

In retrospect, it would be surprising if a plan developed at the height of the Second World War had actually accommodated the economic circumstances of the next quarter century in every significant detail. Bearing this in mind, the ambiguity of the Bretton Woods legal order was a source of strength, not weakness. The Articles established an international monetary constitution of sorts, an overall framework for international monetary relations. They have functioned well as a set of principles and procedures, and rather less well as a collection of specific guidelines – guidelines that were in any case bound to be challenged by events.[68]

Instead, the formal agreement included enough discrepancies and contradictions to permit substantial differences of subsequent interpretation. In this sense, the Articles of Agreement truly were an invitation to struggle. However, these struggles have generally been contained in process and limited in objective. They have resulted in a set of practices that remain consistent with the

---

65 The term is Gilpin's (1987: 134); see also Keohane and Nye (1977: 74).
66 See again fn 2.
67 Ruggie (1982: 404–10).
68 For example, any effort at precise formulation of what constituted 'fundamental disequilibrium' drawn up on the basis of the circumstances and thinking of the 1940s would have looked archaic by the time of the monetary crises of the 1960s and 1970s. For differing views, see Cohen (1977: 91, 185–87) and Mikesell (1994).

primary goals of the signatories at Bretton Woods – that is, to promote trade while preserving autonomy.

These objectives were widely shared; the critical question in 1944 was how restrictive an international financial regime was required to realise them. IMF members were divided on this point, internally and with respect to one another; both beliefs and practices on this matter have since changed. Remarkably, however, the constitutional order agreed at Bretton Woods has proved sufficiently flexible to accommodate these changes while continuing to promote the underlying ambitions of its framers.

References

Bordo, M and James, H (2001) 'Haberler versus Nurkse: the case for floating exchanges rates as an alternative to Bretton Woods?', The Adam Klug Memorial Lecture, *Working Paper 8545*, National Bureau of Economic Research

Cohen, BJ (1977) *Organising the World's Money*, New York: Basic Books

Corwin, ES (1957) *The President, Office And Powers, 1787–1957: History and Analysis of Practice and Opinion*, New York: New York University Press

Eichengreen, B (1996) *Globalising Capital: A History of the International Monetary System*, Princeton, NJ: Princeton University Press

Friedman, M (1953) 'The case for flexible exchange rates', in Friedman, M. *Essays in Positive Economics*, Chicago, IL: University of Chicago Press

Gavin, FJ (2004) *Gold, Dollars and Power: The Politics of International Monetary Relations, 1959–1971*, Chapel Hill, NC: University of North Carolina Press

Gilpin, R (1987) *The Political Economy of International Relations*, Princeton, NJ: Princeton University Press

Gourevitch, PA (1986) *Politics in Hard Times: Comparative Responses to International Economic Crises*, Ithaca, NY: Cornell University Press

Haberler, G (1937) *Prosperity and Depression: A Theoretical Analysis of Cyclical Movements*, London: George Allen and Unwin

Haberler, G (1954) *Currency Convertibility*, Washington, DC: American Enterprise Institute

Helleiner, E (1994) *States and the Re-emergence of Global finance: From Bretton Woods to the 1990s*, Ithaca, NY: Cornell University Press

Hirschman, AO (1945/1980) *National Power and the Structure of Foreign Trade*, Berkeley, CA: University of California Press

Horsefield, JK (ed) (1969) *The International Monetary Fund, 1945–1965; Twenty Years of International Monetary Cooperation, Volume Three*, Washington, DC: International Monetary Fund

James, H (1996) *International Monetary Co-operation Since Bretton Woods*, Washington, DC: International Monetary Fund

Keohane, RO and Nye, J (1977) *Power and Interdependence: World Politics in Transition*, New York: Little, Brown and Company

Kindleberger, C (1973) *The World in Depression, 1929–1939*, Berkeley, CA: University of California Press

Krasner, SD (1976) 'State power and the structure of international trade', World Politics 28: 317–47

Mikesell, RF (1994) 'The Bretton Woods debates: a memoir', *Princeton Essays in International Finance 192*, Princeton, NJ: International Finance Section, Department of Economics, Princeton University

Miller, JN (2000) 'Origins of the GATT: British resistance to American multilateralism', Working Paper No 318, Jerome Levy Economics Institute at Bard College

Milner, H (1997) *Interests, Institutions and Information*, Princeton, NJ: Princeton University Press

Milward, AS (1984) *The Reconstruction of Western Europe 1945–1951*, London: Routledge

Moggridge, D (ed) (1980a) *The Collected Writings of JM Keynes, Volume 25: Activities, 1940–1944: Shaping the Post-War World, the Clearing Union*, Cambridge: Cambridge University Press

Moggridge, D (ed) (1980b) *The Collected Writings of JM Keynes, Volume 26: Activities, 1941–1946: Shaping the Post-War World, Bretton Woods and Reparations*, Cambridge: Cambridge University Press

Moggridge, D (1992) *Maynard Keynes: An Economist's Biography*, London: Routledge

Nurkse, R (1944) *International Currency Experience: Lessons of the Interwar Experience*, Geneva: League of Nations

Polanyi, K (2001) [1944] *The Great Transformation*, Boston, MA: Beacon Press

Putnam, R (1988) 'Diplomacy and domestic politics: the logic of two-level games', International Organization 41: 427–60

Rodrik, D (2000) 'Governance of economic globalisation', in Nye, JS and Donahue, JD (eds), *Governance in a Globalising World*, Washington, DC: Brookings Institution Press

Ruggie, JG (1982) 'International regimes, transactions and change: embedded liberalism in the postwar economic order', International Organization 36: 379–415

van Dormael, A (1978) *Bretton Woods: Birth of a Monetary System*, London: Macmillan

CHAPTER 6

WORK, EMPLOYMENT AND ACTIVITY: REFLECTIONS ON THE HISTORY OF A FICTITIOUS COMMODITY[1]

María Gómez Garrido

Karl Polanyi's ability to grasp the central problems inherent in capitalist societies makes his work indispensable for any contemporary reflection on the issue, and indeed one to which we need to go back time and again. His rich and insightful account comprises various significant theses, one of which has led to the foundations for the development of the institutionalist approach in economics. Polanyi emphasised that capitalism was not an economic system but rather a political form. A glance at the role of institutions such as the European Central Bank or the International Monetary Fund in the present context of global capitalism gives further credit to Polanyi's insight: capitalism has never managed to work as a pure market, since it needs the most rigid regulations.

In effect, Polanyi's reflection was even more radical. Almost anticipating the later constructivist approaches, he showed that there is in the economy nothing inherently natural or governed by immanent laws. It all depends on how we, human beings, organise our life. In that sense his work is most useful today, when we are witnessing a return to an orthodoxy in economics that pretends to represent the iron laws governing human life. As we are going to show in this chapter, in contrast to this recourse to an allegedly timeless order of things, the apparently static and ahistorical categories used in this discipline are in reality historically situated and have had very different meanings depending on the socio-political arrangements sustaining them. The constructivist approach places us in a position to reflect on the consequences of different historically constructed forms for our lives, and to reflect critically on our actions and projects.

Polanyi's second thesis was animated by this critical spirit. We owe him the most lucid reflections on the tragic consequences of capitalism as a system that commodified both the natural environment and human life. His reflections on the fictitious commodities placed this process in the context of concrete historical institutions and regulations, and it gave rise to a critical account of the consequences of commodification.

---

1   This chapter is part of a thesis project on the historical meanings of unemployment. In the process of this work I crossed paths with a diffuse network of women, partly based in Madrid: *precarias a la deriva*. The last parts of this chapter owe much to the discussions held with them.

This chapter focuses on one of those fictitious commodities – labour. In *The Great Transformation* (1944), Polanyi analysed the concrete historical moment in which labour was commodified, and the violence exercised over human life in this process. In his account of this historical process and of the reaction against it (the 'self-defence of society'), he launched a fundamental critique of the anthropological presuppositions of the liberal order, and especially of the allegedly self-sufficient individual. The Polanyian dependent subject, the social subject, is the axis of the reasoning of this chapter.

Here dependence is understood in two senses: at a macro-level, as the impossibility to conceive of an autonomous citizen without defining a series of rights and guarantees that enhance and make possible the realisation of her capacities (Salais 2003); at a micro-level, as the need the individual has of others. As I will argue, this need is manifest in so-called postFordist societies, which have been characterised in the sociological literature as fragmented and exemplifying increasing individualism. The centrality acquired by activities of communication, attention and care in these societies questions those assumptions. These two senses of dependence will be illustrated through a revision of the historically constructed forms of work in western societies over the last century.

The chapter has as its starting point the present crisis of work in its most evident sign, that is, unemployment. This crisis is frequently assumed as an inevitable consequence of globalisation and of the development of new forms of production. Against this economic (and technological) narrative, the chapter analyses the present crisis as the breakdown of a socio-political form of organisation, that of *industrial democracies*. In order to do so, the first part summarises two main movements in the history of labour in western societies. The first is a long political process that lasts from the 19th century to the 1960s. It starts with a conceptualisation of work as a commodity and an attribute of those who have no other option but to sell their labour power, while it arrives at a point in which work had become one of the main conditions of citizenship. In other words, we encounter a movement from *work* to *employment*. The second movement extends from the 1970s to the present, and it consists of a new conceptualisation of work as a commodity. We can call this process a movement from *employment* to *employability*. A review of these historical processes shows that *unemployment* is nothing in itself, but it is rather constituted by the socio-political arrangements around work.

The second part of the chapter explores some processes that have facilitated the crisis of work as it was conceived in industrial democracies and the consequent shift in policies from *employment* to *employability*. In general, this crisis is seen in relation to a weakening of the political critique of liberalism and economics. The attempt is made to relate this weakening of critique to the fragmentation of the social identities sustaining it, while also emphasising the problematic definition of work in industrial democracies constructed around a male breadwinner model of the family.

The third part of the chapter explores new emerging forms of activity in postFordist societies that are normally included under the rubric of *immaterial production*. It is argued that the specific characteristics of these activities present a good opportunity to rethink *work*. Additionally, their importance calls for a general reflection on what it is that we value in our societies. The chapter ends by pointing to alternative ways to enhance public acknowledgment of the importance of the above-mentioned activities for the reconfiguration of citizenship rights.

EMPLOYMENT AND UNEMPLOYMENT: A CONCERN OF ECONOMICS?

Full employment, one of the main objectives of European societies after the Second World War, started going through an acute crisis during the 1970s, when high inflation paralleled high unemployment. Having been both the main indicators of the well-functioning of national economies, their co-existence in high figures put an end to the up to then dominating paradigm. Consequently, monetary policies substituted for Keynesian demand-management, in the attempt to solve the problem of large public deficits.

Persistent unemployment brought new trends in economic theories. Attention increasingly shifted towards labour, in some cases with the explicit aim to put the *blame* on it. In a world perceived as an expanding market, the idea of *flexibility* became the new recipe for efficiency. In relation to the latter, public policies became concerned with the idea of *employability*, which targeted labour supply with the aid of a micro-economic approach. A look at the wider historical context makes evident that employability policies neither *create employment*, nor *reduce unemployment*, at least not if one applies previously held standards in one's judgment. The new policies were actually premised on a revision of the very conceptualisation of employment and unemployment.[2] Behind each economic category lies a political history.

The creation and stabilisation of the employment relation

Concern with unemployment emerged at the turn of the 19th century and it has accompanied us ever since. It is a problem that has never disappeared from the policy agenda and one could even argue that nowadays it has become a more obsessive policy target than ever before. Nevertheless, present policies of *employability* are completely at odds with the concern with unemployment at the turn of the century, and with the idea of *full employment* devised in the decades after the Second World War.

---

2   One of the main representatives of the institutional approach in economics reminded his colleagues of this some years ago. Being so concerned with their equations, economists sometimes forgot that unemployment had not been the result of economic processes. It was a concept historically created in order to cope with employment instability. Unemployment insurance, today identified as one of the causes of unemployment, had been created in the process of the concept's construction in order to deal with lack of work (Piore 1987).

Unemployment is one of various concepts invented in the process of dealing with the *social question* at the end of the 19th century (Salais *et al* 1986). The social reformers of the time engaged in a series of debates on poverty and the place of work whose roots can be traced back to the Enlightenment, and in which political economy and the Marxist critique played a fundamental role in bringing *work* to the centre of attention.[3]

Operating from a productivist perspective that attributed absolute value to wealth, political economists viewed poverty as an illness. Within this conceptual framework, material wealth became one of the main signs of the happiness of a country, and the target of the emergent discipline of political economy. In this formulation, work is a factor of production that, in the same way as capital and land, should be acquired freely. Its value derives from its capacity to become an abstract quantity, and it is in the process of circulation of its product, when work acquires its measure, in the form of *labour*. The texts by Adam Smith, Jeremy Bentham, or David Ricardo marked this fundamental shift in discourse, whose more immediate consequence was that labour became an area of strict regulation.[4]

In reaction to the liberal discourse, for Marx the worker produces *value* in the process of production. The normalising action of political economy, which blurred all distinctions between different crafts and occupations, became thus a political weapon through Marx's reflections. The importance of Marxist theory resided precisely in its connection between political and epistemological critique. By virtue of the diffusion of the Marxist language among the existing forms of social life and association in different countries ranging from craft organisations to popular forms of solidarity, it became possible to create a collective identity that founded the basis for the emerging workers' organisations.[5] The First

---

3   Work had acquired significance in Protestant territories since the 17th century. The Reformation exalted an ethics of work that was accompanied by a program to re-educate the able-bodied that fell into sluggishness. This attitude materialised in paradigmatic institutions, the workhouses (Dean 1991: 35–42; Zimmermann 2001a: 19, 20). The French Revolution (1789) opened a long debate in many European countries on the conditions for political participation that extended throughout the 19th century. The question was whether the Lockean formulation of property as the main condition for political participation could be interpreted – as the Chartists affirmed – as the ownership of one's labour power (Sewell 1980; cf Scott 1988).

4   The inclusion of labour in political economy had policing consequences over human life that we are still suffering from today. Given the concern of the discipline with mastery of a devised world of scarcities that must be reproduced and enhanced, the inclusion of labour in its equations could never bring emancipatory prospects for the workers.

5   This is a process that attracted the attention of a sociologist as alien to Marxian discussions as George Simmel. The author often considered as the founder of symbolic interactionism made these reflections on the processes that could link different working situations: 'united action is only possible when there is a variety of crafts at the same time that a *consciousness* of the unity of all the craft-trades arises, which transcends the specific differences between them ... As has been mentioned, the practical consequences of the formation of higher generalities [concepts, associations, etc] need not always occur in chronological order; frequently these generalities may, in turn, provide the stimulus, which helps to create a consciousness of social solidarity' (Wolff and Bendix 1955: 178–79).

International (London 1864) marked the constitutive moment of a new collective subject.

The workers' movement adopted a discourse based on an ethics that valued the activity of work performance taking place in the elaboration of a product. It praised *homo faber*,[6] clearly evaluating positively male activity.[7] This was coupled with the denunciation of the economic hardship of most of the working population, and of the instability of working life. The politicisation[8] of those areas of life paved the way for the debates in which the reformers approached the so-called *social question* at the end of the 19th century. The first creators of the term *unemployment* became thus concerned with a population that did work, but was still immersed in severe living conditions. This problem was perceived as one of political and social order.[9]

This is the spirit of the Versailles Treaty and the Washington Conference which, only three years after the October Revolution, founded the International Labour Organisation (ILO) (1920). The ILO has as its first explicit aim to define minimum standards for work performance and to safeguard at the international level the creation of a specific area of rights in the signatory states. The recognition of the Rights of Labour is put on a par with the recognition of human rights and constitutes a fundamental condition of citizenship.[10]

---

6 Méda (1995) has explored the tensions between the idea of work as self-fulfilment expressed by *homo faber* and the disciplinary visions of work *qua* obligation and as an element subordinated to the maxim of increase of efficiency.

7 The debate on the specific processes that excluded women from political and social life is long and complex. For some authors it is related to the process of industrialisation, for others to previously established patriarchal structures. A more processual approach that aims at identifying political action has analysed the language developed by the working class movement and its consequences for gender (see Scott 1988).

8 I am using Rancière's concept of *the political* as an action that breaks the common sense assumptions of the *police* [regulative] order, therefore rendering visible subjects marginalised by the hegemonic discourse.

9 Topalov (1994) studies this process in his *Naissance du chômeur (1880–1914)*.

10 One could attempt a comparison between the terms and objectives expressed in the successive meetings and conferences of the International Labour Organisation. At its foundational moment, the protection of labour through the establishment of an area of rights was its prominent objective: 'Considering that there exist working conditions that imply for a large number of people injustice, misery and privations; and considering the urgency to improve such conditions, for example in respect with working hours, ways of recruitment, the fight against unemployment ... considering that the adoption by any nation of a non-human regime of work puts serious obstacles to the efforts of the other nations in improving the condition of the workers, the contracting parts, moved by feelings of justice and humanity ... agree ...' (minutes of the Conference of Paris 1920). However, one decade later, the 1929 crash hit western countries, bringing about this time neither red flags nor romantic dreams, but an economic and technocratic discourse that became the axis of the ILO, changing completely its order of priorities: 'From now onwards regulating working conditions consists more in collaborating in the rational organisation of society than in protecting the worker against abuses. Such is, in sum, the objective proposed today in any economic and social discussion' (Report by Albert Thomas, Director of the ILO in 1933). The ILO was certainly not an organisation towards which the workers could turn to when the 1980s reforms hollowed out labour law, since in some cases it even led such reforms.

The link between rights of work and citizenship had a correlative in a corporatist vision of democracy: the need to include the workers' organisations in all decisions concerning labour regulations. Through a long process of struggle between the employers and the workers' organisations, a general framework for the conditions of work emerged in the middle of the 20th century. Paradoxically, that framework did not abolish dependence in the form of wage labour, but it rather made such dependence a general condition of the majority of the *male*[11] population (Méda 1995). The legislative reforms, however, improved this general situation: limiting the maximum hours of work, providing for paid holiday, penalising dismissals. At the same time, an area of protection was created for the worker outside the strict area of production ranging from health care to pensions. It is by this process in which a series of rights became attached to the wage earner and his family that the notion of work became a synonym of *employment*. The formation of an 'autonomous' subject as devised by liberal economics (a subject that can spend money during his paid holidays, borrow a credit from a bank, and buy a house) depended for most of the population on these series of rights attached to employment.

The concept of unemployment became increasingly stable in parallel with the establishment of the juridical lines of employment. The homogenisation of a series of activities through law established certain standards on a national level that were applied to most employees independently of the particular nature of their activity, skills and so on. This *generalisation* of conditions provided the basis for *equality* and the link between *employment* and citizenship after the Second World War. Employment thus became the basis of *inclusion* in industrial democracies.[12]

European industrial democracy was based on this political construction in which the stability of the labour contract became assumed, and the conflict

---

11 The emphasis on gender is mine and not Méda's. The *workers* were performing an activity yielding a product in exchange for a salary. All the series of activities that did not receive monetary compensation or which failed to realise a clearly defined product were excluded from this definition. This was the case of the activities realised by women in the domestic sphere (and following that logic, in some cases this exclusion applied also to domestic work). 'Working women' were subjected to special legislation, systematically considered workers of inferior status in the working centres. Outside the place of production (the factory, the workshop), those same women were never considered workers, but only wives, daughters and mothers. As a consequence, the female form of citizenship was derived from a woman's links with a family and it was not part of her individuality. We will analyse the consequences of this specific valuation of work in the last section of the chapter.

12 Several remarks should be made on this caricatured picture. First, and as this chapter wants to remark, this condition of citizenship applied only to the male breadwinner (who was considered a sort of *representative* of the other members of society through the family institution). Secondly, *equality* was certainly never achieved in absolute terms. Social stratification was actually recognised through the very same legislation that established different professional categories with corresponding different salaries. However, a general framework (in terms of working conditions, hours, and access to social rights) was established.

between labour and capital could move around the question of wages and contributions to social security. The macro-economic models of this time 'joined law to make possible the projection and intelligibility of homogeneous categories at the national level' (Gautié 2002). This institutional form sustained an idea of work and the worker that was also foundational for the industrial relations literature.

This process of homogenisation and generalisation of different activities delineated clear boundaries of the condition under which someone was *employed*. At the same time, the opposite state of affairs, that is, *being unemployed*, became also very clear to the public. It is under these epistemological and political conditions that *unemployment* became a *thing*, whose shape and *rate* could be easily measured.

Flexibility or 'freedom to work'

The 1980s witnessed the breakdown of the post-Second World War model. After the oil crisis, new theories of efficiency developed, introducing the idea of flexible production in order to cope with the uncertainties of an increasingly open economy. This idea was then also applied to labour.[13] Within this approach, the historical construction of employment was put to an end: blamed for *rigidity*, the new discourses tried to do away with old statutory rights linked with wage labour. The theories of efficiency that emerged in the 1980s charged labour as one of the main causes of the economic crisis. This accusation was based on an alleged non-correspondence of wages to productivity. In order to avoid future crises, it was necessary to increase the productivity of labour. In this way, this approach recovered a forgotten path in economic thought, namely the tradition represented by Alfred Marshall and the marginalists.

At the time of the first discussions on unemployment, Marshall developed a theory according to which unemployment should be studied by its causes which were identified at the micro level. In the marginalist approach, unemployment and low wages are the consequences of the low marginal productivity of each unity of work and the only way to solve it is by an increase in the marginal productivity of the worker. This theory, highly popular with some scholars but completely irrelevant for the social policies of the time, is paradoxically the dominant view one century later. However, labour productivity, which according to many authors, has done nothing but increase constantly, has become something more complex than it was a century ago.

Marshall pointed to the need to invest in education and training in order to increase productivity. Today, this is still a well-considered objective, underlying the theories on *human capital*. Nevertheless, the emphasis has shifted to making

---

13 See Stråth (2000) for a genealogy and case studies of the new flexibility discourse and policies applied to labour.

labour *adaptive* to changing needs. In other words, it is no more a question of forming a *highly skilled* worker, a sort of expert on a particular craft, but rather to make that worker *potentially skilled* for the changing nature of her craft. Such adaptability and continuous training certainly needs the active collaboration of the employee.

The new employability policies emerge within this framework. The First Chapter of the Directive Lines for Employment in 1998 proposes 'to enhance the capacity of professional insertion through four points that put their accent on the idea of opportunities and *incentives to search and accept a job or training'*.[14]

In an alleged struggle against unemployment, employability policies put their accent on the adaptation of labour, ideally putting an end to professional status. This idea of adaptation is also accompanied by the creation of incentives that envisage facilitating the participation of the individual in the labour market. Following the flexibility measures, new forms of contract are created: temporary, intermittent, internship. Many of these forms of contract break with the principles of labour law[15] and most of them are based on the elimination of any costs for the employers.

Participation in the labour market, no matter under what conditions, is presented as a social achievement. Employability policies thus operate through a reconceptualisation of *inclusion* that is completely at odds with the project of juridical protection of labour developed throughout the 20th century. They suffer from an amnesia that ignores that working by itself (that is, participation in the labour market) was never a guarantee of inclusion in a political community nor the source of the well-being of the citizens. This was something that became very clear in the beginning of the 20th century when the severe living conditions of the working population called for a rethinking of the practices related to economic activity. A variety of ideas were devised as a solution to those hard conditions, and the *invention of unemployment* was one of them. The present employability policies have maintained the word unemployment as one of their targets. However, the

---

14 Conclusions de la Présidence lors du Conseil européen extraordinaire sur l'emploi; cf Gazier (1999). The italics are mine.

15 They are the most visible signs of the breakdown of the idea of work that sustained industrial democracies. This breakdown has led to a shift in the discipline of sociology of work from an analysis of *industrial relations* to *employment relations*. In the new epistemological framework it is recognised that the forms of employment (that are now multiple – from temporary to part-time, passing by various forms of internship and even self-employment) can have a stratification effect, sometimes much stronger than the kind of occupation or activity realised (such as the traditional distinction between manual versus non-manual work) (Schnapper 1989; Maruani 1993). This approach is yielding rich results, and it has helped to renew the critical stance that originally underlined the industrial relations approach. Limitations of space, however, do not allow me to go through this literature.

purpose of these policies and hence the very meaning of the word have been reversed.[16]

The question is: how have we managed to arrive at this point? Many economists have their own answer: we have arrived at this point because the previous form of economic performance proved to be quite inefficient. However, it is difficult to talk about the more or less efficient organisation of economic activity when, as we have seen, the concepts used to define such efficiency – indeed unemployment itself – change to denote something completely different. In any case, the main concern of this text is to unravel how economics managed to impose its discourse as a self-evident truth, and to uncover the latent political processes behind this state of affairs.

THE DECONSTRUCTION OF EMPLOYMENT: THE WEAKENING OF CRITIQUE AND THE VANISHING OF A COLLECTIVE SUBJECT

In a long-term perspective, European societies have passed from the construction to the present deconstruction of a particular stable idea of work. The conceptualisation that sustained the model of industrial democracies after the

---

16 The first official definitions of unemployment in the Labor Bureau of Massachusetts recognised as unemployed only those willing to work but not below a certain wage (Keyssar 1986). In Germany, the definition of unemployment recognised also the situation of material need, following the previous assistance practices developed at the municipal level (Zimmermann 2001a). In Great Britain, the attempt by Beveridge (1907) to create an exact definition of unemployment aimed to put an end to casual labour, which for him was the main cause of poverty. In all these cases, unemployment was conceived as a way to devise a rule of employment related to stability, and a certain income. In other words, it was a concept inspired by the social debates related to the precariousness of the workers' lives.
Instead, according to the Fourteenth Conference of Labour Statisticians (1987), the unemployed is seen as someone who: (a) has not worked for at least one hour in the last week. Hence, if the person has worked even only one hour, he or she can be considered to be employed. This definition of employment is perfectly coherent with the idea of 'participation in the labour market' and at odds with the old idea of employment as a stable occupation; (b) is actively seeking a job. This condition has gone through various modifications in the last years that point to a normative project in line with the new liberal policies. The person should 'demonstrate' that he or she has taken active steps to search for a job. From 1987 onwards, registering in a public employment office is not considered an active step, whereas contacting friends, family or acquaintances or 'networking' is considered active. Any person without a job and simply registered in a public employment office is considered *inactive* for the Labour Force Survey. This definition is perfectly coherent with an economic definition of work as the contribution of an individual to the productive process taking place through the market. Strict filters are created to check whether the individual offers him or herself to the market.
It should become clear at the same time that these changes of meaning discredit any economic model based on the statistical linking of unemployment series. No matter how much effort the statisticians devote to adjust their series by passing certain portions from one category to others, it seems to me that the different historically constructed meanings are too heterogeneous to be represented in any mathematical formula.

Second World War entered into acute crisis in the 1980s. Here the attempt is made to link two arguments in order to understand the weakening of that model: one of a symbolic or discursive order, the other more typically sociological. The changes in discourse are thus seen in the light of social processes that result in metamorphoses of the social identities of the actors. I look at two discourses that had sustained the idea of work as stable employment, which have become severely undermined today.

First, we can observe a crisis in the general ideological configuration of western societies, constructed within a liberal framework, but in a continuous dialogue with the Marxist critique. This crisis is related to what Nancy Fraser (1997) has termed the *postsocialist condition*. Secondly, a crisis of a gendered definition of work, which sustained the division of roles rooted in the male breadwinner model of family, and which valued work only as an activity realised for production and in exchange for a monetary reward.

The postsocialist condition

In the last 15 years, there has been a shift in critical thought from questions of equity and redistribution to the problems of multiculturalism and the recognition of diverse identities. This shift has been animated partly by the end of the Soviet regimes, which for decades were a symbol of an alternative to capitalism.

It is a situation that reinforces a dynamic that had started with the 1968 movements, which were highly critical of the hardest modernist part of both social democratic societies and the Soviet model. These movements, characterised by what Boltanski and Chiapello (1999) identify as the *artist critique*, emphasised the idea of creativity and self-expression over standardised forms of work and production and an excessively bureaucratic state. This critique, as the authors show, has been later absorbed by capitalism pervading it with a *new spirit* that grounds the new forms of labour. It is easy to detect the arguments of the artist critique in the new management discourses that seek the active engagement of all workers and not only the directors and chief executives as was the case during the 1960s. The question today is how to make the worker, whatever his or her employment status and salary is, to behave like a 'manager' (Donzelot 1991), a state of affairs which has significant consequences for the intensification of working rhythms (Gollac and Volkoff 1996; Cartron and Gollac 2003).

The effect of such weakening of the political critique of capitalism became exacerbated by the emergence of new actors who fell out of the categories of representation corresponding to the already established modes of employment and who were unable to identify with the main speakers of that model, namely the unions. These new actors are mainly young entrants in the labour market and women. In Europe, these are the social groups that have been most strongly affected by the new deregulative measures. This has created a particular configuration of a segmented labour market in which the lines that separate the stable from the precarious sector are very close to the lines separating the organised workers from the new entrants. In this situation, a legitimacy crisis of the unions was inevitable.

Many of these new entrants, eager to have a job, have accepted a precarious situation, without creating much opposition. To put it in a simplified manner, the loss of rights for one group meant the acquisition of new rights for other social groups. Women and young entrants accepted the new forms of employment motivated by the still dominant value of *employment* as the basis of autonomy. Even if the job found in many cases did not provide the expected salary and social rights, at least it provided social recognition for the individual.[17] Thus, the role of this *industrial reserve army* is complex, given that many of these workers are not only motivated by the material need of a salary. They are rather embedded in the contradictions of the crisis of a social model and the lack of definition of an alternative one.

Being explicitly detached from official labour representatives, most of the new entrants in the labour market have not supported any critique of capitalism articulated along the discursive lines of the unions. This detachment is thus double: from the concrete definition of work that does not represent their situation (work as stable employment), and from the political representation of labour by the unions.[18] This detachment is particularly significant for women who are usually employed under precarious conditions, but also perform a series of activities that were never considered as work proper in industrial democracies.

Critique of the male breadwinner model

The struggles of the labour movement assumed the model of work envisioned by political economy: the activity realised in the market sphere and in exchange for a salary; in other words, the activity performed by male workers only. Many women also worked in exchange for a salary, but they were predominantly seen as holders of specific obligations in the household assumed as part of their gender. The reform policies of the beginning of the 19th century tried to limit the presence of women in the productive centres. The explicit family policies of the mid-20th century (Esping-Andersen 1990) reinforced a male breadwinner model that was almost never questioned by the unions.[19] Women were thus confined to an area and a series of activities that did not receive the public recognition achieved by the specific construction of work as employment.

---

17 This social recognition questions the literature on *the end of work*. It seems that work continues to be sought and highly valued (Moscoso 2002). The importance given to work can be observed, for instance, in the sociological literature on *transitions to adulthood*, which takes employment as one of the main conditions of adulthood.

18 Moscoso (2002) has thus characterised this *crisis of work* as a crisis of democracy.

19 Esping-Andersen has distinguished three different forms in which post-war welfare states were organised: the liberal Anglo-Saxon model, the social democrat and the continental/conservative (which in his later writings has been further divided in a continental and a Mediterranean type). It was only the latter which developed a full family approach. However, notwithstanding important differences, the *family wage* and the explicit exclusion of women from the areas of recognised work was a characteristic of most countries. In that sense, one can keep as a significant *datum* the explicit recommendations to avoid the employment of women and their elimination from unemployment figures in the Beveridge Report (1942).

Since the 1960s, a feminist critique denounced the unequal treatment received by women in so-called 'democratic societies' that were in fact deeply patriarchal. Women, officially recognised by law as citizens, were actually excluded from many areas of participation, given the difficulties to access employment imposed to them. This situation clearly placed them in an unequal status in relation to male citizens. The increasing desire of emancipation led many women to search for a job in the labour market. This was an option related to the images created in the long history of western institutions as described above. In a quest for equality, many women were thus pulled to the labour market.[20]

However, most women still undertook their previous obligations in the household. A more profound feminist critique challenging androcentric models emerged in the context of an increasing pressure for women to become 'professionals' (or recognised workers) and good mothers at the same time.[21] This critique has brought attention to a series of tasks performed in the households that were not socially recognised (under the hegemonic form of recognition, namely *wage labour*), and which were completely alien to the demands of the unions and the lines in which social conflict had been established in industrial democracy.

The centrality attributed to work as an activity realised for the market did not take into account other forms of activities without which the economy and social and political life could not be sustained. Attempting to make them visible, one of the feminist demands has proposed to include these activities in the labour force surveys and as part of the national economic accounts (Waring 1988). Their possible recognition opens a debate on the boundaries that define *work*, as explored in the third and final part of this chapter.

In sum, in the context of a discursive weakening of the critique of economic thought and capitalism, there have emerged new actors (young workers under the rules of precariousness, women searching for equality) who have detached themselves from the notion of work constructed in industrial democracies, and from their main speakers. In my view, the fragmentation of a potential critique of economic thought and capitalism has facilitated the imposition of the neo-liberal approach towards labour supply.[22]

---

20 During the previous decades, however, women belonging to families with low economic resources had always been in the labour market (that is, doing some job in exchange for a salary), but never enjoying employment status. Since the 1960s and 1970s, many women would search for stable employment (full-time job enjoying recognised rights), and not just some job. In other words, they would start searching for autonomy, in the way that western institutions had conceived it.

21 This question has encouraged thousands of publications on the conciliation between work and family life.

22 The only critique with a social content over two decades (since 1979 to the end of the 1990s) was the literature on *social exclusion*. As the negative term implies, this critique was symptomatic of the absence of a collective process through which a series of situations could be represented from within, instead of acquiring the label of an observer's diagnosis. The only social movement that promoted the use of this term was ATD-Quart Monde founded by the priest Joseph Wrésinki. Cf Didier (1996) for the various uses of the term.

THE ECONOMIC FALLACY IN MACRO AND MICRO PERSPECTIVES: WORK IN THE WORLD OF IMMATERIAL PRODUCTION

The new labour policies that seek to stimulate participation in the labour market become a real mockery if we analyse the circumstances of that peculiar form of *participation* for a large sector of the population. The term *working poor*, first used in the US labour market, can now also be applied to significant groups of the European labour markets. They are, namely, those who suffer the consequences of a strict economic definition of work, fully deprived from any rights. Their situation evidences that, beyond a question of economic hardship, the crisis of employment has consequences for citizenship and equality.

To the many political arguments that can be posed, economic orthodoxy replies in its mechanistic fashion that work is a scarce good that can only be provided by adequate 'efficient' measures (such as continuous training, or a level of wages related to productivity). Giving some rights to work would in the long run make it expensive and inefficient. Some technological narratives of postFordist societies have contributed to the creation of an image of work as a scarce good that becomes less and less required in a world of fast technological changes making labour increasingly obsolete.

However, is work really becoming so superfluous in postFordist societies? A close look at the kind of activities highly demanded seems to counter this assumption. Today, we can see the increasing relevance of certain types of activity that require some form of human work: from education to the provision of information to different forms of *care*. These heterogeneous activities are becoming the nodes of western capitalist societies in transformation, a process that has been described by some authors under the term *immaterial production* (Negri and Hardt 2000; Virno 2002). One characteristic of many of these activities is that they were in the past realised in a private/intimate sphere, but they have now become potential goods to be absorbed by the market process.

One peculiarity of these activities is that they in part were previously realised in a private/intimate sphere, but are now becoming potential goods to be absorbed by the market. We can think of the learning of a new language, but also of the capacity to be able to transmit affection, to listen, or to create new signs for communicating (Virno 2002). They share the characteristics of many activities previously realised by women in the household (defined above as *care* activities). Indeed, one could speak about the 'externalisation' of these activities – to use the economists' vocabulary – in the face of the increasing difficulties in their realisation encountered by some women and the weakening of family links.

Many different consequences arise from the centrality attained by these new forms of activity. First, their prominence serves to question the most pessimistic voices about the end of work (as if it were a good that we need to beg for). It seems that our societies can create many different forms of work beyond what one could imagine within a materialist framework.

Feminist groups have claimed the recognition of these activities as work for decades. Ironically, it seems that the value earlier produced in the family has started to be acknowledged and included in statistical accounts only when for many people they have become provided through the market and in exchange for a salary. According to some authors it could not be otherwise: the term *work* (*travail*) does not refer to any particular activity, but to the specific salaried relation created since the end of the 18th century. Additionally, the present demand to recognise as work other series of activities taking place outside the salaried relation (self-work, housework) tends to naturalise a concept that corresponds only to a specific historical and cultural context – that of western societies over the last three centuries (Freyssenet 1993 and 1994).

However, given the historical status of employment as the only main condition for the recognition of rights and social protection, is this attempt to present the most varied types of activities as work nothing but a legitimate demand to expand areas of protection and facilitate the inclusion of different groups in western societies?

The status of these activities, however, is problematic for many reasons. According to some authors, the activities performed in the household and broadly subsumed under the idea of *care* present certain characteristics that do not correspond to the traditional mode of thinking work. First of all, they are 'unproductive' in the sense that they do not yield a product. Secondly, the activity cannot be separated from the person who performs it. In that sense their performance always entails a relation. Seeing them as work would entail a certain reduction (Himmelweit 1995). From family to friendship and various forms of love, these relations were the centres of support, care and affection. Neither *homo oeconomicus* nor *homo faber* could be thought to be within the framework of those relations. Significantly, the disciplines and discourses that devised those anthropological models simply silenced those relations. *Homo oeconomicus* and *homo faber* act individually: the one does his solitary calculations, the other his artisan, solitary work. Both obtain something from their actions: a desired object, a product. The awakening of feminist thought allowed to evidence other forms of subjectivity and understanding of social relations that were fundamental even in our western capitalist societies.

The question then is: do these activities change their status when they are performed outside the domestic sphere? Or, in other words, does the salaried relation transform these activities into proper *work*? If this is the case, does the salaried relation subvert their meaning?

Indeed, some have raised voices of alarm at the expansion of this series of activities into the market sphere. This process could well be seen as a commodification of social relations, another form of colonisation of the life-world. These reservations are certainly justified, while the ambiguity characterising the consequences of this process makes the task of analysis even harder.

There is nevertheless an alternative interpretation of this phenomenon, as the expansion of these activities clearly indicates a demand of communication, attention, care and affection. In that sense, one can possibly arrive at an optimistic perspective: rather than signifying the triumph of the market over all other areas of human life, the prominence of these activities can be taken to prove the failure of the dominant models to adequately capture human action. Instead of the *homo oeconomicus* or the *homo faber*, we have a new 'dependent subject', a subject who needs care and communication. Many of these activities are actually a channel to facilitate social links, and in that sense they are based on an expansion of *sociability* and not on its withering.

Our western societies are overwhelmed today by paradoxes. At a moment where there is a general quest for autonomy by almost all subjects, the need of all those forms of support that political economy and even the Marxist critique had silenced becomes more and more visible. Thus, the importance of these activities not only questions the meaning of work, but it also challenges the anthropological and theoretical assumptions of economic man (Ferber and Nelson 1993) and the entire value system of the discipline of economics. In other words, perhaps we are getting too immersed in this technological and efficiency race to realise that we are desperately seeking many more essential things.

Should all these heterogeneous activities be considered *work*? Whether we call them *work*, or whether we start thinking of a better term to define them, it seems clear that time has come to give them some form of public recognition. However, if we keep in mind the reflections in the first part of this chapter, the need to recognise these activities entails the acceptance of the task to go beyond the actual form of precarious salaried work. As it was argued, doing a job or getting a salary is not a condition that guarantees inclusion or the well-being of the citizens.

Some recent proposals are being elaborated in order to renew labour law at the European level. These proposals are expected to show on the part of public institutions a social recognition of different activities pursued throughout an individual's life, including those 'socially useful activities', such as domestic work, but also volunteer work. Freed from the idea of profession and status, citizens should be entitled to embrace these different activities, performed under different statuses throughout their working lives (employee, entrepreneur, self-employed, or semi-independent worker) without forfeiting the continuity of their social rights. There is one necessary condition for them to be recognised though, namely that they must entail an obligation (Supiot 2000).[23]

Certainly, if we agree that activities such as improving one's education or taking care of one's grandmother are important, we should then also recognise them in the way our societies have organised the most valued form of recognition, that is, the entitlement to social rights that theoretically aims at facilitating democratic participation. We would not go very far if they are just transformed into some sort of a precarious job and it may be the time to start considering other forms of recognition beyond employment, which for decades also functioned as a source of exclusion.

Nevertheless, I am sceptical whether these proposals can acquire their full potential if they are not accompanied by a general politicisation of different areas of life. Technical solutions to policies are often insufficient, and sometimes even

---

23 I would think of the idea of commitment rather than obligation, since the theoretical implications following the adoption of each term differ significantly.

undesirable from the perspective of citizenship. Fortunately, at the turn of the century a political process making visible existing forms of life and the values and objectives shared by citizens and non-citizens has begun, despite being completely silenced by mainstream economic science. This text is indebted to them.[24]

References

Beveridge, WH (1907) 'Labour exchanges and the unemployed' 17(65) The Economic Journal 66–81

Beveridge, WH (1942) *Full Employment in a Free Society*, London: Allen & Unwin Ltd

Boltanski, L and Chiapello, E (1999) *Le Nouvel Esprit du Capitalisme*, Paris: Gallimard

Cartron, D and Gollac, M (2003) 'Intensité et conditions de travail' (58) Quatre pages (Centre d'Études de l'Emploi)

Dean, M (1991) *The Constitution of Poverty*, New York: Routledge

Didier, E (1996) 'De 'l'exclusion' à l'exclusion' (34) Politix 5–27

Donzelot, J (1991) 'Pleasure in work', in Burchell, G, Gordon, C and Miller, P (eds), *The Foucault Effect: Studies in Governmentality*, London: Harvester Wheatsheaf

Esping-Andersen, G (1990) *The Three Worlds of Welfare Capitalism*, Princeton, NJ: Princeton University Press

Ferber, MA and Nelson, JA (eds) (1993) *Beyond Economic Man: Feminist Theory and Economics*, Chicago, IL: University of Chicago Press

Fraser, N (1997) *Justice Interruptus: Critical Reflections on the 'Postsocialist' Condition*, New York: Routledge

Freyssenet, M (1993) 'L'invention du travail' 16(2) Futur Antérieur

Freyssenet, M (1994) 'Quelques pistes nouvelles de conceptualisation du travail' (Hs) Sociologie du travail

Gazier, B (1999) 'Employabilité: concepts et politiques' 67/68 MISEP POLITIQUES, Automne, Hiver

Gautié, J (2002) 'De l'invention du chômage à sa déconstruction' 46 (mars 2002) Genèses 60–76

Gollac, M and Volkoff, S (1996) 'Citius, Altius, Fortius. L'intensificacion du travail', *Actes de la Recherche en sciences sociales*, n 114, septembre

Himmelweit, S (1995) 'The discovery of "unpaid work": the social consequences of the expansion of "work"' 1(2) Feminist Economics 1–19

---

24 The 1990s saw the emergence of a series of movements that created a new language making visible and denouncing forms of precariousness in capitalist postFordist societies. Some examples are the group *chainworkers*, based in Milan, which tries to show the situation of the new proletarians of the 21st century (www.chainworkers.org), the movement of intermittent and precarious workers in France (www.cip-idf.org), and the group *yomango* (www.yomango.org) in Spain, which puts the accent on the forms of discipline created through the consumer norm. The Social Forums have become regular international meetings where different associations and networks are formulating viable alternatives to capitalism, and that place *the social* in the centre of discussion. Discussions on the characteristics of the new immaterial production and the place of care in our societies are linking different groups and creating important networks. One example of these reflections in Spain is *Precarias a la deriva* (2004). See also Bronzini, Chapter 10 in this volume, for the possibilities of creating more democratic channels, taking into account these social demands at the European level.

Jones, GS (1983) *Languages of Class: Studies in English Working Class History 1832–1982*, Cambridge: Cambridge University Press

Keyssar, A (1986) *Out of Work: The First Century of Unemployment in Massachusetts*, Cambridge: Cambridge University Press

Maruani, R (1993) *Sociologie de l'emploi*, Paris: La Découverte

Méda, D (1995) *Le travail, un valeur en voie de disparition*, Paris: Aubier

Moscoso, L (2002) 'Da operai a cittadini e viceversa: la crisi del lavoro nella prospettiva di due svolte di secolo' Anno LXIX – 2001/02. Nuova Serie A – N 53, 4 Studi Urbinati di scienze giuridiche, politiche ed economiche

Negri, A and Hardt, M (2000) *Empire*, Cambridge, MA: Cambridge University Press

Persky, J (1995) 'The ethology of *homo economicus*', Journal of Economic Perspectives 9(2) 221–31

Piore, MJ (1987) 'Historical perspectives and the interpretation of unemployment', Journal of Economic Literature 25(4) 1834–50

Polanyi, K (1944) *The Great Transformation*, Boston, MA: Beacon Press

Precarias a la deriva (2004), *A la deriva por los circuitos de la precariedad femenina*, Madrid: Traficantes de Sueños

Salais, R (2003) 'The risk of social dumping in Europe', paper presented at the workshop *A European Citizenship?* EUI, April 2003

Salais, R, Baverez, N and Reynaud, E (1986) *L'invention du chômage: histoire et tranformations d'une catégorie en France des années 1890 aux années 1980*, Paris: Presses Universitaires de France

Scott, JW (1988) *Gender and the Politics of History*, New York: Columbia University Press

Schnapper, D (1989) 'Rapport à l'emploi, protection sociale et status sociaux' XXX *Revue française de sociologie* 3–29

Sewell, WH (1980) *Work and Revolution in France: THe Language of Labor from the Old Regime to 1848*, New York: Cambridge University Press

Stråth, B (ed) (2000) *After Full Employment: European Discourse on Work and Flexibilit*, Brussels: PIE-Peter Lang

Supiot, A (2000) *Beyond Employment: Changes in Work and the Future of Labour Law in Europe*, Oxford: Oxford University Press

Topalov, C (1994) *Naissance du chômeur, 1880–1910*, Paris: Albin Michel

Virno, P (2002) *Grammatica della moltitudine. Per un analisis delle forme di vita contemporanee*, Derive Approdi

Waring, M (1988) *If Women Counted: A New Feminist Economics*, San Francisco, CA: Harper & Row

Wolff, KH and Bendix, R (eds) (1955) *George Simmel: Conflict and the Web of Group-Affilations*, New York: The Free Press

Zimmermann, B (2001a) *La constitution du chômage en Allemagne: entre professions et territories*, Paris: Éditions de la Maison de sciences de l'homme

Zimmermann, B (2001b) 'Work, labor, history of the concept', in Smelser and Baltes, *International Encyclopedia of the Social and Behavioural Sciences*, Oxford: Pergamon

CHAPTER 7

'ALWAYS EMBEDDED' ADMINISTRATION: THE HISTORICAL EVOLUTION OF ADMINISTRATIVE JUSTICE AS AN ASPECT OF MODERN GOVERNANCE

Peter Lindseth

INTRODUCTION

Legislation is not self-executing but is merely the opening gambit in a complex negotiation between state and society over the substance of regulation. Important normative decisions are made at the summit of the state, of course, in a process that itself entails significant political negotiation between public and private interests. However, once those general policy decisions are handed down, the difficult work then shifts to the administrative sphere. It is there that 'the rubber meets the road', so to speak, because it is in the implementation of specific legislative goals that the 'friction' of social and political resistance is generated. To reduce or override that resistance, the administrative process may effectively reformulate legislative norms in unexpected ways – the ultimate tribute, one might say, to the strength of diffuse 'governance' over hierarchical 'government'.

This chapter focuses on one such avenue of resistance and reformulation – what the French call *le contentieux administratif* – or litigation challenging the legality of administrative action. Through administrative litigation, private interests enlist judges in the counter-effort to check, or at least to participate in, the state's exercise of regulatory power. Given its potential impact on the effective content of legislative norms, the question of administrative justice has, unsurprisingly, been a contested one in the political and constitutional history of modern nation-states. This chapter considers the experiences of two such states, France and Britain (or more specifically England), from the 17th to the 20th centuries. Its perspective is admittedly 'top-down', limiting itself to describing the 'high politics' of administrative litigation rather than the ways in which social interests have, over time, resorted to lawsuits in their effort to control state action. (A micro-level social history of administrative litigation is certainly something that historians might usefully undertake.)

Within these self-imposed limits, the French-English comparison still presents a useful contrast because the elites responsible for articulating the model of administrative justice in each country generally defined their approach in conscious opposition to the other. The guiding idea behind the French system is *juger l'administration, c'est encore administrer* – 'to judge the administration is still to administer'. This phrase alludes to one of the most enduring principles in French public law – one dating, in fact, from the mid-17th century – in which the legal control of administrative action came to be understood as itself an aspect of administration over which ordinary courts should have no control. By contrast, at roughly the same point in history, the English Parliament explicitly rejected a similar effort by the monarchy to establish a non-judicial system of administrative justice. In England, the subjection of crown officials to the jurisdiction of the common law courts, like all other litigants, came to be regarded as a fundamental characteristic of the 'Rule of Law', in which the rights of private property and not the 'general interest' would predominate.

How these contrasting ideological premises were translated into institutional reality over time, however, presents an even more interesting comparison. Despite different ideological starting points, ultimately in England as in France the demands of administrative efficiency prompted a 'dejudicialisation' of administrative dispute resolution. But that is only half of the story. This effort eventually provoked a counter-process of 'rejudicialisation' which, although different once again in form, was arguably similar in its substantive aims, animated by a shared desire to subject official action to traditional norms of justice, whether enforced by common law courts (in England) or the increasingly court-like *juridictions administratives* (in France). As this reference to *jurisdictions administratives* suggests, the initial process of dejudicialisation was clearly more successful in France, leading to the creation of a separate system of administrative justice, at the summit of which sits the Conseil d'Etat. But this historical particularity in the French model should not be overstated; rather, the ultimate survival of the French system depended critically on its institutional separation from the 'active administration' – that is, from the bureaucracy responsible for actual policy implementation.[1] It further depended on the thorough incorporation of traditional notions and forms of justice into the substantive *droit administratif* over the course of the 19th century. The parallel attempt to dejudicialise administrative disputes in England would fail due to Parliament's successful assertion of supremacy over the crown culminating in the Glorious Revolution of 1688. Nevertheless, dejudicialisation would assert itself over the course of the 19th century, albeit *sub silencio* in tribute to the strength of the prevailing rule of law culture. By the early 20th century, with the dramatic expansion of the regulatory capabilities of the state, the ordinary English courts became more aware of reality and began to vigorously contest the preclusion of judicial review of administrative action. Ultimately, English judges were forced to accept separate forms of administrative justice but only after Parliament inscribed in law the general right of appeal to the judicial courts in administrative disputes. Thus, the essence of the old rule of law system was retained.

The broad convergence in the French and English systems, despite their formal differences, is not coincidental. Rather it is directly linked, I would suggest, to the central topic of this volume: the political construction of modern capitalism, particularly through the agency of the state. Dejudicialisation and rejudicialisation of administrative justice are a legal manifestation of the more general 'double movement' described by Karl Polanyi in his classic work on the

1   The definitive history of this process remains Chevallier (1970).

political-historical development of the market economy, *The Great Transformation* (2001 [1944]). Rather than creating a 'self-regulating' market economy by removing it from overtly political control – Polanyi's thesis – dejudicialisation was a political effort to create, in effect, a 'self-regulating' administrative sphere disembedded from traditional values of justice, guided by its own sense of policy rationality and its own estimation of the public interest in the construction and regulation of the market. Rejudicialisation, on the other hand, tracked the political process of 're-embedding' the economy; that is, like the more general 'counter-movement' of which it was a part, rejudicialisation was a concrete expression of the cultural belief that administration, no less than the market economy itself, must remain 'always embedded' in the values of justice and legitimacy inherited from the past.

I will return to this argument later in the chapter. At this point, however, it is useful to note another aspect of Polanyi's thesis that complements my own – one that may shed light on the relationship between the 'varieties of capitalism' and its legal-historical counterpart, the 'varieties of administration'. In *The Great Transformation*, Polanyi effectively claims that the state has served as a neutral instrument, equally available to the 'movement' and the 'counter-movement'.[2] The comparative history of administrative justice in France and England provides some additional support for what we might call the 'state-neutrality thesis'. In France, the effort to dejudicialise administrative justice was directly tied to the movement (state-led in the French case) to construct a national market economy over the course of the 17th to the 19th centuries, whereas in England the effort to dejudicialise would only be taken up in earnest with the emergence of the 'Social State' at the end of the 19th and beginning of the 20th centuries. Although this later quest for dejudicialisation in England would also reflect a desire to make the state a more effective agent of social intervention, that intervention would now be aimed at excluding the judicial courts because they were perceived as excessively attached to prerogatives of *laissez-faire* rather than ancient corporatist privileges, as in France.

In other words, the English experience in the late 19th and early 20th centuries paralleled the French experience from the 17th to the 19th centuries in that each reflected the desire to circumvent the judicial courts in the legal control of administrative action. However, in the earlier French case, administrative dejudicialisation was ultimately in service of very different policy goals, and it is to that experience that I turn first.

THE FRENCH EXPERIENCE

One of de Tocqueville's most important insights in *The Old Regime and the French Revolution* (1955 [1856]) concerned the origins of administrative hierarchy and

---

2 As Block and Somers characterise Polanyi's position: '[T]he state acted in the interests of society as a whole when it passed protective legislation, and yet the same was true when it passed promarket laws; it clearly did not "belong" to either of these forces' (1984: 68).

centralisation in the French tradition. The 19th century model of administration so prevalent in France, with its decision making chain stretching downward from the central bureaucracy in Paris to the prefect, subprefect, and ultimately to the local mayor and municipal council, owed its birth not to Napoleon or the Revolution, as was often supposed in de Tocqueville's time, but to the Old Regime.[3] Faced with the challenges of war, religious and political division, economic decline, and social unrest, the French monarchy in the 17th century created a separate administrative apparatus (members of the Conseil du Roi, the provincial intendants, their subdelegates) unencumbered by corporatist and venal privileges, whose agents did not own their offices and consequently owed their loyalties primarily to the King. Venal office holders could not be 'dispossessed' of their property – that is, removed from office – thus depriving the crown of an essential means of control. The monarchy thus sought to address this principal-agent problem by creating a competing administrative system, internalising administrative functions within the state while also creating an elaborate system of *tutelle*, or the right of administrative approval or control over the actions of corporate bodies, whether communal, ecclesiastical or professional.

There was an important jurisdictional dimension to this phenomenon. To give it a freer hand in achieving its social and political aims, the French monarchy sought to insulate its agents from the legal control of ordinary judicial courts; that is, from judges who were, by virtue of ownership of their offices, judicially independent of the crown. This preclusion found its initial expression in the Edict of Saint-Germain of February 1641, which prohibited the *parlements* and other 'sovereign courts' of the Old Regime from reviewing any matter 'which may concern the state, administration or government', while reserving 'to our sole person and for our successor kings' the right to rule on matters concerning administration and public affairs (Isambert *et al* 1829: XVI, 529–35). This principle of administrative autonomy from judicial control would be reaffirmed throughout the Old Regime, as well as during the Revolution, ultimately attaining expression in the Napoleonic constitution of Year VIII (1799).

Half a century later, de Tocqueville would lament the continued existence of '"exceptional" courts for the trial of cases involving the administration or any of its officers' (de Tocqueville 1955 [1856]: 57). In his hostility to the autonomous French system of administrative justice, de Tocqueville was a 19th century remnant of the 'party of total suppression' of the 18th century – those who objected in principle to separate system of administrative justice and demanded the transfer of all administrative litigation to the ordinary courts – 'as in Anglo-Saxon countries' (Hauriou 1903). The most historically prominent member of this party was Montesquieu, who, in his famous chapter on the English constitution in *De l'esprit des lois* (1979 [1748]), argued strongly against the combination of executive and judicial power as a formula for despotism.[4] In the last decades of

---

3   See the title to Part II, Ch 2 of *The Old Regime and the French Revolution*: 'How administrative centralization was an institution of the old regime and not, as is often thought, a creation of the Revolution or the Napoleonic period.'

4   See Livre XI, Ch VI, 'De la Constitution d'Angleterre' (1: 294–95), and Livre VI, Ch VI, 'Que, dans la monarchie, les ministres ne doivent pas juger' (1: 207–08).

the Old Regime, this theme became a rallying cry of the judicial opposition to the 'administrative monarchy', which had come to symbolise, for the courts, 'unaccountability and inaccessibility to public scrutiny: the secret domination exercised by men who could not be called to account, because they lacked any formal standing within the juridical order of the ancien regime' (Baker 1990a: 161).

This pressure for public accountability and legal legitimation was in direct reaction to the changes in public governance over the prior century, when a fundamental opposition emerged in French public life. That opposition pitted the central government's exercise of police power to remake society in the 'general interest' (through the nascent state bureaucracy) against the judicial power embodied in the *parlements* and other sovereign courts. During this period, the monarchy acquired vast jurisdiction over administrative litigation involving taxation, customs duties, expropriation, public works, administrative *tutelle*, and infractions of police regulations in a whole range of areas (traffic and navigation, agriculture, commerce, and manufacturing) (Mestre 1985: 192–93; de Tocqueville 1955 [1856]: 53). The monarchy's increasing insistence on its exclusive judicial powers in the administrative domain would 'bring us to the very heart of the gravest political and constitutional debates' of Old Regime France (Antoine 1970: 596). After 1750, as one contemporaneous observer described, there was a 'fairly continuous and often too intense war between two powers, the *juridictionnel* and the *ministeriel*'.[5] The *parlements* and other sovereign courts, in a conscious appeal to public opinion, began to challenge the claimed judicial powers of the royal administration with ever greater frequency and ferocity, opening up a crisis of authority from which the crown would never fully recover. The famous remonstrances of Malesherbes, the first president of the *Cour des aides* in Paris (collected in Dionis du Séjour 1779), were the leading example, depicting administrative justice as a fiction and a sham, lacking both publicity and procedural protections for individual claimants that one found in the 'regulated justice' before the judicial courts.

Ironically, even as judges like Malesherbes had done so much to foment public opinion in opposition to the 'despotism' of the crown, the judicial courts of the Old Regime were in fact among the principal institutional victims of the monarchy's eventual downfall during the Revolutionary decade. Their abolition was in part due to the fact that the *parlements* stood for a form of representation antithetical to the absolutist notion of political 'sovereignty' that the Revolution would inherit from the Old Regime. According to this notion, the King (and later the 'Nation' embodied in its representative Assembly) had the sole and exclusive power to determine the 'general interest', free from particularist interference via the courts. As Louis XV declared in the famous *séance de la flagellation* in 1766, the courts could not interpose themselves as 'the judge between the King and his people' (Flammermont and Tourneux 1895, 2: 557). By contrast, the courts saw themselves as the 'representative' of the King to the Nation, as well as of the Nation to the King (Baker 1990b: 228, quoting Flammermont and Tourneux 1895,

---

5   Antoine-Jean-Baptiste Auget de Montyon, A, 'Des agents de l'administration,' Archives de L'Assistance publique de Paris, Fonds Montyon, carton 8: section entitled 'Des intendants de province', quoted in Baker 1990b: 228.

1: 528). The judicial notion of representation, because it effectively recast the courts as the judge not only of private rights and interests *amongst themselves*, but also of rights and interests of private parties *against the state*, would be found as objectionable after 1789 as before.

In the twilight of the Old Regime, enlightened members of the Conseil du Roi nevertheless recognised that the legitimate exercise of state power was in some sense dependent on the perceived fairness and independence of the system of administrative justice, even if that system was organically attached to the executive. This insight would not be lost on Napoleon, particularly after the upheaval of the Revolutionary decade. Although his dictatorship would perpetuate the strict prohibition against judicial control of administrative action, Napoleon's innovations also laid the groundwork for the 'rejudicialisation' of French administrative justice that would gain momentum over the course of the 19th century. By establishing the Conseil d'État in the constitution of Year VIII and later conferring upon it jurisdiction over *le contentieux administratif*, Napoleon hoped to create 'a half-administrative, half-judicial body [to] regulate the exercise of that portion of arbitrary power necessarily belonging to the administration of the state'. Without such a body, Napoleon recognised, 'the government will fall into scorn' (de la Lozère 1833: 191).

With the Restoration, the advocates of outright suppression of the separate system of administrative justice (à la Montesquieu and Malesherbes) would experience something of a revival, but in fact the notion of *juger l'administration, c'est encore administrer* arguably hardened in actual practice. It was not until mid-century that an intermediate view emerged between the extremes of total suppression and the complete autonomy of 'active administration' from legal control. This third view acknowledged the basic validity of the institutional separation of the administrative and judicial courts but also maintained, as one leading member of the Conseil d'Etat famously put it in 1852, that *'juger c'est juger'* (Vivien 1852: 130). This idea – in effect, that 'to judge is to render justice' – meant that even parties to administrative disputes were entitled to a procedurally fair hearing by an independent judge, even if that judge continued to be, formally speaking, attached to the executive. It was under the initially repressive Second Empire that the Conseil d'Etat would refine the various procedural devices used to scrutinise the legality of executive power, most importantly the *recours pour excès de pouvoir*, or the claim that an executive act should be annulled because it fell outside the authority granted under the controlling legislation.[6] This activism on the part of the Conseil d'Etat under the Second Empire would in many respects vindicate the notion of representation defended by the sovereign courts under the Old Regime, in which administrative litigation came to be seen as an important avenue of social representation before the state. A member of the Conseil under Napoleon III, Léon Aucoc, famously characterised the system of administrative justice as a 'safety-valve that should always remain open', a specific allusion to the need to reinforce the legitimacy of the imperial regime in the absence of genuine democratic outlets (Lampué 1954: 380; Auby and Drago 1962: 419).

---

6   The best history of this process remains Laferrière (1896).

With the establishment of the Third Republic in the 1870s, however, the Conseil d'Etat thought it necessary to reassess its role. After the fall of Napoleon III, the Conseil 'asked itself whether the re-establishment of parliamentary control and ministerial responsibility did not remove some of the *raison d'être* from the mission that the Conseil d'Etat had pursued under the Empire, in the absence of guarantees of a political order' (Laferrière 1896, 2: 273). The need to find a proper balance between legal and parliamentary controls of executive power would remain a persistent concern for the remainder of the century. What is significant, however, is how the extreme jurisprudential caution of the Conseil d'Etat in the early years of the Third Republic steadily eroded in the period leading up to the turn of the century. Perhaps the most important historical step (both symbolically and legally) was the *Cadot* decision of December 1889,[7] in which the Conseil declared that it had original jurisdiction to hear any administrative dispute from the moment it arose, thus dispensing with the requirement that a litigant appeal first up through the administrative hierarchy (the so-called doctrine of *le ministre-juge*).

The *Cadot* decision reflects the ultimate realisation on the part of the members of the Conseil d'Etat that there was still a place in the republican order for independent legal control of executive power, and that hierarchical political control by parliament or government ministers was not enough. The result, in the two decades preceding the outbreak of the First World War, was an increasingly sceptical body of case law concerning the 'absolute parliamentarism' of the Radical Republic (Burdeau 1995: 259). It was against this historical backdrop that one of the greatest French administrative scholars of the early 20th century, Maurice Hauriou – whose inclinations would perhaps have otherwise placed him in the tradition of de Tocqueville – called the French system of administrative justice an 'admirable institution' and a 'precious corrective to centralisation' (Hauriou 1903). Even if it was still organically attached to the executive, French administrative justice was no longer to be feared as an instrument of hierarchical political control indifferent to concerns of individual justice.

Indeed, over the course of the 20th century, the French system of administrative justice would gain an almost legendary reputation as a defender of private rights against the state. As one observer put it in the early 1960s: 'Political liberalism has produced two *chefs-d'oeuvre*, both of which result not from the *a priori* elaboration of an intellectual construction, but from the natural and fortunate culmination of a particular historical evolution: parliamentarism in Great Britain and administrative justice in France' (Sandevoir 1964: 11). French administrative lawyers were clearly proud of what they regarded as their distinctive contribution to the development of the modern state. They could take satisfaction that France, in this regard at least, offered a seemingly more advanced model as compared to what was offered across the Channel, the supposed cradle of political liberalism.

---

7   CE, 13 déc 1889, *Cadot, Rec* 1148, concl Jagerschmidt.

THE ENGLISH CASE

Just as the reputation of the French system of administrative justice had fully consolidated itself by the early 20th century, the burgeoning field of administrative adjudication was becoming an increasingly contested question in England. The intensified debate in England coincided with the vast expansion of the British state's control over economic and social life during the First World War and immediately after. It was during this period that Parliament adopted a wide-range of statutes dealing with unemployment, health insurance, housing conditions and local government. Three new ministries were created – Labour, Transport and, perhaps most importantly, Health – the latter acquiring a vast jurisdiction over local housing plans, taxation, local government structure, and a new poor law.

As one commentator summarised in 1933, however, the British administrative state did not emerge out of whole cloth in the aftermath of the First World War; rather, it went through '[a] long period of imperceptible growth' in the 19th century, followed in the early 20th century by 'a quickening to meet the needs of the new Social State', then 'a sudden flowering during the War, and after the War the full fruition ...' (Willis 1933: 5). It was this 'sudden flowering' and 'full fruition', however, which provoked a political response that the 'long period of imperceptible growth' had not. Voices in Parliament were also raised against the evils of 'bureaucracy' but the most vocal source of constitutional opposition came from the British judiciary. Lord Hewart, the Lord Chief Justice of England, famously published a book in 1929 – a kind of modern day remonstrance in the spirit of Malesherbes – provocatively entitled *The New Despotism*. Hewart argued that delegation of legislative and adjudicative powers to the executive posed a grave threat to 'the two leading features' of the British constitution, 'the Sovereignty of Parliament and the Rule of Law' (Hewart 1929: 17).

To grasp why judges like Lord Hewart felt especially threatened by the rise of administrative governance, one must consider certain conventional understandings of English constitutional history (and the place of the courts in that history) from which these views emerged. The political conflict of the 17th century between crown and Parliament that destroyed the 'old despotism' (culminating in the revolution of 1688) definitively established parliamentary sovereignty as the central principle of the English constitution. Bound up in this revolutionary process was a related triumph: the defeat of the crown's attempt to claim a monopoly over administrative disputes, akin to what the French monarchy had successfully established during the same period. In 1641 – the same year of the Edict of Saint Germain in France – the English Parliament abolished the notorious Court of Star Chamber and, in 1688, it abolished the remaining jurisdictions under the control of the Privy Council. This assertion of parliamentary power meant, henceforth, 'the unchallenged dominance of the ordinary courts, the courts of common law' (Mitchell 1965: 97), within which the concept of private property, and not the 'general interest', would be the guiding principle. This revolutionary settlement inherited from 17th century thus involved 'a double control of government activity: control of legality in the courts and political control in Parliament' (Mitchell 1965: 98).

It was this seeming separation of powers, and in particular the separation of executive and adjudicative power, that Montesquieu celebrated as the central feature of the English constitution in *De l'esprit des lois* in 1748. During the 19th century, however, questions were raised regarding how well Montesquieu's construct actually corresponded to the English reality. As FW Maitland would note a century and a half after Montesquieu: 'It is curious that some political theorists should have seen their favourite ideal, a complete separation of administration from judicature, realised in England; in England, in all places in the world, where the two have for ages been inextricably blended' (Robson 1928: 26, quoting Maitland 1911 [1888]: 478). The deeper constitutional reality – despite the seeming achievements of 1688 – was that administrative officers in England, in execution of their legislatively-appointed authority, continued to make inquiries and render judgment on particular sets of facts in light of general legal norms – in other words, to adjudicate in everything but name – often without appeal to the ordinary courts.

This form of autonomous administrative adjudication became even more prominent as government intervention expanded in the 19th and 20th centuries, giving rise to 'a need for a technique of adjudication better fitted to respond to the social requirements of the time than the elaborate and costly system of enforcement provided by litigation in the courts of law' (Robson 1928: 32). While it would be wrong to say that the result was a 'system' of administrative justice akin to what France developed over the 18th and 19th centuries, there was nevertheless a kind of convergence with the French experience, in which a whole range of administrative conduct affecting private interests was excluded from the jurisdiction of the ordinary courts. The adjudicative decisions of English administrative officials were sometimes subject to judicial review but not necessarily; rather, it depended on the regulatory domain and the provisions of the governing legislation. It was the increasing realisation of this state of affairs in the 1920s – 'a growing consciousness that governmental organisation no longer squared with legal theory' (Willis 1933: 29) – that led to the intense criticisms of ministerial powers from the bench.

The persistent notion that England lived under a system of a strict separation of powers, as well as its corollary, the rule of law as enforced by the ordinary courts, was largely due to the extraordinary influence on the legal profession of Albert Venn Dicey's *Law of the Constitution*, first published in 1885. Dicey's position had two principal elements: first, that the powers of the crown in England 'must be exercised in accordance with ordinary common law principles which govern the relation of one Englishman to another' (Dicey 1959: 387); and, secondly, that the very idea of a separate body of principles governing public action – a *droit administratif* – was 'absolutely foreign to English law', because by definition the elaboration of such principles did 'not lie within the jurisdiction of the ordinary courts'. By the end of Dicey's long career, however, even he could not ignore the weight of the evidence that a form of autonomous administrative law was in fact emerging in England, the development of which was taking place largely outside the jurisdiction of the common law courts (Dicey 1915: 148). This realisation did not mean that other lawyers raised on his orthodox teachings were ready to arrive at the same conclusion. Hewart himself, speaking to the American

Bar Association in 1927, continued to assert that the common law did 'not recognize any *droit administratif*. Every person, whatever position he might occupy within the State, is subject to the law of the land, and there are no special tribunals for the trial of matters in which public departments or Ministers of State are concerned' (Robson 1928: 30, quoting *The Times*, 2 September 1927 and 30 September 1927).

It was perhaps Hewart's own uncomfortable realisation that this beloved maxim was no longer valid that led him to write what might still lay claim to being the most famous (or perhaps infamous) book in the history of British administrative law in the early 20th century. What the modern advocates of executive power were trying to pass off as an emergent British system of 'administrative law' *à la française*, Hewart asserted was a system of 'administrative lawlessness' characterised by ministerial prerogatives to define the scope of their own jurisdiction, as well as an absence of procedural protections and rights of appeal to the judicial courts (Hewart 1929: Chapter 4). This intensification of criticism directed at administrative justice resulted, one could argue, from the increasing encroachment of the administrative sphere onto the core province of the ordinary courts – the protection of private property (Jennings 1936: 443–44). English housing law litigation is a good example (Griffith 1993: 18–24). Modern housing legislation interfered with common law rights of property owners (notably the freedom of contract) in any number of ways, imposing duties of repair and obligating landlords to conform to a whole range of standards, indeed even to transfer their property to the local authorities under certain circumstances. More importantly, the prevailing statutes conferred a whole range of legislative and adjudicative powers on local officials, 'sometimes with and sometimes without the consent of the Minister of Health, and sometimes with and sometimes without an appeal to the courts' (Jennings 1936: 437).

Advocates of this approach argued that the 'highly individualistic and conservative' outlook of the courts justified their exclusion from administrative oversight, because the judicial bias in favour of private property and individual rights 'result[ed] in a tendency to give a restricted interpretation to the grant of powers' (Jennings 1936: 434). The debate was thus over not *whether* administration should be subject to legal control but *which judges* could best balance the often conflicting interests of private rights and public welfare – those sitting on the ordinary courts or those who were a part of some hypothetical hierarchy of administrative tribunals in the French tradition. A French-style system had its defenders (notably Robson 1928); indeed, even Lord Hewart begrudgingly acknowledged that the 'Continental system of "Administrative Law"', while 'profoundly repugnant ... to English ideas', was 'at least a system. It has its courts, its law, its hearings and adjudications, its regular and accepted procedure', which stood in stark contrast to the evolving 'administrative lawlessness' in England (Hewart 1929: 12–13).

However, the establishment of a separate system of administrative justice on the French model was never a real likelihood because of the fairly broad-based constitutional attachment to the ordinary courts as enforcers of the rule of law. Evidence of this attachment can be found in the 1932 report of the Committee on

Ministers' Powers, a special parliamentary committee set up in 1929 to examine the entire question of delegated legislation and judicial review in response to the contentious debate that followed the publication of *The New Despotism*. The committee's terms of reference, progressive critics believed, reflected too great a 'devotion to Dicey's memory' (Carr 1941: 27) because they asked 'what safeguards are desirable or necessary to secure the constitutional principles of the sovereignty of Parliament and the supremacy of the Law' (Committee on Ministers' Powers 1932: 1). By emphasising 'the supremacy of the Law', the terms of reference in some sense assumed their conclusion, and perhaps not surprisingly the committee 'without hesitation, advise[d] against adoption' of an autonomous system of administrative justice on the French model (*ibid* 1932: 110).

Nevertheless, the committee also recognised the changing nature of governance in Britain, notably the diffusion of normative power among national and subnational executive and administrative bodies, as well as among public, quasi-public and traditionally private entities (*ibid* 1932: 4). There was a certain inevitability to this phenomenon, the committee claimed, because it emerged out of 'changes in our ideas of government which have resulted from changes in political, social, and economic ideas, and in the changes in the circumstances of our lives which have resulted from scientific discoveries' (*ibid* 1932: 5). The legal and political formula for the legitimation of such diffuse power, the committee asserted, should combine direct legislative oversight, ministerial responsibility, as well as reinvigorated judicial review by the courts of law. Each element, working together, would best ensure that administrative officials remained within the scope of their 'essentially subordinate' authority, while acting reasonably and respecting private rights to the extent possible in the achievement of legislatively-defined public ends.

Although few of the committee's specific proposals would actually make their way into law over the remainder of the 1930s (Carr 1941: 175–76), the committee's report would serve as the point of departure for post-1945 reform discussions on administrative power in Britain (see, eg, Select Committee on Delegated Legislation 1953). In the immediate postwar years, British academic commentators often wrote with embarrassment of the state of their country's system of administrative justice. On the one hand, the prevailing mindset still suffered from the residual influence of Dicey's inaccurate depiction of the administrative law 'as a misfortune inflicted upon the benighted folk across the Channel' (de Smith 1955: 398). On the other hand, there was the reality of 'a plethora of *ad hoc* tribunals', appointed by ministers, not necessarily sitting in public, sometimes excluding legal representation, with often highly informal procedural and evidentiary rules, not always bound to provide reasons for decisions, and not necessarily subject to appeal to a court on questions of law (de Smith 1955: 397). Unfavourable comparisons were made not only with the French system of *droit administratif* but also with the situation that prevailed in the United States, Britain's common law *confrère*, which had passed a far-reaching Administrative Procedure Act in 1946. As an English law professor wrote in the *Yale Law Journal* in 1950: 'American administrative law is so much more developed than the British that there is little for an American lawyer to learn from the British experience – except to be on guard against a weakening of judicial control. Cannot Marshall Plan Aid include "administrative law"?' (Street 1950: 593).

The widely recognised inadequacies of the British system of administrative justice in the late 1940s and early 1950s in fact provided the terrain on which antagonists from the interwar period could now find a point of agreement.[8] The issuance of the report of the Committee on Administrative Tribunals and Enquiries (the Franks Committee) (1957) signalled the consolidation of a new consensus. The general question before the committee was how best to characterise administrative tribunals: are they 'part of the machinery of justice' or are they 'mere administrative expedients'? (Schwartz and Wade 1972: 151). This question – strongly reminiscent of the debate over *juger l'administration, c'est encore administrer* in France – was at the core of the constitutional struggle to stabilise administrative governance in Britain in the first half of the 20th century. Despite the arguments of government witnesses 'that tribunals should properly be regarded as part of the machinery of administration, for which the Government must retain close and continuing responsibility', the Franks Committee emphatically found to the contrary: tribunals were 'part of the machinery provided by Parliament for adjudication', responsible along with the courts for the enforcement of the rule of law (Committee on Administrative Tribunals and Enquiries 1957: 9).

The reforms that grew out of the report of the Franks Committee – notably the Tribunals and Inquiries Act of 1958 (6 Eliz 2, c 66) – marked a key turning point in the emergence of a recognisable body of administrative law in Britain. Although constituted as part of the administrative sphere and structured accordingly, administrative tribunals were now recognised by Parliament as having a basic obligation to dispense justice in an independent fashion.[9] The Tribunals and Inquiries Act also provided for a general right of appeal to judicial courts (reflective of the fundamentally subordinate character of these tribunals on questions of law), as well as a requirement that they publicly provide reasons for their decisions (essential to effective judicial review). Perhaps most importantly, the act served as a 'catalyst for reform' within the courts themselves, which became noticeably 'more active and enterprising' in the development of administrative jurisprudence after 1958 (Schwartz and Wade 1972: 5). A series of major cases would reinvigorate the application of principles of natural justice, impose much stricter judicial limits on ministerial discretion, give a much more

---

8   On the right, see Allen, CK, 'Foreword' to Sieghart (1950), in which Allen concluded that 'the time has come, in view of the great and increasing pressure of administrative problems' to establish a system of administrative tribunals on the French model to hear administrative disputes (p xiii). This suggestion was gladly welcomed on the left by William Robson, who wrote that Allen was simply calling for 'reforms in the direction I have long regarded as essential' (1951: 465).

9   The committee placed a great deal of emphasis on the fact that the term 'tribunal', as it appeared in the statutes, indicated an intent on the part of Parliament 'for a decision outside and independent of the Department concerned' (Committee on Administrative Tribunals and Enquiries 1957: 9). This reasoning is reminiscent of the evolving thinking regarding French administrative justice in the 19th century in which the *juridiction administrative* became distinct from the *administration active*. See Vivien 1852: 130.

narrow reading to preclusive clauses, and more generally use the doctrine of *ultra vires* to review a broad range of administrative illegalities.[10]

Although one could fairly say this was precisely the sort of judicial activism Lord Hewart was demanding in *The New Despotism* in 1929, there were several major differences in the political and legal environment in the late 1950s and early 1960s. After the Second World War, no one in the judiciary any longer seriously questioned the right of the state to intervene actively in social and economic affairs, even if this conflicted with property rights and freedom of contract. Consequently, the greater activism of the British courts at the outset of the 1960s was not seen as a conservative attempt to protect the interests of private property or individual autonomy. Rather, as the Franks Committee put it, the courts were now simply seeking a 'new balance between private right and public advantage' that was necessary to achieve both 'fair play for the individual and efficiency of administration' (Committee on Administrative Tribunals and Enquiries 1957: 2). In other words, the role of the courts in the modern welfare state in postwar Britain was not to impede administrative power but to legitimise it. The courts were to serve as a mechanism to ensure that the British administrative state observed certain basic norms of a constitutional nature, such as natural justice, while also respecting the boundary of authority as established by the enabling legislation itself. Thus, after a decade of quiescence, the British courts had found their place in the constitutional settlement of administrative governance.

RETURNING TO POLANYI

It is appropriate to return to the 'double movement' thesis set out by Polanyi in *The Great Transformation*. The obvious question is whether the legal-administrative phenomenon explored here (dejudicialisation/rejudicialisation) and the political-economic dynamic described by Polanyi (disembedding/re-embedding) are not simply superficially similar but, in fact, causally linked. Passages in the concluding chapter of *The Great Transformation* strongly suggest a causal relationship, particularly where Polanyi celebrates the role of 'tribunals and courts ... [in] vindicating personal freedom' and as 'guarantees against victimization'. Although such judicial interference might inhibit 'efficiency of production, economy in consumption or rationality in administration' – hence suggesting an intimate relation among the three – it was well worth the cost because '[a]n industrial society can afford to be free' (2001 [1944]: 264).

Polanyi, unfortunately, does not elaborate on this point, but several other statements make the linkage between judicial protections and his more general double-movement thesis more evident. For Polanyi, public regulation was the inevitable consequence of the political construction of market capitalism. However, he further states that 'the strengthening of the rights of the individual in society' via the courts was an equally essential (and hopefully inevitable) 'answer to the threat of bureaucracy'. In this effort, '[n]o mere declaration of rights can

---

10 For a summary, see Schwartz and Wade (1972: 299) as well as Griffith (1993: ch 4).

suffice', but rather 'institutions are required to make rights effective' (2001 [1944]: 264). It is here that Polanyi refers to the special role of courts in 'vindicating personal freedom', suggesting that these institutions had already been essential to protecting society from *both* the excesses of the market economy as well as the dangers of an expanding state bureaucracy – a danger that flowed precisely from the 'planning' and other forms of regulatory intervention that he otherwise espoused.

The implication that 'tribunals and courts' were integral to the more general counter-movement was ironic, however, in at least one significant respect. Polanyi insisted that, in *economic* terms, the movement to create a self-regulating market economy, with its attachment to '[f]ree enterprise and private ownership ... [as] essentials of freedom' (2001 [1944]: 265), was a thoroughly utopian undertaking. Nevertheless, in *political* terms, Polanyi seemed to acknowledge these liberal concepts as foundations of precisely the legal culture that was essential to 'creat[ing] spheres of arbitrary freedom protected by unbreakable rules' without which it would be impossible to protect the individual against both market and bureaucratic power (2001 [1944]: 264). In other words, Polanyi acknowledged that his own largely material conception of liberty in the modern era – 'leisure and security that industrial society offers to all' – needed to *build on*, rather than *displace*, these 'old freedoms and civic rights' (2001 [1944]: 265).

This conceptual decoupling of legal/political and economic liberalism seemed also to be an implicit acknowledgment of the potential resilience or, as legal historians put it, the 'relative autonomy', of legal culture in the face of structural-economic change. The historical evolution of cultural categories like 'freedom' or 'rights' – indeed, one might include 'law' writ large – is not, Polanyi's narrative suggests, strictly a function of the corresponding evolution in economic structures. Rather, there is a lack of perfect congruence between the two, and this potential 'lag' in legal-cultural development relative to changes in the economy is a contingency that we must factor into our accounts of political and social history. Polanyi does not focus on this lag in any systematic way (if at all). Rather, in setting out his double-movement thesis, he only thinly describes the cultural-historical underpinnings of the counter-movement, which he depicts primarily as a 'spontaneous reaction ... without any theoretical or intellectual preconceptions' (2001 [1944]: 156–57).[11]

For a better sense of how these underpinnings could motivate the political effort to 're-embed' the market economy, one must look to historians who place the interaction of economic structures and cultural traditions at the centre of their analytical method. The leading example is, of course, EP Thompson. '[H]istorical change eventuates', Thompson argued, 'because changes in productive relationships are experienced in social and cultural life, refracted in men's ideas and their values, and argued through their actions, their choices and their beliefs' (Thompson 1994: 222). The study of this 'experience', in a Thompsonian sense,

---

11 Polanyi could be forgiven for his emphasis on spontaneity because he was responding to conspiracy theories of economic liberals regarding 'collectivism', *trying to* demonstrate the fundamentally defensive nature of the counter-movement.

thus involves two inter-related aspects: first, how those material-structural changes are interpreted (refracted) in the prevailing system of ideas and values; and, secondly, how those interpretations motivate, or give meaning to, subsequent social and political action.

Thompson's approach is one that historians interested in the evolution of legal institutions and structures of public governance in relation to economic change can usefully adopt. Public governance necessarily evolves as societies place new material demands on the prevailing institutions of norm-production and enforcement. These new structures of governance, however, often outpace prevailing understandings of what constitutes a legitimate legal and political order – that is, in the 'refraction' of this reality through ideas or values of legitimacy inherited from the past, the new structures may be found wanting in any number of respects. The gap between socio-institutional reality and historically-embedded conceptions of legal legitimacy thus feeds into a dialectic in which both structures of governance and understandings of a legitimate legal and political order are forced to adjust in the face of the reciprocal influences of the other.[12] In turn, this dialectical process has an impact on subsequent political choices about how the system of governance should be structured in the future.

The effects of this dialectic are revealed most clearly in the evolution of public law, because it is there that modes of governance are 'institutionalised' (Hauriou 1925). As Hauriou argued in his *théorie de l'institution*, this process occurs not simply through the mobilisation of powerful interests in support of a particular governance regime; rather, it requires the 'manifestation of communion in the social group' that necessarily plays itself out over a *longue durée*. Hauriou's theory of institutionalisation perfectly complements Thompson's historiographical approach: it is through the long-term historical 'struggle *about* law, and within the forms of law' (Thompson 1975: 266) that a particular mode of governance achieves durability and legitimacy in an institutional sense. Only after culturally-conditioned 'manifestations of communion' will a structural situation 'of fact' (that is, one established through political or economic power) become culturally one 'of law', thereby achieving a reasonably uncontested social and political existence.

CONCLUSION

It should not surprise us that Hauriou developed his institutional theory after spending nearly all of his adult life devoted to the study of French administrative law as it evolved over the 19th and into the 20th century. In his recognition that the durability of institutions depended on their coming into 'harmony with the

---

12 Cf Hanley (1989: 5–6) describing:

the historical process as a renewable dialogue or cultural conversation, wherein history is culturally ordered by existing concepts, or schemes of meaning, at play in given times and places; and culture is historically ordered when schemes of meaning are revalued and revised as persons act and reenact them over time. One might regard this process of reordering as one that 'counterfeits culture'; that is, as a process that replicates the perceived original but at the same time (consciously or unconsciously) forges something quite new.

conscience of jurisprudence' over time (Hauriou 1918: 816), he almost certainly had in mind, *inter alia*, the French system of administrative justice. Created by force under monarchy of the Old Regime (over the intense opposition of the sovereign courts) and consolidated in the constitution of Year VIII by Napoleon as part of his dictatorial regime, the French system of administrative justice nevertheless became, as he put it, an 'admirable institution' and a 'precious corrective to centralisation' (Hauriou 1903). The historical 'party of total suppression' – Montesquieu, Malesherbes, de Tocqueville – was defeated by the system's own eventual recognition that a complete dejudicialisation of administrative justice was untenable – politically, legally, and culturally. The response was partial rejudicialisation over the course of the 19th century.

In 20th century England, Lord Hewart was the leading member of a similar 'party of total suppression', and his polemic in *The New Despotism* led directly to the formation of the Committee on Ministers' Powers, which in turn marked the beginning of the process of rejudicialisation of the English system of administrative justice that had developed *sub silencio* over the 19th century. As in the French case, the traditional legal system in England was ultimately forced to make significant adjustments in the face of the new realities of governance – but, importantly, it did not completely surrender to them. Eventually, the system of administrative adjudication, even if intimately bound up with the work of administration, was acknowledged in law as part of the machinery of 'justice' traditionally conceived. Parliament eventually recognised that administrative tribunals served as a sort of 'junior partner' with the judiciary in the enforcement of the Rule of Law (hence the general right of appeal to the common-law courts), a decisive step in the reconciliation of the new forms of administrative governance with older legal-cultural ideals in England. Once this settlement was achieved, the English courts could get on with the difficult task before them: the development of a genuine body of 'administrative law' – something Dicey claimed was an impossibility – to govern the actions of a state deeply engaged in the regulation of the market economy.

EPILOGUE

It would perhaps be wise to end there. However, I would like to add one final thought – a kind of epilogue – and an extremely brief one at that. Its purpose is to suggest a relationship between the material covered here (and more particularly the historiographical theory I have just outlined) and debates over the current state of governance in the European Union.[13] The historical evolution of administrative justice is directly tied to the diffusion and fragmentation of normative power in the modern regulatory state, and, in turn, to the evolution of the expanding market economy. Over the course of the 20th century, to make the state a more effective regulator of that economy, significant amounts of power were shifted away from the constitutional *trias politica* (legislative, executive, and judicial) that had been originally envisioned in the 18th and 19th centuries, into a

---

13   See, eg, the contribution of Christian Joerges and Michelle Everson in this volume.

complex and variegated administrative sphere. As we proceed into the 21st century, and as market capitalism continues to evolve (globalise), this shift in power continues, not simply to 'independent' agencies within the state but also to institutions operating outside its confines, whether private, semi-private or, most importantly, supranational – a phenomenon especially pronounced in Europe.

To many observers, this shift in the locus of governance to the supranational level in Europe appears historically *sui generis* and thus in need of entirely novel forms of legal legitimation. There is some truth in this claim but one might also query whether the current situation is merely a 'new dimension to an old problem' (Lindseth 1999: 629). Throughout history, political-economic demands have pushed governance in new directions. The difference today is that, in Europe at least, those demands are increasingly pushing governance outside the confines of the nation-state, into a complex system of governance operating at multiple levels and through multiple types of actors. As in the past, the durability of these new structures will depend heavily on society's capacity to reconcile them with notions of a legitimate legal and political order inherited from the past. This raises a question: might it be that, just as the pursuit of administrative efficiency through complete dejudicialisation ultimately gave way, at least in part, to a rejudicialisation over time, so too will supranational efficiency give way – despite the ardent hopes of many European federalists – to a significant degree of 'renationalisation' of the legitimation of European norm-production?

My view is that this is probably already the case. Despite the seemingly supranational form of Community (and now Union) institutions, it is difficult to deny that national systems continue to provide the critical source of legitimation for European integration. The driving force behind this persistence of national oversight and control (even if often indirect) is the widespread cultural attachment to national constitutional structures as the foundation of a legitimate legal and political order in Europe, something that the progress of European integration to date has only marginally altered. Even as significant normative power has shifted to the supranational domain in certain areas, there is a discernible legal-cultural resistance toward the creation of a supranational system of norm-production constitutionally 'disembedded' from the nation-state (that is, fully autonomous). The result, in institutional terms, is that norms produced at the European level still need to be mediated in meaningful ways through national institutions, a position I have explored elsewhere and will not revisit in detail here (see both Lindseth 2001 and 2002).

Europe is living, in other words, through a period of increasing historical disconnect: socio-institutional realities of 'governance' are moving in a supranational direction but legal and political culture remain wedded to national constitutional structures as expressions of legitimate 'government'. Given the need to bridge this disconnect, it thus seems likely that, for the foreseeable future, the struggle to reconcile supranational governance with specifically national constitutional structures (perhaps under the rubric of 'transnationalism') will be the real focus of European public law, rather than the creation of a supranational 'constitutional' order that is 'disembedded' from its national foundations (Lindseth 2003).

References

Antoine, M (1970) *Le Conseil du roi sous le règne de Louis XV*, Genève: Droz
Auby, J and Drago, R (1962) *Traité de contentieux administratif*, vol 2, Paris: LGDJ
Baker, K (1990a) 'Science and politics at the end of the Old Regime', in Baker, K, *Inventing the French Revolution: Essays on French Political Culture in the 18th Century*, Cambridge: Cambridge University Press
Baker, K (1990b) 'Representation redefined', in *Inventing the French Revolution: Essays on French Political Culture in the 18th Century*, Cambridge: Cambridge University Press
Block, F and Somers, M (1984) 'Beyond the economistic fallacy: the holistic social science of Karl Polanyi', in Skocpol, T (ed), *Vision and Method in Historical Sociology*, Cambridge: Cambridge University Press
Burdeau, F (1995) *Histoire du droit administratif (de la Révolution au début des années 1970)*, Paris: Presses Universitaires de France
Carr, C (1941) *Concerning English Administrative Law*, New York: Columbia University Press
Chevallier, J (1970) *L'Elaboration historique du principe de séparation de la juridiction administrative et de l'administration active*, Paris: LGDJ
Committee on Administrative Tribunals and Enquiries (1957) *Report of the Committee on Administrative Tribunals and Enquiries*, Cmnd 218, London: The Stationery Office
Committee on Ministers' Powers (1932) *Report*, Cmd 4060, London: The Stationery Office
de Smith, S (1955) 'Rule of law' [book review], 69 Harvard Law Review 396–400
de Tocqueville, A (1955) [1856] *L'Ancien régime et la revolution*, in Gilbert, S (trans), *The Old Régime and the French Revolution*, New York: Doubleday
Dicey, A (1915) 'The development of administrative law in England' 31 Law Quarterly Review 148–53
Dicey, A (1959) *An Introduction to the Study of the Law of the Constitution*, 10th edn, London: Macmillan
Dionis du Séjour (ed) (1779) *Mémoires pour servir à l'histoire de droit public de la France en matière d'impôts*, Bruxelles
Flammermont, J and Tourneux, M (eds) (1895) *Remontrances du parlement de Paris au XVIIIe siècle*, Paris: Imprimerie Nationale
Griffith, J (1993) *Judicial Politics since 1920: A Chronicle*, Oxford: Blackwell
Hanley, S (1989) 'Engendering the state: family formation and state-building in early modern France' 16(1) French Historical Studies
Hauriou, M (1903), 'Note on the *Terrier* decision of the Conseil d'Etat of 6 February 1903, *Recueil Sirey*', 25 March 1903, reprinted in Hauriou, M (1929) *La jurisprudence administrative de 1892 à 1929*, Paris: Librairie du Recueil Sirey
Hauriou, M (1918) 'An interpretation of the principles of public law' 31 Harvard Law Review 813–21
Hauriou, M (1925) 'La théorie de l'institution et de la fondation' 4 Cahiers de la nouvelle journée 2–45
Hewart, L (1929) *The New Despotism*, London: Ernest Benn
Isambert, F et al (eds) (1829) *Recueil général des anciennes lois françaises*, Paris: Belin-Leprieur
Jennings, W (1936) 'Courts and administrative law – the experience of English housing legislation' 49 Harvard Law Review 426–54
Laferrière, E (1896) *Traité de la juridiction administrative et des recours contentieux*, 2 vols, 2nd edn, Paris: Berger-Levrault (reprinted Paris: LGDJ, 1989)

Lampué, P (1954) 'Le développement historique du recours pour excès de pouvoir depuis ses origines jusqu'au début du XXe siècle', 2 Revue internationale des sciences administratives 359–92

Lindseth, P (1999) 'Democratic legitimacy and the administrative character of supranationalism: the example of the European Community' 99(3) Columbia Law Review 628–738

Lindseth, P (2001) '"Weak" constitutionalism? Reflections on comitology and transnational governance in the European Union' 21(1) Oxford Journal of Legal Studies 145–63

Lindseth, P (2002) 'Delegation is dead – long live delegation: managing the democratic disconnect in the European market polity', in Joerges, C and Dehousse, R (eds), Good Governance in an 'Integrated' Market, London: Oxford University Press

Lindseth, P (2003) 'The contradictions of supranationalism: administrative governance and constitutionalization in European integration since the 1950s' 37 Loyola-Los Angeles Law Review 363–406

de la Lozère, P (1833) Opinions de Napoléon, Paris: F Didot

Maitland, F (1911) [1888] 'The shallows and silences of real life', in The Collected Papers of Frederic William Maitland: Downing Professor of the Laws of England, vol 1, Cambridge: Cambridge University Press

Mestre, J (1985) Introduction historique au droit administraif français, Paris: PUF

Mitchell, J (1965) 'The causes and consequences of the absence of a system of public law in the United Kingdom' Public Law 95–118

Montesquieu, C (1979) [1748] De l'esprit des loix, 2 vols, Paris: Flammarion

Polanyi, K (2001) [1944] The Great Transformation, Boston, MA: Beacon Press

Robson, W (1928) Justice and Administrative Law: A Study of the British Constitution, 1st edn, London: Macmillan & Co

Robson, W (1951) Justice and Administrative Law: A Study of the British Constitution, 3rd edn, London: Stevens & Sons

Sandevoir, P (1964) Études sur le recours de pleine juridiction, Paris: LGDJ

Schwartz, B and Wade, H (1972) Legal Control of Government: Administrative Law in Britain and the United States, Oxford: Clarendon Press

Select Committee on Delegated Legislation (1953) Report, Together with the Proceedings of the Committee, Minutes of Evidence and Appendices, London: The Stationery Office

Sieghart, M (1950) Government by Decree: A Comparative Study of the History of the Ordinance in English and French Law, London: Stevens & Sons

Street, H (1950) 'Book review' 59 Yale Law Journal 590–93

Thompson, E (1975) Whigs and Hunters: The Origins of the Black Act, New York: Pantheon

Thompson, E (1994) 'History and anthropology, lecture given at the Indian History Congress (30 December 1976)', in Thompson, E, Making History: Writings on History and Culture, New York: New Press

Vivien, A (1852) Etudes administratives, 2nd edn, Paris: Guillaumin et cie

Willis, J (1933) The Parliamentary Powers of English Government Departments, Cambridge, MA: Harvard University Press

RE-EMBEDDING PUBLIC POLICY: DECENTRALISED COLLABORATIVE GOVERNANCE IN FRANCE AND ITALY[1]

Pepper D Culpepper

INTRODUCTION

One of the most prominent innovations of policy-making in the advanced industrial countries over the past 20 years is the proliferation of institutions of decentralised collaborative governance (OECD 2001 and 2003). Institutions of collaborative decentralised governance are defined by three distinctive characteristics: they promote routine interaction in a given policy domain among governmental and non-governmental actors; they operate primarily at the sub-national level; and they involve no monopoly by state actors of either problem definition or methods of implementation. These institutions embody the trends identified in the introduction to this volume toward both a territorial diffusion of policy-making responsibility (away from national governments) and a blurring of organisational roles between public and private actors. Institutions like these, which involve decentralised sharing of policy-making authority among the private and public sectors, are now established in a majority of the advanced industrial countries.[2]

Decentralised collaborative governance, however, is more likely to be instantly recognisable to bureaucrats and lawyers than to political scientists, because little work in political science has linked these developments to existing theories of politics.[3] This is startling, since decentralised collaborative governance entails a rethinking of both components of the state-society dyad; it alters the level and character of state intervention and oversight, and it foresees an increased role for societal engagement in public governance institutions. The theoretical properties of state-society relations have long been a central topic of interest in comparative

---

1   The author thanks Felipe Barbera, Tito Bianchi, Archon Fung, Gary Herrigel, Richard Locke and Peter Hall for comments on earlier drafts of this chapter; thanks also to Elena Fagotto for research assistance and the Weil Program at the Kennedy School of Government at Harvard University for financial support.
2   Such experiments are currently established in Austria, Belgium, Canada, Denmark, Finland, France, Germany, Ireland, Italy, the Netherlands, Norway, Poland, Spain, Sweden, the United Kingdom and the United States (Balloch and Taylor 2001; OECD 2001 and 2003).
3   The silence of political science on these institutional innovations contrasts sharply with the close attention they have received in legal scholarship. See eg Freeman (1997); Dorf and Sabel (1998); Ayres and Braithwaite (1992).

politics. If these institutions are indeed reshaping the way the public and private actors work, as several contributions in this volume suggest they are, then the relevant question for political scientists is whether or not existing theories can account for the variation in outcomes between successful and failed instances of decentralised collaborative governance.

Success is a meaningless metric if left undefined. I define the success of institutions of decentralised collaborative governance by two characteristics: *durable* establishment of institutions that promote regular exchange among actors in the public and private domains; and an *observable change in the co-operative propensities of local actors*. These institutional experiments are established with an eye to resolving various real policy problems (lowering unemployment, increasing investment, etc). Whether or not they achieve those policy goals is indeed an important question. However, it is one that also depends on the suitability of the tool of decentralised collaborative governance for solving those policy problems, which will vary across policy areas. *Qua* institutions, however, the claim of their proponents is that they succeed in getting competing actors to talk to each other, and that by so doing they positively improve their likelihood of co-operating with each other. In this chapter I am interested in the preliminary question of what distinguishes those institutions that meet those goals from those that do not. Their suitability for solving various policy problems is an open question for future research.

Two prominent literatures in political science seem most likely to account for empirical developments in this new field of policy-making. First, these arrangements may be viewed as another instance of sectoral neo-corporatism, about which we know a great deal already (Berger 1981; Goldthorpe 1984; Cawson 1985; Keeler 1987). This, in fact, is the most likely alternative, since institutions of decentralised collaborative governance are found most frequently in the areas of local economic development and active labour market policy, two policy domains familiar from work on neo-corporatism (Lehmbruch 1984). If these apparent institutional innovations show the same organisational and political regularities predicted by sectoral corporatist theory, then that increases our confidence in the findings of that literature and generates clear expectations about the conditions under which decentralised collaborative governance should thrive. There is a second strand of analysis whose findings may explain variations in collaborative decentralised governance: recent work on 'empowered participatory governance' (EPG), a literature most closely associated with the work of Archon Fung and Erik Olin Wright, who examine the correlates of success in institutional experiments in deliberative democracy (Fung and Wright 2003; Fung 2004; Heller 2000). The EPG literature looks from school reform in Chicago to decentralised development planning in the Indian province of Kerala and sees a similar set of design principles focused on the devolution of formal decision making power to institutions that foster sustained citizen participation and deliberation. EPG theorists explicitly delimit their findings to proposals whose aim is to empower local citizens to participate in policy-making, and few of the innovations that fall under the rubric of decentralised collaborative governance take increased participation as their unique goal. It is, however, worth considering whether the findings of EPG theorists in the narrow set of cases that genuinely aim to increase individual participation generate portable expectations about other policy innovations that share a similar institutional architecture.

This chapter examines the propositions of these literatures in light of two of the most sweeping instances of collaborative decentralised governance observed in Europe in the 1990s: the attempted revolution in French vocational training policy and the successful revolution in Italian economic development policy. To foreshadow the argument that follows, these literatures fail in interestingly antagonistic ways when confronted with concrete cases of decentralised collaborative governance. Sectoral corporatism is too cynical. It expects success when organisations are insulated from membership discontent and when states compensate these organisations by aiding them materially against rival groups (Keeler 1987: 9). Organisations in decentralised collaborative governance are not in fact most successful when they demobilise their members, but when they are able to promote local cooperation by mobilising their members and promoting internal deliberation (Baccaro 2002a). EPG, however, is too dismissive of the old-fashioned organisational resources emphasised in sectoral corporatism. For the EPG authors, secondary associations carry with them the old, adversarial ways of doing things (lobbying parliaments and rallying supporters), and these associations 'have to acquire entirely new kinds of organisational competencies in order to function effectively in collaborative governance arrangements' (Fung and Wright 2003: 281). However, decentralised collaborative arrangements that are constructed without the pre-existing organisational capacity of secondary associations are likely to fail, because only such existing organisational capacity allows individual participants to overcome the (inevitable) cases of free-riding that they observe among other participants in the early stages of institution building.

In the next section of this chapter I explore in more detail the characteristics of decentralised collaborative governance and the expectations with respect to it of both sectoral corporatism and of empowered participatory governance, arguing that the polarised debate between these two literatures obscures the fruitful theoretical ground that lies between their extremes. In the following two sections I then present evidence from the two national episodes studied, those of French training reforms and Italian territorial pacts, comparing the observed experiences with theoretical expectations. The final section concludes.

THEORIES OF STATE AND SOCIETY

Policies establishing decentralised collaborative governance institutions aim to use collaborative institutions at the sub-national level as the new instruments for local actors to devise solutions to overcome their joint policy problems. They differ from more traditional sectoral corporatist arrangements in two principal ways: the scope of private actors involved and the level of delegation of policy autonomy to these actors. Sectoral corporatism explicitly involved the incorporation of a *limited* number of groups into the policy-making process; these groups received 'certain benefits in exchange for their cooperation and their restraint in the articulation of demands' (Keeler 1987: 9). In contrast, many of the reforms based on decentralised collaborative governance – which usually attempt to overcome information and coordination problems in local labour markets or economic development –actively involve multiple actors from civil society and from business (Giguère 2003; Greffe 2002). Secondly, groups involved in sectoral corporatism received seats on administrative bodies charged with implementing the details of policies decided by state policy-makers (Lehmbruch 1984; Keeler 1987). New instances of collaborative decentralised governance are empowered not merely to implement policies decided at the centre, but to develop their own analyses of local problems and proposed responses to them. They are not merely bodies of decentralised implementation, but of decentralised policy design, in which 'public and private actors share responsibility for the creation of public goods' (Considine 2003: 60).

The two institutional reforms examined in this chapter shared a common set of objectives: to build institutions of public/private collaboration that could provide collective goods at a local level and to change the cooperative propensities of local actors. Their significance lies in the stark reversal of direction they represented in state society-relations in two centralised policy-making systems previously considered poor social terrain for the establishment of corporatism: France and Italy (Cameron 1984; Regini 1984). The first case is the 1993 French reform that created multipartite institutions to develop proposals for regional education and training initiatives that aimed to spur private investment in human capital. The second is the institution of territorial pacts as the cornerstone of Italian development policy in the 1990s. The development pacts sponsored the participation of local secondary associations and politicians in proposing territorial development plans, with the goal of promoting ongoing cooperation among these actors at the territorial level.

In both cases, the goal of overcoming past failures of private cooperation was primary: national policy-makers posited that failures of private cooperation were central causes of the problems of youth training policy in France and of economic development in disadvantaged regions of Italy (Comité de coordination 1996 and 1999; Barca 2001). The cooperative problem at the heart of apprenticeship training is well known but difficult to solve (Soskice 1994). Individual employers have no incentive to invest in the general skills of their own workers, when they could just as easily hire an apprentice trained at another company, thereby depriving the training company of its investment in the general skills of its apprentice. Thus, firms underinvest in general skills and then complain of skill shortages that impede their productivity (Becker 1964). The cooperative problem here is convincing employers simultaneously to move from an equilibrium based on high-poaching, low skills, to one based on low-poaching, high skills. In southern Italy (the so-called Mezzogiorno), small companies have shown a systematically lower propensity to develop institutions that provide collective goods, which is the comparative competitive strength of industrial districts in northern and central Italy (Signorini 2000). This failure is often attributed to the weak propensity of economic actors to trust each other in the Mezzogiorno.[4] The explicit

---

4   Famously in Putnam (1993).

goal of the development pacts was to change the orientation of the economic actors so as to create the trust necessary to support this collective good (Cersosimo 2000: 288).

The proliferation of these institutions represents a challenge for comparative politics only if they infirm the expectations of existing theories of state-society relations. The most prominent theoretical work that should apply to these institutional innovations is that on sectoral corporatism and empowered participatory governance, but the fit of each is imperfect. As noted above, decentralised collaborative governance involves a greater number of actors from civil society and a wider delegation of state policy authority to these actors than is foreseen in classic works on sectoral corporatism. Empowered participatory governance takes as one of its defining characteristics the ambition to empower private individuals through the creation of deliberative fora for policy-making, and this goal is not explicit in either reform studied here (nor in most of the economic and social policy reforms that fit this paradigm in the OECD countries).[5] Nevertheless, work in these two theoretical traditions comes closest to approximating these new institutional configurations, and their prior expectations of the preconditions of success must be the null hypotheses for any investigation of them.

Neo-corporatism has long been the theoretical foil to pluralism in comparative politics and thereby the obvious referent for American observers looking at European systems of interest intermediation (Schmitter 1974). The ideal typical corporatist interest group system was defined by Schmitter as one in which interest groups are 'organised into a limited number of singular, compulsory, non-competitive, hierarchically ordered and functionally differentiated categories recognised and licensed ... by the state and granted with a deliberate representational monopoly within their respective categories' (ibid: 93–94). Within this body of theory, it was particularly the peak associations of employers and labour unions that were designated by states as privileged interlocutors. While we have seen that decentralised collaborative governance breaks this representational monopoly, in practice it almost always includes the sub-national representatives of unions and employers' associations. Moreover, unlike income policies (in which the competition is often zero-sum), the sorts of labour market and economic development policies in which we observe the development of collaborative decentralised governance across the industrialised countries are those in which sectoral corporatism proved stable over time, given the greater potential convergence of interest among actors (Lehmbruch 1984: 63).

---

5   Fung and Wright (2003: 39), however, posit broad applicability of the institutional principles of EPG as a means to solve contemporary problems of policy-making: 'the diversity of cases – across policy areas, levels of economic development, and political cultures – discussed in this volume suggests that EPG would usefully contribute to a large class of problem-solving situations ... [P]erhaps the burden of proof lies on those who would oppose more participatory measures.' It is these sorts of problem-solving situations, in which contemporary states in the OECD are turning to greater civil society involvement, that this chapter seeks to assess the ability of EPG tenets not just to increase participation but to solve public problems.

The keys to success in sectoral corporatism are twofold: organisations must be able to discipline their members so as to restrain them, and states have to provide organisational benefits to compensate organisations for their potential loss of membership (Keeler 1987: 9). Organisations that restrain their members' demands are vulnerable to competition for members from more radical groups, excluded from corporatist arrangements, which are not bound by the deals made through those arrangements (Sabel 1981). Thus, the organisational mechanism that makes the corporatist machine go is hierarchy, and the state mechanism that keeps it going is insulating those organisations from membership discontent, whether through material resources or legal preferences.

This is a very different set of prerequisites for success than that argued for in the literature on EPG. In addition, it is worth noting that the institutional fit between the tenets of EPG and the characteristics of the collaborative governance experiments undertaken in France and Italy during the 1990s is quite striking. Fung and Wright enumerate three design features of EPG institutions: devolution, centralised supervision and coordination, and state-centrism. In its first feature, the devolution of power, EPG institutions aim to bring local knowledge to answer public policy problems: this 'entails the administrative and political devolution of power to local action units ... charged with devising and implementing solutions and held accountable to performance criteria' (Fung and Wright 2003: 20). The aforementioned performance criteria foreshadow the continuing role of the central state in observing performance and circulating information among these devolved actors. The third characteristic is that these institutions 'colonise state power and transform formal governance institutions', formalising these deliberations rather than keeping them *ad hoc* (*ibid*: 22). To be clear, neither Fung and Wright nor any of their collaborators hold that these conditions of institutional design are *sufficient* to promote the deliberative democratic practice that they espouse. However, their tentative suggestion is that these features – which are also the core institutional features of the decentralised collaborative governance arrangements adopted in France and Italy – might be the backbone of EPG arrangements in a variety of settings.

In EPG, the prescriptions for success are the exact opposite of those in sectoral corporatism. Existing interest organisations are said to be hamstrung by their adversarial interest group capacities. In other words, they are generally skilled at trying to 'influence peak policy and legislative decisions [by swaying policy-makers, while] participatory collaboration requires competencies of problem-solving and implementation' (Fung and Wright 2003: 281). Why are the organisational capacities of collective problem-solving fundamentally different than those of contestation? This appears to be a problem both of organisational practice and of cognitive framing. The capacities of arm-twisting and contestation do not directly translate into those of having local knowledge and using it to bridge local political divisions. Established interest organisations, especially those that are federated affiliates of national organisations, are the least likely to be able to play these roles because of their ongoing history of adversarial practices. Just as they discount existing organisational capacities, so too do EPG theorists constantly seek to encourage 'popular involvement as a counterweight to entrenched officialdom' (Isaac and Heller 2003). Thus, the only way that the state has a useful role under EPG is in circulating information among existing (decentralised) experiments and in setting accountability standards (Fung and Wright 2003: 21–22). The state as network centre replaces the state as bureaucratic apparatus under EPG.

Both sectoral corporatist and EPG arrangements are observed in a wide variety of political and cultural settings. Each has a core set of design principles that establish the conditions under which policy areas can effectively be governed by such arrangements. However, these are very different principles from each other, and it is worth considering why. Sectoral corporatism focuses almost entirely on the ability of organisations to coordinate the quiescent response of their members – that is, to persuade them to accept government policies, in return for benefits to their representative organisation. Lucio Baccaro has recently launched a trenchant critique of corporatism for this approach: 'what the corporatist literature missed entirely is that organisational concentration and hierarchy are two possible mechanisms of coordination, perhaps even the most widely diffuse, but not the only possible mechanisms ... Democracy is [also] a powerful mechanism of coordination and dispute resolution' (2002a: 332). Baccaro demonstrates in his work that Italian unions, which are exactly the sort of adversarial organisations whose ability to promote deliberative-solving is denigrated by EPG theorists, are effective both at problem-solving *and* at traditional contestation (Baccaro 2002a and 2000b; cf Regini 2000). If collective problem-solving and public good provision are the indices on which we want to assess organisational capacity, the organisational antinomy between sectoral corporatist views of hierarchical, adversarial organisations and EPG views of democratically deliberative ones may be empirically inaccurate. Established organisations may be good at both things.

The role of states and public policy presents a similarly stark dichotomy between sectoral corporatism and EPG. The effective sectoral corporatist state is essentially making side-payments to social actors: buying off their quiescence for a degree of control over implementation and organisational resources. Frequently, as in the paradigmatic case of French agriculture, the state is using its corporatist social relays to euthanise all but a fraction of an obsolete sector (Keeler 1987). For EPG, the state is to be feared not for its execution of a sector, but for the tendency of bureaucrats and established politicians to strip politics of its deliberative, participatory character (Isaac and Heller 2003). The state can promote the success of experiments in empowered participatory governance, but only when it limits itself strictly to the role of information and accountability clearinghouse. Greater state involvement, in the EPG view, is likely to sap the participative life out of an institution by bureaucratising it. There is a wide gulf between institutional principles enunciating the neo-corporatist state as cynical provider of resources and the new age network state of EPG. Is there an intermediate role for public policy in the promotion of effective decentralised governance experiments?

I will argue in this chapter that the organisational and state policy dichotomies posed by these two literatures are over-stylised, revealing an undeveloped middle ground that is likely to be fertile for many experiments in decentralised collaborative governance. Decentralised collaborative governance calls on the distributed intelligence of actors close to local problems, as EPG theorists argue. *Pace* the literature on sectoral corporatism, rigidly hierarchical organisations have difficulty managing and mobilising information like this, given their top-down structure. However, existing adversarial organisations solve a variety of collective action problems and pay the start-up costs in experiments that provide public goods. Against the expectations of EPG theorists, we expect such groups to be the prerequisite to effective experiments in decentralised governance. With respect to state involvement, sectoral corporatism suggests that state aid will be devoted primarily to insulating groups from competition. However, when they are not managing decline but trying to solve local problems, organisations do not suffer principally from membership discontent. They suffer from their tenuous, uninstitutionalised position – they require resources and protection from politicians who would divert resources to other experiments. This is a very conventional role for politics – elected officials fighting for constituents in higher level representative bodies – but it is the sort of conventional politics that EPG theorists deride. Without such protection, though, experiments in decentralised collaborative governance are not likely to survive over time.

Why are these two elements necessary for success? Existing organisational infrastructure is the primary functional requisite of successful collaborative governance. Existing organisations with collective capacities bring together members to pursue a socially preferred goal, even one that requires actors not to pursue opportunities for short-term gain at the expense of social optimality. Such organisations can credibly pay some of the start-up costs of a new cooperative endeavour (Marwell and Oliver 1993). Even if these organisations do not have an effective sanctioning capacity to prevent free-riding by their members, their existing organisational infrastructure allows them to commit to pursue cooperative goals even in the face of occasional free-riding. No group, obviously, will continue to play the cooperative game for long if no one else is reciprocating a cooperative move. However, in trying to persuade local actors to pursue new patterns of cooperation, organised groups can both pay some start-up costs and absorb some free-riding in the early period of a new cooperative initiative (Culpepper 2003). Note that this is not a claim that social capital, as represented by local density of sports and civic clubs, is necessary for collaborative governance to succeed (cf Putnam 1993). Successful decentralised collaborative governance does not require lots of organisations that are important for their representation of generalised norms of reciprocity. Success requires only one or two capable organisations that provide what might be called organisational leadership in the early phases of experimental reform (Cersosimo and Wolleb 2001). Rather than trying to build up organisations *de novo*, therefore, governments that want to support collaborative governance would be wise to build their institutional architecture around existing organisational capacity in the political economy.

The second necessary condition for collaborative governance to succeed is political: namely, political leadership to protect fragile new governance arrangements from budgetary axes and to provide a direct link to the arena of electoral politics and policy-making. Collaborative governance arrangements, like those associated with EPG, are often adopted to deal with difficult policy problems that central states have conspicuously failed to solve. This was certainly the case of French training and Italian development policies. Given that new arrangements are being adopted to address difficult problems, it is reasonable to expect that some fine-tuning will be required. If these new arrangements are not merely to function as methods for central politicians to shift blame for problems they cannot solve, they will need to have electorally legitimated backers to allow for this fine-tuning of policy instruments to take place. This argument echoes the finding of Elinor Ostrom and Arun Agrawal (2001: 505) that decentralisation initiatives are often launched without strong local demands for them, but that the long-term effectiveness of these initiatives depends on the development of local pressures and lobbying to support them.

REGIONAL GOVERNANCE INSTITUTIONS IN FRANCE

The French government adopted an ambitious project of decentralised collaborative governance in 1993 as a means to overcome low levels of employer investment in vocational training. This law had both an institutional and a policy objective: it aimed to establish institutions of public-private collaborative governance at the regional level as a way to overcome the co-operative dilemmas that had previously impeded companies from investing in youth training contracts (Culpepper 2003). The decentralisation laws of 1982–83 had first ceded power to regional governments over the area of youth training, but 1984 laws that created new contracts governed at the national level had limited the effect of the reform. The 1993 Five-Year Law on Work, Employment, and Professional Training attempted to overcome past governmental failures by bringing together the various affected societal actors under the auspices of regional governments to work out the details of how to improve France's poor record of company investment in youth training contracts.

As with most reforms, this law had an expressly political catalyst: the election of the centre-right RPR/UDF coalition government in 1993, which brought to power many partisans of reinforced decentralisation. Chief among these was Charles Millon, president of the parliamentary group of the UDF and also the president of the regional council in Rhône-Alpes.[6] As regional president, Millon had since 1988 made Rhône-Alpes the region that had most vigorously attempted to assume the governance power over youth training conferred by the 1982–83 decentralisation laws. Millon had commissioned a non-partisan study to evaluate the progress of the regional reforms, and the reports had concluded that the reforms in Rhône-Alpes had failed in reaching their training goals because of the poor articulation between the region and private actors, underlining 'the fatal gap between the UFA program's central protagonists [regional government and employers' associations] and the micro-economic agents whose decisions underpin the effectiveness of the policy: especially the youth and the companies

---

6   Politicians in France can hold numerous offices at once, thus allowing Millon simultaneously to be a member of the national assembly and the president of a regional council.

tied by a labour contract, but also the decentralised actors of the educational system' (Brochier *et al* 1995: 115). Thus, one of the major political architects of the Five-Year Law came to power with the goal of empowering the regions by developing governance institutions that could enable collaboration among government, employers, unions and educational authorities.

However, for neither unions nor employers in France is the region a constituent level of organisation.[7] Most of the associations have territorial (sub-regional) organisations with a strong central peak association in Paris. One commonality of both French employers' associations and French unions is their weak organisational capacity at the grassroots (Howell 1992; Bunel 1995). Their major orientation therefore is sectoral and national, not regional and intersectoral. However, the new collaborative governance institutions developed by the Five-Year Law *were* regional and intersectoral: the COREFs.[8] The Five-Year Law, which had excluded secondary associations from its design phase, thus attempted to build collaborative governance institutions at the regional level, where French economic associations have the weakest collective capacities.

The law foresaw the COREF as a regional centre for consideration of projects by the representatives of employers' associations, labour unions, chambers, teachers' unions and parents. The regional governments, in consultation with the private actors assembled in the COREFs, were then to develop regional plans for how best to respond to the needs of employers and of the youth within the area of the region. This would allow policy to be elaborated by regional councillors in close consultation with all the relevant social actors with little oversight from Paris, and as such represented a radical departure from past patterns of policy-making in France.

The attempt by national politicians to establish functioning institutions of regional collaborative governance was undermined by the weak capacities of interest groups to circulate information among their members and to promote their engagement in the new policy initiative. Employers and unions, not typically close allies in France, worked together in most regions to marginalise the COREFs and to empower an alternative body (the COPIREs[9]) where only they were represented – thus cutting out the other representatives of civil society included in the COREFs. However, even in consultations with the COPIREs, regional administrators discovered that unions and employers at the regional level lacked the information-gathering and mobilising capacities to be useful interlocutors over policy-making (Culpepper 2003: 153–56).

Across France, the inability of regional associations to deliver useful information about the private economy to regional governments subverted this experiment in collaborative governance. The prime ministerial report that

---

7   The only exception to this rule is the CFDT, one of five officially recognised unions, which has a stronger regional capacity than its competitor unions and thus saw the 1993 law as an opportunity to improve its competitive position vis à vis those other unions.

8   Comité régional de la formation professionnelle, de la promotion sociale, et de l'emploi.

9   Commission paritaire interprofessionelle régionale de l'emploi.

evaluated the reforms in 1996 caustically observed that the uneven informational capacity of secondary associations at the regional level was a serious barrier to the successful functioning of the new institutions (Comité de coordination 1996: 117). The whole experiment of the Five-Year Law was premised on the idea that actors within society had local information that could inform policy, if that policy was sufficiently decentralised and allowed a strong enough role for private actors. However, the attempt to construct such institutions on the weak regional organisational capacity of the French social partners was unsuccessful, and the law foresaw no particular way to build capacity.

What was the impact of this institutional failure on the objective of increasing company investment in youth training contracts – that is, in increasing patterns of local cooperation? In short, French regional policies failed to convince companies to invest in youth training contracts. One good metric of firm training investment is the retention of employees in regular work contracts after their training period. Those companies that have invested heavily in general skills training should be loath to lose that investment by not hiring the trainee (Soskice 1994). There were two major youth training contracts in France in the 1990s: the apprenticeship and qualification contracts. In the mid-1990s, only 10% of apprentices and 29% of youths in qualification contracts were hired into regular work contracts after their training by the firm that trained them, which suggests that very few companies were heavily investing in the training of their young workers (Charpail and Zilberman 1998: 50; Vialla 1997). With few exceptions, the French reforms failed to stimulate local cooperation among employers (Culpepper 2003). In aggregate, French firms clearly used the subsidies associated with the training reforms to lower their labour costs, rather than to invest in developing the skills of their future workers.

The French experiment suggests that states are very likely to fail when they adopt institutions of decentralised collaborative governance that do not take into account the organisational structure of society. In the case of French training, this would have been the territorial employers' associations and unions.[10] Moreover, the French case is indicative of the problems of reforms that lack support from local politicians. The political force behind adopting decentralised collaborative governance was a political party (UDF) that wanted to strengthen the regions, despite the fact that regions were *not* the level most likely to succeed in facilitating the resolution of collective training problems. Thus, the political support for the project came from national politicians and their regional allies (and often, as in the case of Charles Millon, national politicians also held important regional offices). As long as the problem was how to support regional power through the expansion of collaborative governance, regional political entrepreneurs such as Millon were willing to invest their political capital in the regional project (Verdier 1995). However, as the failure of regional secondary associations became manifest, there was no political incentive for these leaders to solve the problem by changing the level of associational governance to correspond better to the capacities of

---

10 However, even at this level, that of their strongest constituent unit, French employers are on the whole still poorly organised; cf Bunel (1995).

French secondary associations. Regional politicians, in other words, were hardly likely to exert themselves to have power delegated to territorial levels below the region.

Consider in this light the proposition of EPG theorists that a central state needs to set effective performance criteria and circulate information about what works and what does not in collaborative governance. Such a design element was fundamental to the design of the Five-Year Law in France; an independent evaluative committee (the Comité de coordination) was administratively attached directly to the prime minister's office to assess progress in the reforms and circulate information about regional reforms to the regional actors and to parliament. The weakness of associations and the consequent hobbling of the collaborative institutional architecture is apparent in the reports of this evaluative committee (Comité de coordination 1996 and 1999). However, this diagnosis of problems had no political advocate with a vested interest in making collaborative governance work, if it was not going to work at the regional level. Without such a voice from electoral politics to initiate change in the French reform, the supervision from the centre proposed by EPG's advocates is likely to have little real effect in improving the structures of collaborative governance. Technical corrections are likely to be implemented only if they are harnessed to the interest of sub-national politicians in making a reform succeed.

TERRITORIAL PACTS IN ITALY

The institutional innovation of the Italian territorial pacts grew out of sub-national experiments that converged with several dramatic developments in Italian national politics in the early 1990s. First, 1992 marked the end of the 'extraordinary interventions' as the primary economic policy for the under-developed south of Italy. The extraordinary interventions had been extraordinarily ineffective in promoting the catch-up of the south with the more developed north, but they had been costly, transferring large amounts of money from Rome to governments in the south with little apparent effectiveness in promoting economic growth (Trigilia 1992). Secondly, the Tangetopoli (Bribesville) scandal of the early 1990s, which decimated the old political class in Italy, involved many corruption scandals linked to southern development money. Finally, the signature of the Maastricht treaty and its substantial budgetary demands in the run-up to the introduction of the euro put fiscal pressure on a process seen as ineffective and frequently corrupt. Such a programme based on high investments with low returns was an easy target for post-Maastricht budgetary rigour.

The character of the development policy that was to succeed extraordinary interventions – the territorial pacts – was however adopted for some clear political reasons.[11] The extraordinary aid had been a helpful benefit for central politicians to strengthen their machines and their supporters in the south. One of the

---

11 The pacts were not the only measure that replaced the old model of development aid. There were also a set of financial incentives for individual companies that ran as a concurrent policy to the pacts (Law 488/92).

electoral beneficiaries of this crisis was Umberto Bossi's Lega Nord, which decried the redistribution of money from the prosperous north to the under-developed south (Cersosimo 2000: 210). Thus, as in France, the ambition to build new institutions of public-private collaborative governance was born partly of a federalising push to empower the regional governments. However, regions have not historically been the most important level of sub-national government in Italy. That distinction belongs to communal governments (Dente 1997: 192–23). The forces of decentralisation thus had consequences for both communal government and regional government. The large change for communal governments came first, in the form of law 81/1993, which provided for the direct election of local mayors. This change led to a wholesale turnover of the local political class, as new political leaders from outside the old system were able to win office in local elections (Dente 1997: 184). Italian decentralisation was not developed as a uniquely regional phenomenon.

Moreover, the territorial pacts were not invented as a *regional* measure. They were not regional pacts, but territorial ones, aimed at incorporating actors from a local area (whose ambit was left undefined) rather than from the political-administrative unit of the region. The pacts that emerged varied in scale, but most were larger than a single local labour market and smaller than a province (a sub-regional administrative unit in Italy) (DPS 2003). The choice of the territory as the unit of the pact responded to the recognition by Italian policy-makers that the most successful organisational units of the Italian political economy were local: the industrial districts of the centre-north (Trigilia 2001). In contrast with the French policy discussed previously, the Italian policy was designed to take advantage of the existing organisational infrastructure of secondary associations.

The confluence of these three factors – failure of the extraordinary methods, collapse of traditional national political parties, and growing political recognition of the local base of the Italian economy – were the context within which the territorial pacts emerged in the mid-1990s as a tool for development. Once the government recognised the pacts in 1995, the possibility of state funding increased the number of applications, challenging the previously 'bottom-up' character of the pacts. In order to formalise the legal stature of the pacts and to distinguish them from other forms of negotiated policies in Italy ('programmazione negoziata'), the government clarified the juridical conditions of official pact recognition in March 1997.[12] Pacts were officially agreements signed by local actors that defined development objectives, apportioned expenditures toward meeting those objectives among state and private actors, and suggested regulatory changes in the legal development or industrial relations

---

12 In this chapter I discuss only the territorial pacts, leaving aside other elements of 'programmazione negoziata' in Italy: the area contracts (contratti di area), the institutionalised programme agreement (intesa istituzionale di programma), the programme contracts (contratti di programma), and the neighbourhood contracts (contratti di quartiere). The increase in these programmes has been substantial, and they suppose different models of private-public interaction. Among observers of the different development interests, the territorial pact has been identified as the 'instrument of programmazione negoziata that applies most clearly the principle of social partnership' (CNEL 1999: 53). As such, it has also been the subject of the most attention by researchers. For details of the various instruments, see CNEL 1999: 39–83.

provisions that could stimulate local economic growth. In practice, four types of actors were central to these agreements across Italy: the provincial administration, the communal leaders, industrial employers' associations, and the unions (Cersosimo 2000: 232). Other societal and governmental actors – such as chambers of commerce, banks, and regional governments – were involved in some pacts but not in others.[13]

Although signed by local actors, the territorial pacts were equally importantly a form of agreement between territories and the central government; when approved, they opened the way for money to flow from central coffers to the periphery (Trigilia 2001). Thus, rather than a central state devising the disbursement of development money, territories competed with each other to put forward their own 'endogenously grown' development plans. They competed with other territories for funding, which putatively incentivised them to put forward the best possible plan. Certainly this is a logic close to the heart of EPG, which sees the central government as a source of information circulation and accountability standards.

Besides devising a more efficient way to distribute money from the centre to disadvantaged regions, the territorial pacts also aimed to promote two changes in the character of interaction among territorial actors (DPS 2003: 14–15): first, to promote a sense of common identity and purpose among local collective actors; and, secondly, to reverse destructive patterns of weak inter-actor cooperation, particularly in the Mezzogiorno (Cersosimo and Wolleb 2001: 383–85). Through a new instrument, then, the government hoped to allocate development resources more efficiently while promoting the development of cooperation whose absence was seen in the past to have retarded common collective action, and perhaps economic development (Putnam 1993).[14]

What has been the experience, thus far, of the territorial pact experiment? Of the so-called first- and second-generation pacts (signed between 1997 and 1999), there were 51 Territorial Pacts, plus a further 10 financed under different rules by the European Union. It is obviously too early to draw a comprehensive balance sheet of the pacts – the more modest goal in this chapter is to try to understand what regularities have been observed across pacts, based on existing case studies and the comprehensive governmental evaluations of the pacts.[15] Looking over the

---

13 The absence of regional governments from most pacts is notable in light of recent discussions of Italian regionalism. In a sub-sample of 18 pacts, a department of the treasury study found that only four (22%) had regional signatories (Cersosimo 2000: 232).

14 Development pacts, and the aid that accompanied them, were made available to disadvantaged regions throughout Italy, whether under-developed or de-industrialising. They have not been limited to the Mezzogiorno.

15 The results on performance of the pacts are drawn from three main studies of the first and second generation pacts and 10 European pacts for employment (those signed between March 1997 and April 1999): the evaluative report of the department of development and cohesion policies of the Italian treasury (DPS); a study of 18 pacts conducted by Domenico Cersosimo and his collaborators (Cersosimo 2000; Cersosimo and Wolleb 2001); and a study of 46 pacts commissioned by the DPS through Sviluppo Italia (Sviluppo Italia 2001). This information is supplemented by comparative case studies conducted by Filippo Barbera (2001) and Anna Carola Freschi (2001). Thanks to Fabrizio Barca of the DPS for providing me access to the governmental reports.

51 nationally-subsidised pacts, one study suggests the typical pact comprises roughly 40 separate new initiatives, with financing split between public and private sources, mobilising roughly 700 million euros in new investments and creating about 530 additional jobs (Cersosimo 2000: 215–17). If these estimates are correct, then the direct job-creation effect of the pacts is modest at best. Indeed, a government evaluation of the national and European pacts shows very little difference in the public cost per job created of the pacts in comparison with the costs of the policy of direct incentives to companies (DPS 2003: 11–13).[16]

Which pacts succeed in promoting public-private cooperation and why? Existing research points to two 'moments' that are crucial in determining success or failure in changing the cognitive orientations of local actors. The first critical moment comprises the early period of creating confidence in the process of negotiated policy-making, while the second moment moves from the initial project phase to the institutionalisation phase (DPS 2003: 50–51). Success in the first moment – that is, successful transformation of the cognitive orientations of local actors toward a higher propensity to trust former antagonists – is invariably correlated with '*institutional leadership* that is credible and reliable, from actors who by experience or specific competences are able to aggregate, organise, and lead local coalitions made up of people who had scarcely communicated with each other in the past ...' (Cersosimo and Wolleb 2001: 395).[17] Two types of actors possessed the institutional resources to play this local leadership role: political actors (from provincial or municipal administrations) and social partners (the industrial employers' association and the major unions) (Cersosimo 2000: 232).[18] In pacts characterised by positive concertation processes – that is, those that have generated new cognitive orientations among previously competing actors – it seems that either an entrepreneurial local political figure (as in the pact of Appenino Centrale) or an entrepreneurial association (such as the union leadership in the pact of Locride) paid the start-up costs and provided the leadership to create local level concertation (Freschi 2001: 465; Cersosimo and Wolleb 2001: 397). While Appenino Centrale is located in the heart of the third Italy celebrated by Putnam, Locride is deep in southern Italy. As suggested by other case study research, social capital measured as pure associational density is neither a necessary nor a sufficient condition for successful concertation to emerge (Barbera 2001). What is necessary in the first phase is some actor with the

---

16 'At the level of mere financial outlays, the pact does not provide specific advantages [compared to past development policies]: its true comparative advantage is to act simultaneously on the double lever of direct incentives and amelioration of the firm's external context, on the financing of investment and the reduction of ambient diseconomies' (Cersosimo and Wolleb 2001: 387).

17 In pacts characterised by collusive behaviour and little behavioural change, by contrast, 'concertation is an "empty, virtual" process that does not change the game of traditional system of relations, but only a pretence necessary to apply for public money. Frequently these are inclusive coalitions, which means agreements formally signed by a multiplicity of local actors, institutional and not, which have nothing in common, nor do any want to share, but who are together with the lone goal of intercepting, for the use of their own organisation or its members, financial or non-material resources tied to the pact' (Cersosimo 2000: 223).

18 By contrast, representatives of regions have rarely been serious actors in the pacts that have emerged.

institutional wherewithal to pay many of the start-up costs of cooperation itself.[19] This wherewithal includes better technical training of administrators, better ability to diffuse information to local economic actors, and the ability to withstand some non-participation (defection) by uncertain local actors. The hierarchical organisational attributes characteristic of stable sectoral corporatism are not particularly useful in the engendering new co-operative relations at the local level.

The transition to the second stage represents the move from initial overtures of cooperation to *institutionalisation*. As foreseen by the EPG literature, the institutionalisation stage is the prerequisite to a durable change in standard operating procedures of private and public actors involved in the project of development. However, this moment is inherently fraught with risks for the co-operative actors, because institutionalisation always involves the channelling of resources among organisations.

In other words, organisations that may have begun to co-operate, in view of the possibilities of achieving new development policies, are almost certain to battle with each other over the resources that institutionalisation makes possible. Politicians like to control resources, and organisations need resources to survive and continue to attract members. The fact that they may have been willing to bear the start-up costs of local cooperation does not mean that they will foreswear the future material benefits to be acquired through such a new system. 'The problem of transition and linkage between the concertation phase and the management phase is very present in local discussions, indeed in certain cases it is the ground on which tensions and rifts between actors are created, to the point of compromising the positive concertative climate of the first phase' (Cersosimo and Wolleb 2001: 403).

What does this mean in practice? Many of the most ardent advocates of the 'bottom-up' development strategies have been disappointed by the process of institutionalisation as inimical to the local process they originally advocated. In their disappointment they echo the concerns of EPG theorists, observing that the project has been undercut by (re)introducing politics and bureaucracy into the local development policies (De Rita and Bonomi 1998: 11). This is an observation shared by many local participants, who frequently demanded a streamlining of the bureaucratic procedures in releasing money once the local actors met their benchmarks (DPS 2003; Sviluppo Italia 2001). At this stage what differentiated failed pacts from successful ones – successful ones being those that were able to institutionalise the newly co-operative relationships at the local level – was the presence of local political actors with either personal or political links to higher

---

19 The recent comprehensive governmental evaluation of the experience of early pacts suggests that the relatively better performance of first generation pacts than of second generation pacts may result from the greater local leadership provided in the first case than in the second. Among the second generation pacts, the tendency was to copy earlier pacts rather than to identify the needs of local participants (DPS 2003: 40–41). Note that the first generation pacts were all located in (social capital poor) southern Italy, while many of the second generation pacts were also located in northern and central Italy.

levels of power; notably, the treasury in Rome (Freschi 2001: 465–66). Where these actors were absent, or where they were divorced from the earlier concertation process, the transition from 'exceptional concertation' to 'routine management' was more difficult to achieve. Thus, as for example in the case of the pact in Brindisi, early gains in achieving local concertation were squandered, to the point where the various parties wound up taking each other to court (Cersosimo 2000: 241). If the risks of bureaucratic institutionalisation are great, the alternative appears to be worse for maintaining local development strategies.

DECENTRALISED COLLABORATIVE GOVERNANCE AND TERRITORIAL POLITICS

Experiments in decentralised collaborative governance have been under way in the advanced industrial countries for about 20 years, and they proliferated during the 1990s (OECD 2001). The cases examined here are two of the most prominent attempts to develop decentralised public-private collaborations, and they span the policy areas where many of these experiments have taken root: in active labour market policy and in local economic development. Just as the literature on neo-corporatism only began in the 1970s to analyse a social phenomenon in state-society relations that had long belied the assumptions of pluralist theory, it may be time for contemporary comparative politics to confront the realities of collaborative public-private governance. This chapter has taken one step in that direction.

The observation that the old tenets of corporatism no longer hold in the face of new policy challenges is consistent with other recent findings about the correlates of success in concertational economic policy-making (Regini 2000; Baccaro 2002a). The hierarchical insulation that was associated with stable governance arrangements in neo-corporatist theory does not translate to organisational effectiveness under decentralised collaborative governance. The failure of the French reforms, and the variation observed in the fate of Italian reforms, results from the capacities of groups to circulate information and to bear some of the early organisational costs involved in establishing new institutions. However, these organisations are not mere information networks; they are, importantly, organisational and technical relays that in the Italian cases proved to be crucial in paying some of the start-up costs of collaborative experiments. Thus, while the state under neo-corporatist arrangements helped insulate organisations from discontent, the most effective role of public policy may be in paying some of the costs of early institution-building. Clearly in these new experiments of policy-making, old-fashioned organisational attributes and material resources still count for a great deal.

It is exactly these attributes that EPG theory discounts too heavily. The findings in this chapter contradict the claim by Fung and Wright that 'participatory collaboration requires organisations with very different skills, sources of support, and bases of solidarity' than do adversarial interest organisations (2003: 266). In fact, the Franco-Italian comparison discussed here suggests that organisational resources are fungible. Where organisations are weak and adversarial – as in French industrial relations – they prove unable to carry out the roles devolved to them through collaborative governance, and they fall back on adversarial practices. However, with the strong and adversarial organisations of Italian industrial relations, groups that had not previously cooperated were able to engage productively in institutions of decentralised collaborative governance. This was particularly difficult in the moment of institutionalisation, when their tenuous cooperation sometimes broke apart given conflict over the distribution of resources. However, new organisations seldom had the organisational wherewithal to participate widely in the new institutions of collaborative governance (Cersosimo 2000). Some unions and employers' associations were able to change their functioning from adversarial to co-operative – and back again – relatively easily. It seems that organisations with the most developed collective capacities are likely to be strong in both adversarial and collaborative arenas.

Sub-national institutions of collaborative governance, in order to be effective and stable over the long run, need political protection and social capacity. In neither case studied here was this protection provided by a constitutional grant of power. The policy-making authority transferred to collaborative institutions was delegated by the central government, and it could be taken away by the central government. In France, the effectiveness of the institutions was undermined by social actors that did not have strong capacity at the grassroots level. Moreover, the reforms were not self-correcting, because there was no actor with an incentive to lobby politicians in favour of strengthening the observed weaknesses of collaborative institutions. Policy-makers at the regional level had few political allies to combat the weaknesses they encountered in dealing with the social partners, so they opted out of trying to create societal cooperation. Instead, they focused their attention on trying to develop their own governmental capacities, rather than the capacities of those social partners that they needed in order for the reform to succeed. While there is common agreement in France on the reasons regions have not been successful in taking control of this policy area, there is no strong political actor with an incentive to promote the building of social capacity that will be necessary if the French training reforms are ever to work as originally planned.

The change in Italian development policy was, like the French initiative, stimulated by a changing national political landscape. However, unlike the French initiative, the Italian territorial pacts had two attributes likely to increase both their resilience and their effectiveness in promoting local cooperation. First, the development pacts built essentially on a territorial logic, responding to the existing organisational architecture of the social partners. This reflected the bottom-up (rather than top-down) nature of their development. Rome did not invent the territorial pacts and bring them to the less developed territories; actors in those territories fashioned them themselves and then pushed for the politicians in Rome to use them as the central instrument of development policies. Secondly, the territorial pacts were invigorated by the 1993 law that had allowed for the direct election of mayors. As observed in the previous section, local leadership was the critical variable distinguishing successful pacts from failed pacts. The development of new institutional leaders at the local level not only provided this leadership; it also simultaneously provided a set of actors that was active in promoting (and protecting) the tool of the territorial pact to national politicians.[20]

When social scientists try to draw lessons from these institutional experiments, the analysis in this chapter suggests that they need to look at social capacities as much as at institutional rules when drawing lessons about the correlates of good governance. We are still far from identifying with the sort of precision and explanatory power of the neo-corporatist literature the characteristics and limits of decentralised collaborative governance institutions. It is likely that building on social capacities will, even where it creates net improvements for public good provision, also create the possibility for private rent-seeking. The nature of this trade-off, and the ways in which it varies across different political and cultural settings, are the sorts of issues that will require much additional research.

References

Ayres, I and Braithwaite, J (1992) *Responsive Regulation: Transcending the Deregulation Debate*, New York: Oxford University Press

Baccaro, L (2002a) 'The construction of 'Democratic' corporatism in Italy', 30 (June) Politics & Society 327–57

Baccaro, L (2002b) 'Negotiating the Italian pension reform with the unions: lessons for corporatist theory', 55(3) Industrial and Labour Relations Review 413–31

Balloch, S and Taylor, M (2001) (eds) *Partnership Working: Policy and Practice*, Bristol: Policy Press

Barbera, F (2001) 'Le politiche della fiducia: Incentivi e risorse sociali nei patti territoriali', 63 (March) Stato e Mercato 413–49

Barca, F (2001) 'New trends and the policy shift in the Italian Mezzogiorno' 28 (Spring) Daedalus 93–113

Becker, G (1964) *Human Capital*, New York: Columbia University Press

Berger, S (ed) (1981) *Organising Interests in Western Europe*, New York: Cambridge University Press

Brochier, D, Causse, L, Richard, A and Verdier, E (eds) (1995) *Les Unités de formation par alternance (UFA): Une co-opération Éducation nationale-professions dans la région Rhône-Alpes (1988–1993)*, Marseille: CEREQ Documents

Bunel, J (1995) *La Transformation de la représentation patronale en France: CNPF et CGPME*, Paris: Commissariat Général du Plan

Cameron, D (1984) 'Social democracy, corporatism, labour quiescence, and the representation of economic interest in advanced capitalist society', in Goldthorpe, J (ed) *Order and Conflict in Contemporary Capitalism*, New York: Oxford University Press 143–78

Cawson, A (ed) (1985) *Organised Interests and the State*, London: Sage

Cersosimo, D (2000) 'I patti territoriali', in Cersosimo, D and Donzelli, C (eds) *Mezzogiorno: Realtà, rappresentazioni e tendenze del cambiamento meridionale*, Rome: Donzelli Editore

---

20 As demonstrated in the French region of Rhône-Alpes, this strong local leadership with links to the centre represents a necessary condition, not a sufficient condition, for successful decentralised collaborative governance (Culpepper 2003).

Cersosimo, D and Wolleb, G (2001) 'Politiche pubbliche e contesti istituzionali. Una ricerca sui patti territoriali', 63 (March) Stato e mercato 369–411

Charpail, C and Zilberman, S (1998) 'Diplôme et insertion professionnelle après un contrat de qualification', in *Bilan de la Politique de L'Emploi 1997*, Paris: Direction de l'animation de la Recherche, des Etudes et des Statistiques

CNEL (1999) *Labouratori Territoriali: Rapporto sulla concertazione locale*, Rome Consiglio nazionale dell'economia e del lavoro (CNEL)

Considine, M (2003) 'Local partnerships: different histories, common challenges – a synthesis', in OECD, *Managing Decentralisation*, Paris: OECD 253–72

Comité de coordination (1996) *Évaluation des politiques régionales de formation professionnelle*, Paris: Prime Minister's Office

Comité de coordination (1999) *Évaluation des politiques régionales de formation professionnelle*, Paris: Prime Minister's Office

Culpepper, P (2003) *Creating cooperation: How States Develop Human Capital in Europe*, Ithaca, NY: Cornell University Press

Dente, B (1997) 'Sub-national governments in the long Italian transition', 20(1) West European Politics 176–93

De Rita, G and Bonomi, A (1998) *Manifesto per lo sviluppo locale: Dall'azione di comunità ai Patti territoriali*, Torino: Bollati Boringhieri

Dorf, M and Sabel, C (1998) 'A constitution of democratic experimentalism', 98 (March) Columbia Law Review 267–473

DPS (2003) 'La Lezione dei Patti Territoriali: Sintesi e Conclusioni', Rome: Department for Development and Cohesion Policies (DPS), Italian Ministry of Economics and Finance

Freeman, J (1997) 'Collaborative governance in the administrative state', 45 (October) UCLA Law Review 1–98

Freschi, C (2001) 'Capitale sociale, politica, e sviluppo locale: l'esperienza dei patti in Toscana', 63 (March) Stato e Mercato 451–85

Fung, A (2004) *Empowered Participation: Reinventing Urban Democracy*, Princeton, NJ: Princeton University Press

Fung, A and Wright, E (eds) (2003) *Deepening Democracy: Institutional Innovations in Empowered Participatory Governance*, New York: Verso

Giguère, S (2003) 'Managing decentralisation and new forms of governance', in OECD, *Managing Decentralisation*, Paris: OECD 11–27

Goldthorpe, J (ed) (1984) *Order and Conflict in Contemporary Capitalism*, New York: Oxford University Press

Greffe, X (2002) *Le Développement Local*, Paris: Éditions de l'Aube

Heller, P (2000) 'Degrees of democracy: some comparative lessons from India', 52 (July) World Politics 484–519

Howell, C (1992) *Regulating Labour: The State and Industrial Relations in Post-War France*, Princeton, NJ: Princeton University Press

Isaac, T and Heller, P (2003) 'Democracy and development: decentralised planning in Kerala', in Fung, A and Wright, E (eds) *Deepening Democracy: Institutional Innovations in Empowered Participatory Governance*, New York: Verso 77–110

Keeler, J (1987) *The Politics of Neo-corporatism in France*, New York: Oxford University Press

Lehmbruch, G (1984) 'Concertation and the structure of corporatist networks', in Goldthorpe, J (ed) *Order and Conflict in Contemporary Capitalism*, New York: Oxford University Press 60–80

Marwell, G and Oliver, P (1993) *The Critical Mass in Collective Action: a Micro-social Theory*, Cambridge: Cambridge University Press

OECD (ed) (2001) *Local Partnerships for Better Governance*, Paris: OECD

OECD (ed) (2003) *Managing Decentralisation: A New Role for Labour Market Policy*, Paris: OECD

Ostrom, E and Agrawal, A (2001) 'Collective action, property rights, and decentralisation in resource use in India and Nepal', 29(4) Politics & Society 485–514

Putnam, R (1993) *Making Democracy Work*, Princeton, NJ: Princeton University Press

Regini, M (1984) 'The conditions for political exchange: how concertation emerged and collapsed in Great Britain and Italy', in Goldthorpe, J (ed) *Order and Conflict in Contemporary Capitalism*, New York: Oxford University Press 124–42

Regini, M (2000) 'Between deregulation and social pacts: the responses of European economies to globalisation', 28(1) Politics & Society 5–33

Sabel, C (1981) 'The internal politics of trade unions', in Berger, S (ed) *Organising Interests in Western Europe*, New York: Cambridge University Press 209–44

Schmitter, P (1974) 'Still the century of corporatism?', 36(1) Review of Politics 85–131

Signorini, L (ed) (2000) *Lo Sviluppo Locale: Un Indagine della Banca d'Italia sui distretti industriali*, Rome: Meridiana Libri

Soskice, D (1994) 'Reconciling markets and institutions: the German apprenticeship system', in Lynch, L (ed) *Training and the Private Sector: International Comparisons*, Chicago, IL: University of Chicago Press 25–60

Sviluppo Italia (2001) 'Caratteristiche e potenzialità dei patti territoriali', Report Commissioned by DPS, 2000

Trigilia, C (1992) *Sviluppo senza autonomia: Effetti perversi delle politiche nel Mezzogiorno*, Bologna: Il Mulino

Trigilia, C (2001) 'Patti per lo sviluppo locale: un esperimenta da valutare con cura,' 63 (March) Stato e mercato 359–67

Verdier, E (1995) 'L'accord fondateur d'une politique régionale: une ambiguïté créatrice?', in Larceneux, A and Kabantchenko, E (eds) *La stratégie des acteurs locaux dans les politiques de formation*, Marseille: CEREQ Documents 96–110

Vialla, A (1997) 'Apprentissage: ruptures, enchaînements de contrats et accès à l'emploi', 97(22) *Note d'Information*, Ministère de l'Education Nationale 1–4

THE EUROPEAN TURN TO GOVERNANCE AND UNANSWERED QUESTIONS OF LEGITIMACY: TWO EXAMPLES AND COUNTER-INTUITIVE SUGGESTIONS

Christian Joerges and Michelle Everson

INTRODUCTION

The European Union is ever more often seen as a *sui generis* order, with *sui generis* problems and modes of tackling those problems all of its own. This is a false impression. Europe's struggles and tussles, say, in the matter of reconciling efficient (non-political) economic management with sometimes conflicting (politically formulated) demands for social justice and redistribution, not only mirror the old, if obscured, conflicts carried on behind the edifice of the traditional national constitutional settlement,[1] but are also increasingly being set in a far wider, globalised, context. Today, many formerly avowed Europeanists are accordingly turning their urgent attentions to the embeddedness of Europe within globalisation processes. However, and against this trend, this paper also seeks to take a closer look at European peculiarities. Even if Europe is not unique, it has nonetheless presented the world with one of the clearest examples of the limits to notions of 'disembedded' markets and also proves itself, under the eponymous title of 'European governance', to be a fascinating laboratory for the creation of new forms of interrelations between market processes, governing power and civil society.

The story of 'the sting in the tail' of a seemingly deregulatory and liberal process of European market integration, the renewed need for market direction and the plethora of re-regulatory solutions and institutions brought to bear on a European scale, is not simply an old, if surprising, story. Instead, it is also startling proof of Fred Block's assertion that distinctions made between liberal market economies and co-ordinated market economies,[2] as well as the general tendency

---

1   That is, in legal terms, the underlying constitutional tension between the primacy of democratic direction and the need for 'polity restraint' in matters such as the efficient pursuit of economic expansion (see Everson 2004b).

2   We do not assert to have considered the whole range of alternative theoretical approaches striving for an understanding of 'markets as polities' such as those offered by the 'varieties of capitalism' literature or contributions from the risk and knowledge societies debate (see Stehr 2003: 222–44 on the 'moralisation' of markets), or from systems theory (Teubner 2004). Our references to Fred Block's inspiring analysis emphasise one core insight that these approaches share, namely that what happens in markets cannot be understood by stimulus-response mechanics or any modelling which does not take the 'political' (communicative/moral) dimensions of markets seriously.

to analyse modern market developments in terms of how much a state should or should not intervene in a seemingly autonomous market sphere, are, if not wholly false, nevertheless largely misleading. Along with Karl Polanyi, Block notes that:

> Once it is recognised and acknowledged that markets are and must be socially constructed, then the critical question is no longer the quantitative issue of how much state or how much market, but rather the qualitative issue of how and for what ends should markets and states be combined and what are the structures and practices in civil society that will sustain a productive synergy of states and markets. (Block, Chapter 1 in this volume; see also Amstutz 2001: 16–21)

Europe's re-regulatory tendencies, the set of 'fictitious commodities' (most notably 'knowledge' and 'risk') upon which Europe's market is founded, and which have necessitated societal re-intervention within economic processes, are a clear indicator of the existence of Polanyi's 'always embedded market'. The days of the gloriously isolated autonomous European market sphere were short indeed: judicial activism and negative integration soon succumbed to social constructionism and a welter of new institutional responses to demands for the embedding of the European market in a European civil society with its own *sui generis* modes of 'poststatal' intervention. Accordingly, as its title indicates, this paper is somewhat reductionist, concentrating largely upon two fields of transnational 'social regulation', but only one transnational level of governance. The European market may well be only one segment within a densely interwoven patchwork of national, supranational and international 'always embedded markets'. It is, however, instructive. Just as it took EU policy-makers years to understand why their market integration project required not just the opening of markets and the 'abolition' of non-tariff barriers to trade, but a broad re-regulatory effort (Majone 1989), the years of re-regulation have also seen very varied institutional efforts to re-embed the European market and, in the absence of clear statal direction, evolve structures and practices in (a European) civil society that will sustain a productive synergy of (European) society and markets. In this respect then, the European examples of standardisation and food safety are particularly useful, not only allowing us to detail the always embedded nature of the European market, but also to assess efforts to reconnect, society, 'governing' or 'governance' power and economic processes for their effectiveness and legitimacy.

The turn to governance is central to the analysis. Europe, so political-science integration research has been telling us for some years now, must also be understood as a 'multi-level system of governance', a heterarchy rather than a hierarchy, an only partially integrated polity without a government, which needs to ensure the co-operation of semi-autonomous political and administrative bodies. Although also a far broader term (see for detail below), governance can thus also, and in the specific terms of the 'always embedded market', be understood as an effort to structure civil society and market relations beyond our traditional understandings of state-market dichotomies. A first section accordingly examines the career of this concept in two disciplines, political and legal science, and explains why the turn to governance occurred at all levels, the international, the European and, last but not least, the national level. Section two then presents an overview of European 'modes of governance'. It is not just descriptive but also addresses legitimacy issues and, more particularly, the role that modern law plays or should play in maintaining a productive and legitimate synergy, societies, polities and markets.

This final point is determinative. Practical European developments and the praxis of European re-regulation not only betray the always embedded nature of markets, but also expose the weaknesses in our traditional statal constitutional approaches to the legitimate control of embedded markets. In a new supranational polity, law is accordingly called upon to develop new modes of civilising market-society relations, either through a 'conflicts of law mechanism' that establishes the joint principles that various relatively autonomous polities and partial polities will adhere to, or through the vexed question of the 'constitutionalisation of (partially privatised) transnational governance mechanisms'. It is with respect to such governance arrangements that the tough questions are raised. To whom are the authors of these regimes accountable? On what grounds can their claims to validity be justified? We cannot and do not offer a comprehensive answer to these questions. Nonetheless, on the basis of our limited examples, we do offer some (counter-intuitive) suggestions.

THE TURN TO GOVERNANCE

The new millennium in Europe appears to be host to an all-pervasive allergy: everybody seems to be talking and writing about governance. This all began with a speech by the President of the Commission delivered on 15 February 2000 in Strasbourg to the European Parliament. On this occasion, Romano Prodi, still smarting under the impact of the BSE crisis and its negative impact on the reputation of the European 'regulatory state', announced far-reaching and ambitious reforms. This was a message spoken in a new vocabulary, announcing a fresh agenda and a novel working method. Prodi envisaged a new division of labour between political actors and civil society, and a more democratic form of partnership between the layers of governance in Europe. This was a package of innovation, openly admitting of the need better to embed the European market in European society and launched strategically into a legally undefined space that is located somewhere between administrative[3] and constitutional reform.[4] The Commission followed up on the rhetoric of the speech. A 'governance team', composed of Commission officials under the leadership of Jérôme Vignon, the former director of the Forward Studies Unit, was entrusted with the task of elaborating the reform agenda.[5] It co-operated with eminent academics and

---

3   Cf *Reforming the Commission – A White Paper*, COM(2000) 200 final of 1 March 2000; cf http://europa.eu.int/comm/reform/index_en.htm.

4   Which was set in motion by the EU Charter of Fundamental Rights, solemnly proclaimed at Nice on 7 December 2000 ([2000] OJ C346/1 of 18 December 2000), followed by the Laeken Conference of 14–15 December 2001 with its concluding declaration on the future of the Union and the setting up of a constitutional convention, which took up its work in March 2002.

5   Enhancing democracy in the European Union. Working Programme, SEC (200) 1547/7 final of 11 October 2000 (http://europa.eu.int/comm/governance/work/en.pdf).

experts. Remarkable essays were produced (De Schutter *et al* 2001). A website disseminated the work to the outside world (http://europa.eu.int/comm/governance/index_en.htm). A White Paper was published in July of 2001.[6] Although not well received in academic circles (see Joerges *et al* 2001), 'governance' retained its prominence. European academics are scrambling to investigate the concept, whilst American observers confirm the significance of the shift from government to governance, the move from regulatory reform to 'new modes of governance'.[7] However, how do you know governance when you see it? This depends, of course, on where you look.

International relations

Neither the European Union nor the American Federation invented the term. Its career began at international level and in international relations theory, most prominently with James Rosenau's seminal 1992 article (see Rosenau 1992). What Rosenau brought to the attention of international relations scholarship was the disjunction of governance from government, the delegation of governmental authority to non-governmental bodies. He stated: 'To presume the presence of governance without government is to conceive of functions that have to be performed in any viable human system' (see above). This was a functional definition and was not linked to the public-private dichotomy. Nonetheless, at this time governance was still conceived as an intentional activity, a connotation that the German term *Regieren* still carries with it (see Jachtenfuchs and Kohler-Koch 2003). In the meantime, however, attention has appeared to have shifted to the composition of the actor configurations that produce such activities; meanwhile, and unsurprisingly for lawyers, the debate has extended ever more intensively to encompass prescriptive queries about the nature of 'good' governance (see Jachtenfuchs and Kohler-Koch 2003).

By the same token, however, it has now become difficult to clearly identify the contours of the concept. To take two recent examples: the reactions of the US Department of Agriculture to an individual case of BSE in Washington State are an example of traditional regulatory policy as we know it. However, the *ensemble* of actions taken by governmental and non-governmental bodies around the globe, and their subsequent impact upon the USA(!), are of a different quality. The East Asian poultry issue is even more dramatic: the simple fact that markets are always embedded, even far beyond the borders of the traditional state, gives rise to interventionist efforts to prevent 'market cascades' (see Block, Chapter 1 in this volume), or combat risk to human health, by a huge variety of actors worldwide, by *officials* at all levels of governance and by non-governmental organisations (Commission on Global Governance 1995: 2 and 4). Governance, in short, would seem to refer to those somewhat indistinct cases of 'spontaneous unco-ordinated

---

6   *European Governance – A White Paper*, COM(2001) 428 final of 25 July 2001, OJ C287, 5.
7   See, for example, the contributions to the Workshop on the Open Method of Co-ordination and Economic Governance in the European Union, organised by the European Union Centre at the University of Wisconsin, Madison in April 2003. The contributions are available at http://eucenter.wisc.edu/Calendar/Spring03/harvardomc.htm.

action' between public and private actors at all national, supranational and international levels.

National level

A brief remark on the national level: German administrative law scholarship tends to avoid use of the term (although 'public and private partnerships' are accepted) but nonetheless discusses the topic intensively (see, for example, Trute 1996; Franzius 2003; Mehde 2002). Private law scholars are no less curious.[8] One, in our view, particularly interesting contributor to the discussion in the US is Jody Freeman (see Freeman 2000). She defines 'governance' as a 'set of negotiated relationships between public and private actors' (Freeman 2000: 546). These negotiations concern 'policy-making, implementation and enforcement' (Freeman 2000: 548). Examples are manifold. She points to a broad variety of administrative contexts, including standard-setting, health care delivery, and prison management (Freeman 2000: 581, 592 and 594). Some of them are clearly a public responsibility. Does this mean that any involvement of non-governmental actors is inconceivable? The reply to this objection is the core argument. To cite from her most recent article (Freeman 2003): privatisation (the inclusion of private actors into governance arrangements) 'might extend public values to private actors to reassure public law scholars that mechanisms exist for structuring public-private partnerships in democracy-enhancing ways' (Freeman 2003: 1290).[9]

Constituting governance arrangements: bringing the 1980s back in

Let us summarise and add one point. At international level, the term governance denotes 'policy arrangements' which emerge outside the administrative system of a single nation state (government) but which, nevertheless, have a significant impact on a globally or regionally defined set of recipients. 'Governance' is like 'government' in so far as it stands for the regulation of the economy and social relations. It is distinct in so far as it relates to European, international, transnational or global activities, which are not exclusively public and involve experts and knowledge pools. It is not hierarchical, but heterarchical and typically 'organised in networks'.

---

8 Their focus is, of course, on the governance arrangements within the economy. See, for example, Teubner (2004).

9 One counter-intuitive example was already mentioned in the NYU article just cited (Freeman 2000): 'The "American correctional association" (ACA) is an association of correctional professional dating back to 1870. It sets standards for every aspect of prisons, including security and control, food service, sanitation, medical and health care, inmate rights, work programmes, etc ... The ACA is widely regarded as a leading progressive standard-setting body in correctional policy and, in the prison reform cases in the 1960s and 1970s, the ACA manual became an important resource for Federal Courts' (fn 183).

At a more particular level of governing the embedded market, 'knowledge management' is vital. In the view of some commentators (see Block, Chapter 1 of this volume), a 'fictitious commodity' joining together with Polanyi's famous triad of money, labour and land to furnish the socially constructed building blocks upon which markets are founded, knowledge is not always easily found within simple statal administrative structure. Instead, at national and international level, governance arrangements typically respond to the need to integrate the expertise and organisational responses of non-governmental actors (civil society) into the management of public affairs. Where this is the case, their achievements reach beyond what governmental actors and bureaucracies can accomplish. In this sense, 'governance' could be called a productive activity.

It would be premature, at this point, to take a stand as to the legitimacy of these developments. It is important, however, to recall that such phenomena are not so new, at least to lawyers (for an elaboration of the following observations, see Joerges 2005: 226–35). They have been on the legal theory agenda ever since lawyers became aware of implementation problems and joined the critique of welfare state interventionism that gave rise to particularly intense debate in the 1980s. Broad disappointment with 'purposive' legal programmes of economic management and a new degree of sensitivity towards 'intrusions into the lifeworld' through social policy prescriptions mirrored the understanding that economic processes were embedded within societies in far more complex ways than a simple market-state dichotomy might suggest, further triggering a search for new modes of legal rationality to replace formalist intervention and doing away with the destructive myth that law might get a grip on social reality through the simple application of 'grand theories' such as, for example, economic theories of law (see Teubner 1983; Wiethölter 1989). At the same time, however, proceduralisation and 'reflexive law' were also concerned with very practical issues such as the improvement of implementation and compliance. Discrepancies were clear between grand purposive legal programmes and their real world social impact: it became a core concern of legal sociology to establish soft-law and regulatory alternatives to command and control regulation (famously summarised and analysed by Teubner 1987). In other words, law, concerned both to ensure the practical effectiveness of economic regulation, as well as its wider social legitimacy, was drawn very early on into the refashioning of constitutional and administrative legal spheres in order to overturn the myth that the 'state' might simply choose (or not choose) to direct the economy through control mechanisms. With this, law (even at the national level) was evolving a far more differentiated view of the constructive and legitimate synergies between markets and civil societies.

NEW AND NOT SO NEW MODES OF EUROPEAN GOVERNANCE

Governance seems thus to have a long and seemingly successful history both at national and international level. This, of course, begs the question of why Europe has been so tardy in applying the term explicitly to its own regulation. Clearly, especially those governance strategies which recognise the social and institutional complexities of always embedded markets, and in particular, the limited effectiveness of directive 'state' regulation should have been an immediate and urgent blueprint for internal market regulatory strategies, furnishing the cure for both the Community's output deficiencies and its legitimacy malaise. Nonetheless, matters were never and still are not that simple at European level. Most pertinently, Europe's design, perhaps influenced by economic theories championing the self-regulatory powers of economic processes, did not foresee the administrative powers and resources that the administering of the European market project would require. This gap in administrative law perfectly complements Europe's so-called democracy deficit and its 'social deficit';[10] implying, on the one hand, that Europe might never be in a position to develop uncontested institutions that might create an effective synergy between its market and its civil society, and determining, on the other hand, that governance within Europe is more a matter of praxis, rather than determined design. In other words, the malaise may be clear, but the cure is not. A broad variety of responses to the lack of steering capacity are nonetheless conceivable in the abstract.

(1) Administrative powers should, in principle, remain national. This is what the German government suggested in its complaint against the General Product Safety Directive (Directive 92/59/EEC [1992] OJ L228/24). This argument is unsurprising. It projects Germany's federalism, which reserves administrative powers to the *Länder* onto EU law. That would be, so the ECJ has explained, unacceptable.[11] (2) Alternatively, Europe should bravely shoulder its tasks and develop an equivalent to the US Administrative Procedure Act, not only in areas that are traditionally characterised as administrative law (such as foodstuffs regulation), but even in the legal structuring of standardisation (see Vos 1999; see also Harlow 1996; Dehousse 1999). (3) Finally, the EU is not a federation; it can neither follow the German nor the US model. Instead, the EU has to learn how to 'administer' a multilevel system of governance in which the Member States retain some autonomy while the Community has neither the competences nor the resources that 'good' administration would require.

This third position is our chosen positive and normative background for our review of Europe's modes of governance. It is positive background because the configuration of interests within the European polity can plausibly explain why the dynamics of market building and the hesitancy of the Member States to grant new competences and finance their exercise have generated such a plethora of institutional innovations outside the legal frameworks of the EC Treaty. The normative aspects of these institutional innovations are inextricably linked to these processes, and the continuities within the various normative agendas are fascinating. Again and again, the proponents of European state-building have sought to strengthen supranational powers. Again and again, the intergovernmentalists have renewed their objections. There is much continuity in these complex and dynamic developments. In addition, to be sure, the disputes over the *gestalt* of

---

10 One more statement that would deserve substantiated explanations. Suffice it here to underline that the present EU is no longer the European Economic Community which could plausibly reject quests for 'social' integration. For an elaboration of this argument, see Joerges and Rödl (2005).

11 See the rejection of Germany's argument by the ECJ in Case C–359/92, *Germany v Council (General Product Safety Directive)* [1994] ECR I–3676.

Europe were never purely aesthetic. They were always political contests as well, in which many stakeholders raised concerns and defended interests.

The new approach to technical harmonisation and standards

The so-called new approach, which has just celebrated its 20th birthday, is a regulatory innovation that still fascinates. Summarising a well-known story (see Joerges *et al* 1991, Chapter 3; Schepel 2005, 37–76 and 101–44), the new approach is the clearest European institutional expression of the always embedded nature of the European market. The dual needs to guard against market cascades (risks to public health and safety) and manage information within a European market seemed to dictate that market integration could only follow upon the 'positive' harmonisation of countless regulatory provisions. Harmonisation, however, was always difficult to achieve, even after the old unanimity rule of Article 100 of the EC Treaty was replaced by qualified-majority voting (Art 100(a), as introduced by the Single European Act of 1987) and even following the by now legendary *Cassis de Dijon* decision of 1979, introducing mutual recognition of national regulatory provisions as a founding regulatory principle within the European market.[12] The 'fictitious commodities' (the need for the regulation of risk and information) of the always embedded European market both mitigated against a simple deregulatory integration strategy and remained politically and normatively highly sensitive, acting as a honey pot around which a host of economic interests swarmed. Accordingly, it was very difficult to achieve legislative harmony as amongst the Member States. By the same token, under the 'traditional approach', legislative directives required a high level of technical detail and sophistication.[13] Somewhat paradoxically, self-regulation, a technique widely used in Germany in particular, was by no means easier to live with either. Voluntary product standards were 'private' obstacles to trade that the Community legislature could not overcome by legislative *fiat*. How could the Community exit this *impasse*?

These were the answers of the new approach:

(1) European legislation confines itself to laying down 'essential safety requirements'. Only products complying with these requirements may be placed on the market. If they do, they circulate freely within the Community.

(2) The 'concretisation' of the requirements is a task not for legislatures and/or public law, but for the experts working in European and national

---

12 Case C-120/78 *Rewe Zentrale v Bundesmonopolverwaltung für Branntwein* [1979] ECR 649 (*Cassis de Dijon*).

13 For an admirably careful and thoughtful recent reconstruction, see Schepel (2005), especially Chapter 2.4. Schepel points to Directive 84/438/EEC on the permissible sound power level of lawnmowers, [1984] OJ L183/9, adopted six years after the Commission's proposal, [1979] OJ C86/9, and Directive 84/526/EEC on seamless, unalloyed aluminium and aluminium alloy gas cylinders, [1984] OJ L300/20, adopted a full 10 years after the Commission's proposal, [1974] OJ C104/75.

standardisation organisations. The standards that they elaborate are to be published in the *Official Journal* and transposed into national standards. Products complying with such standards are presumed to be safe.

(3) Legally speaking, such compliance is voluntary. Manufacturers remain free to develop alternatives, which must, however, respect the mandatory essential requirements.

The 'new' approach was thus complemented by the 'global' approach that dealt with conformity assessment procedures. Further refinements and complementary legislation were necessary, and important problems were never addressed. Harm Schepel (2005: 65) cites a widely shared perception of the proponents of the new approach:

> If the basic characteristics of the new approach had to be summed up in a single sentence, it could be said that this method, in fact, makes it possible better to distinguish between those aspects of Community harmonisation activities which fall within the province of the law, and those which fall within the province of technology, and to differentiate between matters which fall within the competence of public authorities and those which are the responsibility of manufacturers and importers. (Nicolas 1995: 94)

Neither a wonderful, nor a real world. This comment will be substantiated below.

The committee system and comitology

European committees, charged with elaborating European standards, were born out of a strong national desire to retain control over both the setting and the consequences of European regulatory standards. Thus, as innovative European mechanisms of market governance, they best embody the functional and structural tensions, which characterise internal market regulation. First, being made up both of technical experts and (political) governmental and social interests, they hover between 'technical' and 'political' considerations, between the functional needs and ethical/social criteria, which inform European regulation. Secondly, their often very fluid composition not only reflects upon the regulatory endeavour to balance the rationalisation of technical criteria against broader political concerns, but also forcefully highlights the schisms that exist among the political interests of those engaged in the process of internal market regulation. Even where they are explicitly established to support and oversee the implementing powers delegated to the Commission, committees are deeply involved in political processes and often resemble 'mini-councils', in that they are the forum in which the balancing of a European market-integrationist logic against a Member State interest, in terms of the substance and the costs of consumer protection and cohesive national economic development, has to be achieved.

Agencies

Moving on to further European governance mechanism, however, the functional and compositional divergence between European agencies and committees seems all the more striking. Charged with regulation on market entry and exit, or more general informal, and policy-informing, information-gathering duties, the new European agencies meet a purely technical demand for market-corrective and sector-specific regulation. The most prominent proponents of agencies submit the type of arguments we have just heard in their defence: agencies perform primarily technocratic functions. This is what they accomplish best, and semi-autonomous status gives implicit voice to private market interests and much credence to the lingering notion that internal market regulation has more to do with the 'neutral' sustenance of individual economic enterprises (preserving the 'disembedded market') than with the imposition of (collective) political/social direction (managing the 'always embedded market'). Their placement under the Commission's institutional umbrella and the presence of national representatives within their management structures notwithstanding, agencies are largely shielded from explicitly political processes by their founding statutes (Council directives and regulations), permanent staff, organisational independence, varying degrees of budgetary autonomy, and direct networking with national administrators. The most recent creature in the line is the European Food and Safety Authority (see Regulation 178/2002 [2002] OJ L31/1), a particularly important and instructive example, to which we will return.

Agencies were the core institutions in Giandomenico Majone's design of the European 'regulatory state'(see Majone 1994). This design, however, was not fully implemented. What European agencies are or will become is controversial. That much is uncontested.[14] Agencies are emphatically not self-sufficient bureaucratic entities. They must co-operate with a web of national authorities in accomplishing the tasks laid down in European legislation and, because of these relationships, it is virtually impossible to allocate responsibility for policy decisions to one set of civil servants or another. Decision-making is national, infranational, and supranational, all at the same time.

Mutual recognition and regulatory competition à la européenne

The idea that regulatory competition might become a substitute for political governance in the EU was once nurtured by the Commission's deliberate over-interpretation of the ECJ's *Cassis de Dijon* judgment.[15] The contrast between the expectations raised and the processes to be observed are again striking. The mutual observation of stakeholders in all the areas concerned and the processes of interaction between legal systems are becoming increasingly intense. A conceptualisation of these developments in terms of a competitive search for efficiency as suggested by many must refer to very heroic assumptions.[16] Not even in the field of company law, it seems, is an interpretation of the ECJ's recent

---

14 For an analysis of the example at first sight closest to American examples, see Feick (2002).
15 See the Communication from the Commission in [1980] OJ C256/2.
16 The most thorough study we are aware of is by Tjiong (2002).

jurisprudence convincing. The freedoms that the ECJ allows the parties to exercise are not without limits. What the recent ECJ jurisprudence, at least in our benevolent interpretation (see Joerges 2002), has achieved is the opening of national legal systems for internal critique based on the viewpoints of other jurisdictions. National legislatures must justify the wisdom of their laws. European law, it might be suggested, thus oversees a process whereby judiciaries constantly review the appropriateness and 'civility' of national legislation, furnishing a basis for the balancing of an integrated market against legitimate national regulatory concerns.

The Open Method of Co-ordination (OMC)

The Treaty of Amsterdam witnessed the insertion of a new Title (VIII) on employment as well as a novel mode of governance, namely, a national and Community co-ordination of employment strategies in Article 125. The European Council in Lisbon in 2000 then recommended that the OMC be extended to encompass social policy. The OMC broke with the old 'Community method' for three reasons: first, it permitted the taking of action even outside the area of competences that had been expressly transferred to the Community; secondly, it upgraded the Council; and, thirdly, it renounced the conventional 'juridification' of Community policies. The OMC has become the object of intensive discussion and hopes. It is perceived as a chance to overcome Europe's 'social deficit'; in other words, the OMC, it is argued, is the 'new missing link', the evolutionary fulcrum re-establishing a direct relationship between Europe's disembedded market and a European populace's demands for embedded redistributive action.

American political scientists, legal sociologists and economic historians are the most active proponents of this idea (see Sabel and Zeitlin 2003). They have found followers in Europe, both among political scientists and lawyers (see Eberlein and Kerwer 2002). The idea of 'constitutionalising' the OMC was taken up in pertinent working groups in the European Convention (see de Búrca and Zeitlin 2003). However, even strong OMC proponents can only point to weak or ambivalent empirical evidence.[17] So far, the effects of the OMC have not been easy to grasp in any of the fields in which it has been tried, and this is particularly true in the field of employment policy. It is difficult to find reliable information on the mechanisms that define it. Is the autonomy the Member States enjoy in their search for the means to achieve the agreed upon targets really being used innovatively? Have criteria been discovered and defined which enable 'benchmarking' which competitors will find convincing? Do political and societal actors really expose themselves to learning processes that they then convert without further pressure? Or does the OMC erode core principles of constitutionalism, such as the regulative idea that governance should adhere to

---

17 This is of course a point the sceptics underline; see eg Chalmers (2003); even stronger Offe (2003): the OMC is effective, but does not achieve the effects its proponents advocate.

legal principles and the rule of law?[18] Whether this risk comes to pass depends on how the Member States synchronise their actions, and whether they find principles and rules to distinguish such co-ordination from pure political competition. More surprisingly and damning, however, is the fact that the OMC itself remains isolated from European market processes. Not only has there been no real attempt to apply this novel methodology to the regulatory core of the European market sphere (the only exception we are aware of being Scott 2004). There also has been no effort to co-ordinate application of the OMC mechanism within social and labour spheres with possibly contradictory market regulatory actions. As such, the OMC's claim to re-embed a disembodied European market remains hollow, whilst its relevance both to this paper and a real-world process of European market socialisation remains questionable.

PROBLEMS OF LEGITIMACY AND MARKET GOVERNANCE

More variants of European governance mechanisms exist. Independently conceived, innovatively created out of the non-existent administrative provisions of European Treaties, all such institutions nonetheless share one thing in common: they are institutions of 'governance' rather than 'government and administration'. This is the new European 'praxis', but it is ultimately also the problem, at least for law. Mechanisms of governance within the European market, the institutional effort to encapsulate and foster the necessary and inevitable synergies between economic processes and a European civil society, can, at the level of political science, be analysed and categorised in phenomenologies, complete with explanations of their genesis and analyses of their effectiveness. Lawyers, however, have a harder task. They are not necessarily ill-equipped to deal with the complexities of the normative dimension of the new modes of governance but, as a brief glance at the legal theory of the 1980s reminds us, they cannot avoid such issues, especially where they remain true to their doctrinal duty not just to create institutions of market management, but also to legitimise them.

Europe is a laboratory, not necessarily as unique a one as the widely deployed sobriquet a multilevel system *sui generis* might insinuate, but a highly instructive one nonetheless, especially in view of its postnational constellation. What lessons can we draw from the European experiments with new modes of governance for a more general construction and oversight of those transnational governance arrangements that have overtaken the traditional nation state role in guiding and overseeing synergetic relations between the market and civil society? The following represents a preliminary and experimental effort to find answers to these questions. In brief, law it seems must, in efforts to ensure creative synergy between markets and society, increasingly take on a dual co-ordinating function: (1) mediating between the regulatory competences of operationally restricted, but still autonomous partial polities; and (2) re-establishing and overseeing relations

---

18 See Scheuerman (2004) in his discussion not of the OMC, but its theoretical basis in 'democratic experimentalism'.

between plural public regulatory institutions and an increasingly vivid and vibrant private regulatory sphere.

Two qualifications of the multi-level governance analysis: the pedagogical legacy of methodological nationalism and the new importance of arguing

The qualification of Europe as a 'multilevel system of governance' has become widely accepted. In order to also link this characterisation to the globalisation debate, we would like to add two further, albeit not so widely accepted, qualifications.

The first is primarily analytical and originated in international relations theory. Michael Zürn (2001) uses two key concepts of 'denationalisation' and 'methodological nationalism' in his analysis of globalisation. Three dimensions of statehood, so Zürn argues, which the nation state had once integrated, are presently subject to a process of disaggregation:

(1) nation states are no longer autonomous in determining political priorities but need to co-ordinate their policies within international institutions;

(2) national political actors (including private actors) must strive for recognition, but not just from their own national constituencies; their practices are increasingly exposed to evaluation at international level;

(3) the nation state retains significant resources, which are indispensable, for the implementation of internationally agreed upon policies.

This scheme has been designed for the analysis of globalisation processes. However, it is illuminating at all levels of governance. Take, for example, the controversy over the compliance with the Maastricht criteria of fiscal policy. The nation states have demonstrated their residual powers, dispensing with (albeit questionable) stability criteria, but are nonetheless still being called to account by international regulatory institutions such as the Commission and ECJ. (We rely here on Eichengreen 2003.)

Our second qualification is from the world of lower politics. There, we can observe the strength of arguing. To generalise: exactly because of the non-hierarchical network character of the European system, and exactly because powers and also, to some degree, the resources for political action, are located at various and relatively autonomous levels, successful forms of governance must be in a position to organise communication between actors who are genuinely competent in their various domains. This is what, at least, some political scientists can accept, albeit in limited fields (Neyer 2003 and 2004).

What form of law is in a position to bring about such miracles? What form of law can hope to reintegrate the three functions of the nation state, organising communication between autonomous (national and international) actors and providing for effective and legitimate synergy between market and civil society within this fragmented form of polity? An argument has made been elsewhere in support of a law founded in 'deliberative supranationalism' (Joerges and Neyer 1997; Joerges 2002).We would like here further to refine that argument into two forms of law: (deliberative supranationalism I), a law that should seek to respond to the interdependence of autonomous polities by identifying rules and principles that can organise their interdependence (conflict of laws); and (deliberative supranationalism II) a law that seeks to address the dangers of an apparently irresistible transformation of institutionalised government into under-legalised governance arrangements (Mehde 2002: 683), through the creation of the normative criteria under which such arrangements *deserve recognition*.[19] In other words, the time has come for law to constitutionalise governance, not only through the structured procedural interconnection of fragmented polities, but also through the direct oversight and legitimation of interactions between different polities, that are also themselves increasingly disturbed by private regulatory actors (public-private governance arrangements).

Preserving autonomy and strengthening the community: deliberative supranationalism (I) and comitology

Our terminology is more idiosyncratic than our argument: deliberative supranationalism is a critique of, and an alternative to, orthodox notions of supranationalism, which have underlined the autonomy of European law and its supremacy over national law. It is a response to economic interpenetration and interdependency, to the unavoidability of extra-territorial effects of the decisions and omissions of democratic polities, to the irrefutable insight that nation states still retain operational powers but cannot act wholly democratically where those operations impact upon other national and international communities. Deliberative supranationalism is supranational in that it invokes principles and rules that ensure the respect of 'foreign' concerns, and imposes the obligation on formerly sovereign states to search for mutually acceptable answers in cases of conflict: it demands that still sovereign polities dialogue with one another.[20]

To summarise: the normative core message of deliberative supranationalism is that Europe, through its supranational rules and principles, should give voice to 'foreign' concerns and should insist that Member States mutually 'recognise' their laws (that they 'apply' foreign law) and refrain from insisting on their *lex fori* and domestic interests. This is the principle. The discipline imposed on a Member State's political autonomy is limited. The principle and its limitations can be discovered and studied best in the jurisprudence of the ECJ on Article 28 (ex

---

19 This one term would require extensive explanations. All we can do here is to refer to Habermas (2001: 113).

20 The authority of such answers need not be deduced from some principled supremacy of European law. European law should rather be understood as 'conflicts law'. This term has a well-defined meaning in the discipline of private international law. There it denotes rules prescribing which legal order should be applied where a 'case' touches more than one legal system. Our use of the term is different in that we also use it for conflicts *within* national legal systems, and do not restrict conflicts law to the choice of a given law (for a related view see Teubner 1999). Quite to the contrary the resolution of the conflict will require productive answers – hence, our resort to 'deliberation'.

Art 30). This jurisprudence has repeatedly documented how mediation between differences in regulatory policies and the diverse interests of the concerned jurisdictions can be accomplished (see Joerges 2002). These examples, we argue, represent a truly European law of conflict of laws. It is 'deliberative' in that it does not content itself with appealing to the supremacy of European law; it is 'European' because it seeks to identify principles and rules that make differing laws within the EU compatible with one another.

The Committee system institutionalises this form of problem solving. It establishes a framework within which the implementation of secondary legislation can be ensured. The comitology process is distinguished from adjudication by virtue of the nature of the tasks that it must accomplish. The positive characterisation of these activities is a more delicate task. We are, however, particularly hesitant with the use of the label 'administration' for three interdependent reasons. First, the traditional somewhat restricted European (especially the continental) understanding of this term is hardly compatible with the creative problem solving activities that the 'administration' of the European market undertakes. Secondly, the networks of national and European actors organising the 'implementation' of European legislative frameworks do not have the degree of unity that such an administrative machinery presupposes (see Olsen 2003).

Last, but not least, the European multilevel system is not the type of hierarchy constitutional theorists presuppose when they seek to reconcile the ideals of constitutional democracies with the emergence of the administrative state (see Joerges 2002).

Be that as it may, as long as the comitology process can be understood as the search for answers that the concerned polities can accept, it represents a conflict of laws regimes – and the defenders of democratic governance need not be alarmed.

The normative challenges of transnational governance: deliberative supranationalism (II)

The committee system, however, has also itself been overtaken by the praxis of European governance. As private actors have joined within the task of standard-setting and European agencies have inexorably been woven into the committee system fabric, comitology has lost its deliberative innocence, and instead given birth to hybrid transnational governance arrangements, structured neither in purely private law nor in purely public law terms, neither nationally nor European, neither purely governmental nor non-governmental, in which societal and governmental actors adapt to a transnational reality that is no longer 'controllable' at national level. Transnational governance arrangements do not just mediate between different given policies and law, but elaborate genuinely transnational responses to transnational problem constellations. This type of governance cannot be rejected as being illegal or illegitimate outright, not only because of its factual importance, but also because of its normative potential. The term 'political administration (*politische Verwaltung*)', an oxymoron in the German understanding, may convey the problematics quite well.

Is the 'constitutionalisation' of such hybrids at all conceivable? Can we conceive of consistent legal principles and mechanisms through the application of which law might ensure that such arrangements 'deserve' recognition? One may, of course, mobilise widespread and convincing panaceas: more transparency, more pluralism, opening to broader public debates, a gradual juridification of procedures, exit options in cases of legitimate normative and ethical concerns, regular and focused parliamentary oversight, and a separation from distinct regimes dealing with distributive implications – such topics need to be addressed and they can only be addressed in radically procedural perspectives.

TWO EXAMPLES

Rather than examining these very abstract perspectives further, we return to concrete examples. Again, it must be emphasised that suggestions can only be explorative; Europe's governance laboratory remains radical and experimental.

The European Food Authority: beyond comitology?

In its White Paper on Governance, the Commission had announced that it would seek to establish new EU agencies, entrusted with autonomous powers on the basis of a clearly defined mandate. The agencies' mandate should remain restricted to individual decisions that involve neither 'political discretion nor complex economic assessments'.[21] Such powers should remain the province of the Commission, which, thanks to the new agencies, would be able to focus on its 'core tasks'. We have criticised this (see Joerges et al 2001) but did not take these announcements too seriously. How could the Commission ever successfully portray itself as the apex of an 'administration' of the internal market, as though it were carrying out the will of a European sovereign, as if, to put it in the metaphorical language of American administrative law, it were acting as a mere 'transmission belt' (Stewart 1975: 1674) in a 'unitary polity'? How could it ever believe that an 'executive agency' would act as a sort of assistant, subject to strict control by the Commission? We were nevertheless wrong. The first really important new body, namely the European Food Safety Authority (EFSA – Regulation 178/2002 [2002] OJ L31/1), is both allotted far greater regulatory functions and, in justification of this, is deemed to be nothing more than a body collecting and distributing expert knowledge on food safety (see Krapohl 2003).

Some commentators have indeed pointed to idiosyncrasies in the new authority. In this analysis, it is neither a return to a traditional national command model of regulatory nor is it a reassertion of the primacy (regulated solely by market internal logics founded in expertise) of disembedded European economic processes. As Damien Chalmers comments:

---

21 *European Governance – A White Paper* (see note 6) at 46. These are the formulae used in the age old *Meroni* judgments, Case 9/56, *Meroni and Co Industrie Metallurgiche SpA v High Authority of the ECSC* [1958] ECR 133, Case 10/56, *Meroni and Co Industrie Metallurgiche SpA v High Authority of the ECSC* [1958] ECR 157.

> With regard to the Authority's institutional make-up, it is impossible to locate it along any conventional national-supranational continuum. It is rather a transnational governance regime which cuts across national/supranational and public/private distinctions, and which both guides and is accountable to scientific communities, national food authorities and civic society. As these networks inform its constitution, it cannot be seen as something starkly autonomous from them, but something that both contributes to their constitution and is constituted by them. (Chalmers 2003)

Nonetheless, whatever the FSA becomes, the White Paper governance logic within which it is founded is both pure fantasy and a poor answer to the demands that European governance be legitimated. The agency is an institutional tautology: the demand for the productive re-embedding of a European market, the constant and sensitive treatment of normative and political issues with distributional implications, cannot be met through the creation of an institution that is itself legitimated by its seeming expertise-led and technocratic isolation from a politicised civil society.

Standardisation: societal constitutionalism in the shadow of public governance

As underlined above, standardisation as institutionalised under the 'new approach' is the most 'private' form of transnational governance. The paradox is, however, that 'private transnationalism', standardisation, is far more 'regulated' than public transnationalism. Harm Schepel (2005: 6) summarises many years of research in the following way:

> Standardisation procedures have developed into a remarkably consistent set of truly global principles of 'internal administrative law'. Partly influenced by legal instruments, partly by the ethics of the engineering and other professions and structured by an extensive process of global reciprocal normative borrowing between the public and private spheres at various levels, these procedures provide *at a minimum* for:
>
> (1) Elaboration of draft standards in technical committees with a balance of represented interests (manufacturers, consumers, social partners, public authorities).
>
> (2) A requirement of consensus on the committee before the draft goes to.
>
> (3) A round of public notice and comment, with the obligation on the committee to take received comments into account.
>
> (4) A ratification vote, again with the requirement of consensus rather than a mere majority, among the constituency of the standards body.
>
> (5) The obligation to review standards periodically.

Likewise, in addition to its private, but starkly proceduralised, character, standardisation within the EU has adopted many of the characteristics of comitology. The non-unitary network character of standardisation in the EU ensures that national delegations will represent their national positions, mobilise national expertise and, so it seems, provoke meaningful discussions among interested circles on the national level, which are then 'channelled' into the standardisation process on the international one. Further, as in comitology, public institutions, such as administrative executives and courts are always present within proceedings; being called directly into the process of the negotiation of standards or being (courts) the final body of procedural adjudication. In short, standardisation both integrates and co-ordinates private governance actors across national and international levels, and reconnects with national and international public spheres, functioning all the while, not under their direction, but in their shadow.

CONCLUSIONS

Harm Schepel's move towards – his version[22] of – 'societal constitutionalism' is thus a move away from a famous philosopher of legal theory he nevertheless highly appreciates:

> When faced with political decisions relevant to the whole of society, the state must be able to perceive, and if necessary assert, public interests as it has in the past. Even when it appears in the role of an intelligent adviser or supervisor who makes procedural law available, this kind of law-making must remain linked to legislative programmes in a transparent, comprehensible, and controllable way. (Habermas 1996: 441)

'Good' governance, as we observe it in standardisation, or arguably, in comitology, is not political rule through institutions as constitutional states have developed them. Instead, it is innovative practices of networks, horizontal forms of interaction, a method for dealing with political controversies in which actors, political and non-political, public and private, arrive at mutually acceptable decisions by deliberating and negotiating with each other (see Eriksen and Fossum 2004). The crux of this observation is a paradoxical one within traditional democratic theory and counterintuitive within our analysis. In short, productive and legitimate synergy between market and civil society cannot be furnished within traditional democratic theory, be that theory majoritarian (working with a *demos*) or deliberative (dispensing with the *demos*, but placing a 'governing' emphasis on the primacy of a public sphere). In our two examples, 'private transnationalism' scores better than a White Paper-style transnational administration. How can this be? Let us once again cite Harm Schepel (2005: 223):

> The paradox is, of course, that the mechanism through which to achieve this is, well, politics. Due process, transparency, openness, and balanced interest representation are norms for structuring meaningful social deliberation. They are not obviously the appropriate vehicles for revealing scientific 'truth' or for allowing room for the invisible hand.

The primacy is with politics, but lies outside a public sphere. This is a message with many theoretical premises and practical provisos. In our language: the

---

22 'Societal constitutionalism' is a term Gunther Teubner has borrowed from *Sciulli (1992)*, and then recrafted (see Teubner 2004). Schepel prefers the notion of 'legal pluralism' – also claiming, however, that non-statal norms should be recognised as 'law'.

modern economy and its markets are 'politicised' in the sense that politically important processes are taking place there. The political system cannot reach into that sphere directly. These two steps of the argument claim some plausibility. The third thesis is the critical one: there are constellations in which the political processes within society seem perfectly legitimate. Legitimate in what sense? There the proponents of societal constitutionalism and legal pluralism accentuate different aspects. The form of legitimacy claimed for (constitutionalised) comitology rests upon the epistemic and political potential of deliberative processes to achieve fair compromises between conflicting interests, to integrate a plurality of expert knowledge, to make use of the management capacities at different levels of governance and to remain open for revision where new insights are gains or new concerns are raised by politically accountable actors (see Joerges and Neyer 1997; Joerges 2002). Constitutionalised comitology is a legalised (proceduralised) endeavour operating in the shadow of democratically legitimated institutions. Similarly, the legitimacy and autonomy Harm Schepel ascribes to standardisation rests upon the compatibility of its institutionalisation with the legal institutions surrounding it: it is not so surprising that standardisation organisations seek to establish procedures in which society as a whole can trust and that sufficiently self-critical law-makers and regulators realise they would not be able to substitute for what standardisation accomplishes.

Consider again the separation of politically accountable discretionary decision making (through the European Commission) and the proliferation of objective expert advice (through an executive agency). That is a 'public' alternative. Once more, a return to the 'classical' separation of legislative and administrative powers is unconceivable. What we have to realise is that the model of public governance as we see it in the *Official Journal* is very uncomfortable.

References

Amstutz, M (2001) *Evolutorisches Wirtschaftsrecht*, Baden-Baden: Nomos

Chalmers, D (2003) '"Food for thought": reconciling European risks and traditional ways of life', 66 Modern Law Review 532–64

Chiti, E (2003) 'On European agencies', in Eriksen, EO, Joerges, C and Neyer, J (eds) *European Governance, Deliberation and the Quest for Democratisation*, Oslo: Arena: Arena Report 2/2003 271–322

Commission on Global Governance (1995) *Our Global Neighbourhood*, Oxford: Oxford University Press

de Búrca, G and Zeitlin, J (2003) 'Constitutionalising the open method of co-ordination: a note for the Convention', Madison, WI/Florence (on file with authors)

De Schutter, O, Lebessis, J and Paterson, J (eds) (2001) *Governance in the European Union*, Luxembourg: European Commission

Dehousse, R (1999) 'Towards a regulation of transnational governance? Citizens' rights and the reform of comitology procedures', in Joerges, C and Vos, E (eds) *EU Committees: Social Regulation, Law and Politics*, Oxford: Hart 109–27

Eberlein, B and Kerwer, D (2002) 'Theorising the new modes of EU Governance', 6: 5 *European Integration Online Papers* http://eiop.or.at/eiop/texte/2002-005a.htm

Eichengreen, B (2003) 'Institutions for fiscal stability' http://emlab.berkeley.edu/users/eichengr/index.html

Eriksen, EO and Fossum, JE (2004) 'From government to governance?', in Joerges, C, Sand, I-J and Teubner, G (eds) *Transnational Governance and Constitutionalism*, Oxford: Hart 115–46

Everson, M (2004a) 'Accountability and law in Europe: towards a new public legal order?' 67 Modern Law Review 124–38

Everson, M (2004b) 'A "political" administration? Executive "deliberation" in "regulatory" agencies', contribution to the Workshop on 'Good Governance in Supranational Market Regulation', University of Bamberg, 16–17 January 2004

Feick, J (2002) *Regulatory Europeanisation, National Autonomy and Regulatory Effectiveness: Marketing Authorisation for Pharmaceuticals*, Köln: Max-Planck-Institute for the Study of Societies (MPIfG Discussion Paper 02/6)

Franzius, C (2003) 'Der "Gewährleistungsstaat" – ein neues Leitbild für den sich wandelnden Staat?' 42 Der Staat 493–517

Freeman, J (2000) 'The private role of public governance', 75 New York Univ L Rev 543

Freeman, J (2003) 'Symposium: public values in an era of privatisation: extending public law norms through privatisation' 116 Harv L Rev 1285

Habermas, J (1996) *Between Facts and Norms: Contributions to a Discourse Theory of Law and Democracy*, Cambridge, MA: MIT Press

Habermas, J (2001) *The Postnational Constellation*, Cambridge: Polity

Harlow, C (1996) 'Codification of EC administrative procedures? Fitting the foot to the shoe or the shoe to the foot', 2 European Law Journal 3–25

Jachtenfuchs, M and Kohler-Koch, B (2003) 'Regieren und Institutionenbildung', in Jachtenfuchs, M and Kohler-Koch, B (eds) *Europäische Integration* (2nd edn), Opladen: Leske & Budrich 83–218

Joerges, C (2002) 'The law's problems with the governance of the European market', in Joerges, C and Dehousse, R (eds) *Good Governance in Europe's Integrated Market*, Oxford: Oxford University Press 3–31

Joerges, C (2005) 'Compliance research in legal perspectives', in Joerges, C and Zürn, M (eds) *Governance and Law in Post-National Constellations: Compliance in Europe and Beyond*, Cambridge: Cambridge University Press 218–61

Joerges, C, Falke, F, Micklitz, H-W and Brüggemeier, G (1991) *European Product Safety, Internal Market Policy and the New Approach to Technical Harmonisation and Standards*, Florence: EUI Working Papers Law Nos 91/10–14 (www.iue.it/LAW/WP-Texts/Joerges91/chap.41.htm)

Joerges, C, Mény, Y and Weiler, JHH (eds) (2001) *Symposium: Mountain or Molehill? A Critical Appraisal of the Commission White Paper on Governance*, Jean Monnet Working Paper No 6/01, New York: NYU (www.jeanmonnetprogram.org/papers/01/010601.html)

Joerges, C and Neyer, J (1997) 'Transforming strategic interaction into deliberative problem-solving: European comitology in the foodstuffs sector', 4 Journal of European Public Policy 609–25

Joerges, C and Rödl, F (2005) '"Social Marker Economy" as Europe's social model?', in Magnusson, L and Stråth, B (eds) *A European Social Citizenship? Preconditions for Future Policies from a Historical Perspective*, Brussels: Peter Lang 125–58

Joerges, C and Vos, E (1999) *EU Committees: Social Regulation, Law and Politics*, Oxford: Hart

Krapohl, S (2003) 'Risk regulation in the EU between interests and expertise: the case of BSE', 10 Journal of European Public Policy 189–207

Majone, G (1989) 'Regulating Europe: problems and perspectives', 3 Jahrbuch zur Staats und Verwaltungswissenschaft 159–77

Majone, G (1994) 'The rise of the regulatory state in Europe', 17 West European Politics 77

Mehde, V (2002) 'Kooperatives Regierungshandeln', 127 Archiv des öffentliches Rechts 655–83

Neyer, J (2003) 'Discourse and order in the EU: a deliberative approach to multilevel governance', 41 Journal of Common Market Studies 687

Neyer, J (2004) *Postnationale politische Herrschaft: Vergesellschaftung und Verrechtlichung jenseits des Staates*, Baden-Baden: Nomos

Nicolas, F (1995) *Common Standards for Enterprises*, Luxembourg: Office of Official Publications

Offe, C (2003) 'The European model of "social" capitalism: can it survive European integration?', 11 Journal of Political Philosophy 437–69

Olsen, J (2003) 'Towards a European administrative space', 10 Journal of European Public Policy 506–31

Rosenau (1992) 'Governance, order, and change in world politics', in Rosenau, JN and Czempiel, EO (eds) *Governance without Government. Order and Change in World Politics*, Cambridge/New York: Cambridge University Press 1–29

Sabel, C and Zeitlin, J (2003) 'Active welfare, experimental governance, pragmatic constitutionalism', New York/Madison, WI (on file with authors)

Schepel, H (2005) *The Constitution of Private Governance: Product Standards in the Regulation of Integrating Markets*, Oxford: Hart

Scheuerman, WE (2004), 'Democratic experimentalism or capitalist synchronisation? Critical reflections on directly-deliberative polyarchy', 17 Canadian Journal of Law and Jurisprudence 101–27

Sciulli, D (1992) *Theory of Societal Constitutionalism*, Cambridge: Cambridge University Press

Scott, J (2004) 'International trade and environmental governance: relating rules (and standards) in the EU and the WTO', European Journal of International Law 15: 307

Stehr, N (2003) *Wissenspolitik: Die Überwachung des Wissens*, Frankfurt a M: Suhrkamp

Stewart, R (1975) 'The reformation of American administrative law', 88 Harv L Rev 1671

Teubner, G (1983) 'Substantive and reflexive elements in modern law', 17 Law and Society Review 239–85

Teubner, G (1987) 'Juridification – concepts, aspects, limits, solutions', in Teubner, G (ed) *Juridification of Social Spheres*, Berlin/New York: de Gruyter 3–48

Teubner, G (1999) 'After privatisation? The many autonomies of private law', in Wilhelmsson, T and Hurri, S (eds) *From Dissonance to Sense: Welfare State Expectations, Privatisation and Private Law*, Dartmouth: Aldershot 51–82

Teubner, G (2004) 'Societal constitutionalism: alternatives to state-centred constitutional theory?', in Joerges, C, Sand, I-J, and Teubner, G (eds) *Transnational Governance and Constitutionalism*, Oxford: Hart 3–28

Tjiong, H (2002) 'The political economy of regulatory competition', PhD Thesis, Stanford, CA

Trute, H-H (1996) 'Die Verwaltung und das Verwaltungsrecht zwischen gesellschaftlicher Selbstregulierung und staatlicher Steuerung' Deutsches Verwaltungsblatt, 950–64

Vos, E (1999) *Institutional Frameworks of Community Health and Safety Regulation- Committees, Agencies and Private Bodies*, Oxford: Hart

Wiethölter, R (1989) 'Proceduralisation of the category of law', in Joerges, C and
    Trubek, DM (eds) *Critical Legal Thought: An American-German Debate*, Baden-
    Baden: Nomos 501
Zeitlin, J and Trubek, DM (2003) *Governing Work and Welfare in a New Economy:
    European and American Experiments*, Oxford: Oxford University Press
Zürn, M (2001) 'Politik in der postnationalen Konstellation', in Landfried, C (ed)
    Politik in einer entgrenzten Welt, Opladen: Westdeutscher Verlag 181–204

PART III

RE-EMBEDDING CAPITALISM:
TWO PERSPECTIVES

CHAPTER 10

THE EUROPEAN SOCIAL MODEL AND THE CONSTITUTIONAL TREATY OF THE EUROPEAN UNION

Giuseppe Bronzini

> From its first moment, a constituent practice introduces into the social Community the nucleus of a euphoric idea. In the light of this idea of the self-constitution of community of free and equal members, the usual practices of law production, application and implementation are unavoidably exposed to critique and self-critique. (Habermas 1996a)

This chapter analyses the work of the Convention for the Future of Europe and its Draft Constitutional Treaty as modified by the Intergovernmental Conference of June 2004. We believe that these documents represent an important and necessary step in the constituting of a political and social counter-weight to the hegemony of market dynamics on the old continent, a form of solidaristic 'cement' between the citizens of the EU, even though it may be neither sufficient nor conclusive. Whether an efficacious model of social guarantees will emerge depends ultimately on the ability of the public sphere to interpret this project, a project for which the text that the European governments approved last June after painful negotiations will only offer a problematic, although important, platform of support.

THE CONSTITUTION AS AN INSTITUTIONAL PLATFORM FOR A EUROPEAN WELFARE STATE

An eminent French economist (Fitoussi 2003) recently underlined that: 'certainly no technical answer can be given to the question about the future of a social Europe. The point is not to determine which form of social organisation will show greater economic efficacy, but to act so that the model of the society of the future will be the object of a democratic choice that is taken by political means.' Fitoussi concludes: 'In our normal hierarchy of values, the social question indeed refers to the one about sovereignty, that is, to the Constitution of Europe.' Fitoussi's analysis seems to be secondary to the debate about the constitutional future of Europe. Conflicts within the Convention and broader discussions were always dominated by the 'institutional' question and by the division of power between 'intergovernmental' and 'supranational' organs.

The 'social question' and 'the institutional question', however, are so deeply intertwined that it is misplaced to address the one without the other, at least on the conceptual level. A more subtle form of interpretation that is free from the temptation to categorise phenomena in hierarchical scales (of norms or values) is needed in order to address a 'constitution' that has introduced an even more controversial institutional and juridical panorama for the Union. Scholars have heralded a constitution without the people (Scoditti 2002; Dellavalle 2002), without the state (Bonacchi 2001; Torchia 2001), and without the nation (Shaw 1999; von Bogdandy 1994). Must we now add a 'constitutionalism' without an authentic constitutional charter to the list? The EU has engaged deeply with these first three images of its institutional future. The text approved by the IGC will now challenge in a yet more radical way the innovative and imaginative capacity of democratic legal theory. The preface to the proposal drafted by the Convention described the unresolved issue: 'the Laeken declaration raised the question whether the simplification and reordering of the Treaties should not open the way to the adoption of a constitutional text. The work [of the Convention] has culminated in the elaboration of a draft treaty that institutes a Constitution for Europe.' The draft of the Convention (and, despite everything, also the modified text) describes a *quid novi*, a novelty, that locates it at a great distance from any treaty that has hitherto been approved. This is the case not only because of the revolutionary method of its formulation (with the work on the Charter of Fundamental Rights as the only precedent), but also because the treaty gives structure to a system of powers, rights and objectives that can no longer reasonably be traced back to the will, be it even a converging one, of the single states that form the European Union; a union that represents, as is now commonly recognised, the greatest juridical invention of the postwar period. In sum, the treaty seems to represent the renewed institutional reinforcement of an entity *supra partes*, a postnational entity with numerous potentially generalisable norms of its own. Anticipating future conclusions we might now identify the European constitution not as an accomplished text, but rather as a public process, in terms of the gradual formation of a constitutionalised society; a process that would nonetheless receive a decisive consolidation impetus with the final approval of the text. Together with Peter Häberle, we might speak of 'an open society of constituents', or of a 'plurality of actors who participate in the drafting of the European constitution as political parties, groups, individual intellectuals, organs of the states and of the European Union' (Häberle 2003).

Such a perspective, however, must also take care not to forget the substance that is at stake: the issue is not simply one of institutional dynamics. The process will only reach a successful conclusion if it is founded in a social substratum, an original idea about the regulation of the relations between individuals and groups that is worthy of translation into 'constitutional form'. It would evidently be inadequate to reduce the whole matter to the issue of a relocation of powers between supranational and intergovernmental organs. The European Constitution as a project and as a process can only prevail if it gives birth to a 'European social model' that invites the involvement of the radical collective and political subjects of the old continent in a struggle for the constitution, and that lays the basis for the solidification of an alliance between such radical forces and newer federal and democratic elites characterised by their adherence to a form of continent-wide nationalism that has occasionally masqueraded as *the defender of* the constitutional identities of the individual countries (Weiler 2002; critically Negri 2003a; Friese and Wagner 2003).

In his latest noteworthy intervention into the constitutional debate, Jürgen Habermas (2003) writes: 'The economic benefits from European unification count as an argument in favour of a further development of the Union only in the context of a force of cultural attraction that goes far beyond the economic dimension. The threat towards a certain form of life [...] – characterised by the post-war welfare state as the foundation of well-being and security – and the prospect that it can be preserved drive towards the development of a vision of the future Europe that would again know how to address the current challenges with innovative solutions.' In other words, at stake is the continent-wide reinvigoration of a welfare state that furnishes the vital mediatative fulcrum between competing logics of social and systems integration, as well as its renewal and adaptation to the radical transformations in productive processes and life-styles that have occurred since the 1970s.

Such a demand – namely that the European Union should be dedicated to satisfying the demand for social policies that counter-balance market dynamics – is implicitly federalist since nation-states haven been the 'masters' not only of sovereignty but also of solidarity ever since the end of the 19th century. The idea, as also suggested by Habermas, that social exclusion can be combated at the European level by introducing 'a minimum income regardless of the employment situation' is as subversive of national sovereignty as is the principle of qualified majority decision making (Ferry 2000). If one assumes that, at least on the old continent, a consolidated exchange between the obligation of political loyalty and the guarantee of a minimum of social benefits is at work (Offe 2001), the relocation of such substantive legitimacy at EU level could solidify a postnational commitment that would inevitably also have healthy hollowing-out effects in relation to individual state identities.

From an historical perspective that is largely shared by progressive labour lawyers within Europe, a reconstruction of the constitutional process has recently emerged that is inspired by Polanyian categories. Social policies in Europe (Giubboni 2003) can be broken down into three phases: the first was dominated by a model of 'embedded liberalism' marked by a compromise between the building of a single transnational market with its gradual implementation of the four Community liberties and the erection of solid systems of social protection at the national level. During this phase, social rights were inscribed within the constitutions of the individual states, whilst economic integration did not compromise the efficiency and the autonomy of individual welfare states. The second phase was one of crisis within and subversion of the first model. Market logic and law undermined national systems of *droit social*. The right to compete began to infiltrate bodies of labour and social law, weakening or emptying out national constitutional guarantees. This second phase is encapsulated as follows: 'the state is not sovereign, but it has a sovereign; by means of the treaties, this sovereign is the market.' The Maastricht Treaty represented the apex of the process of increasing autonomisation of market rules as budgetary constraints prevented national states from pursuing social policies, sometimes even those that they were constitutionally obliged to do so. The most recent phase of 're-embedding-liberalism' is now host to the laborious and still uncertain reconstruction of a viable balance between 'negative' and 'positive integration' by means of a steady communitarisation of labour law, the evolution of European social cohesion policies, the widening of the objectives of the Union, juridification of collective agreements at EU level and the elaboration of a Charter of Fundamental Rights, also known as the Nice Charter. Just as the compromise enshrined in the national welfare states found its consecration in post-war constitutions, this current phase should ideally also find its conclusion in the constitutionalisation of a European system of social security. In analogy to Polanyi (1974), tomorrow's scholars of integration might then comment upon the reaction of nation states to a 'self-regulated' capitalism by asserting that that it was 'inevitable that society take measures to defend itself'. Such a transition will necessarily induce the birth of a new political form of a federal entity, even if debate might remain as to whether this entity should be inspired by a 'solidaristic federalism' of the German kind which preserves all the institutional features of the modern state, the high degree of territorial and normative autonomy of 'federated' components notwithstanding, or by a 'co-operative' solidarism, which would maintain the truly original features of the EU, such as the traits of polyarchy and of institutional pluralism (Streeck 1999).

In the remainder of this chapter, we will first briefly analyse the theoretical significance of the Convention. Subsequently, we will examine the most important elements of the proposed institutional solutions. Thirdly, we will assess the significance of the current draft treaty from a social point of view. We will then conclude by identifying some examples of how social movements can take a 'constituent' attitude towards this process, 'taking seriously' some of the formulations in the higher law elaborated in Brussels in order to pursue social consolidation.

A SUCCESS OF THE CONVENTION: THE EVOCATION OF A CONSTITUENT POWER

Displaying a certain lack of style, the 105 members of the Convention afforded themselves 'recognition' for having elaborated the 'constitution'. However, their real merit is a different one. With its dense work over one and a half years, its strongly controversial debates and its consultation of civil society (even though within clear limits), the convention brought about an event that was unexpected and maybe even undesired: the evocation of constituent power.

We must begin with the failure of the Nice summit. When following the night of the long knives Nice failed, the explosion of nationalistic competition between the (predominantly smaller) states made the immediate realisation of Joschka Fischer's courageous federalist aspirations seem far-fetched, despite the success of the Charter of Fundamental Rights (founded upon the first application of the 'conventional' procedure) and even though European public opinion was minded to support them. However, the founding countries at least obtained the last minute attachment of a declaration to the Nice Treaty that assured that the question of the future of the Union would be taken up again, and soon. The envisaged reform of the EU, however, was at that time described in terms of a clearer distribution of competences between the Member States and the Union and of a simplification of the treaties, with only generic allusion to the question of the status of the Nice Charter and to the role of the national parliaments in the European institutional architecture.

It was then left to the second convention established by the Laeken Declaration to confront the question of the 'future of the Union' in all its dimensions. The 105 members of the Convention on the Future of Europe were given 56 questions concerning the entire European institutional architecture and all aspects of the distribution of competences, which were then grouped into four categories. The first and the second categories addressed the reordering and simplification of the treaties, the third related to the mode of giving full recognition to the Nice Charter, and the final category concerned the eventual adoption of a 'constitutional' text. In the case of an affirmative response to the last question, the convention was asked to determine 'what should be the values that the Union cherishes, the fundamental rights and obligations of the citizen, and the relations between the States in the Union'. This mandate needless to say left ample discretion to the Convention, with a vast range of possible outcomes stretching from a simple face lift for the treaties to the creation of a full scale federal arrangement, including economic government and comprehensive social security policies.

Today we can say that no 'minimalist' perspective has been adopted, even though the original proposal has been somewhat downsized, in particular with regard to qualified majority voting. The Convention proceeded 'as if' it was writing a constitution, just as the preceding Convention had proceeded 'as if' it was writing a bill of rights endowed with full legal validity. While one can certainly not claim that there is general agreement on such a perspective, the issues at stake have become much clearer: a democratic, social and federal – or, according to a recent suggestion by Ulrich Beck (2003), cosmopolitan – Europe versus a Europe as a space of free economic activity. In this light – as we will discuss in more detail below – the federalist option is the only acceptable one for all those who aim at conserving at least the basic rationale that stood behind the creation of the welfare state in European societies.

That is why the taking up of problems of this order means exercising a power that is of a constituent nature. No-one imposed 'conceptual' limits on the work of the Convention, and it is now clear that the process it embarked upon has not yet reached its conclusion with the draft or the IGC text. At best, we now have a 'dilatory compromise' that might be further interpreted and rendered concrete by its utilisation within the juridical and institutional spaces opened up by the 'European Constitution'. The innovative spirit that liberates itself in historical moments of radical juridical transformations, as well as a subordination of the European states to a higher authority, will be pivotal in order to make of this a truly fruitful epochal dimension. Habermas and Derrida expressed this interest well when they asserted in their public intervention of June 2003 that 'a European public sphere has shown itself in the demonstrations for peace held on

15 February 2003 and has demanded to be listened to and to be given space and power' (Liberation, 1 June 2003). Or, to use the words of Joseph Weiler (2003): 'the future of Europe in its true and profound sense will not be decided by the Convention or by the Intergovernmental Conference. In moments like this one the notion of a Convention "out there" is fallacious. The citizens and the intellectuals are also part of the Convention and have a role in "constituting" Europe. [...] They are, we are part of the Convention in as much as we contribute to define, through our thoughts, passions and responses, precisely the political culture that forms through the values it carries our identity and the way in which our polity and its society will be constituted.'

If there is a victim of the 'conventional' method, it is the 'no-demos thesis'; that is, the idea that democratic participation is confined to settings in which the citizens are linked to each other by pre-political bonds, at least bonds of language and of culture. Virtually every European political party, trade union or association has expressed its position on the reform of Europe, and vitally such interventions cannot be ordered nationally. The scope of the debate unleashed following the Convention demonstrates that it is no longer possible to argue that Europeans cannot decide together about the definition of Europe because they do not share cultural or linguistic traditions. Ten years on, the wound that was inflicted on the ongoing construction of a political Europe by the German Constitutional Court's Maastricht judgment is now healing. That verdict, while laudably aiming at a strengthening of the mechanisms of democratic participation and control, made dangerous and arbitrary demands that turned cultural homogeneity into a presupposition for the transformation of a population into a demos. This imprudent realigning of the ethnos and the demos was rendered anachronistic not only by the struggle over the ideas of the convention, but also by the more profound emergence of what might be termed a 'clash of civilisations' between the US and the EU over key themes such as the International Criminal Court, the Kyoto Protocol and means of international conflict resolution, as well as over the future of the welfare state.

Given this broader context, the Convention's success in casting a final (also formal legal) verdict on juridical archaisms that still make use of concepts of 'people' and 'nation' is highly significant. The Brussels assembly was the first to take note of the turn that the emergence of a European public sphere will mark for the evolution of the Union institutions. Article 1 initially described the 'current Constitution' as being 'inspired by the will of the peoples and the states of Europe'. In a wise and far-reaching amendment, the term 'peoples' was replaced by 'European citizens', thus demonstrating how a postnational demos can be the repository, in parallel to the Member States, of a will destined to express itself in the institutions of the Union – and this even though the existing mechanisms that allow public opinion impulses to reach concrete levels of political decision making must be strengthened.

However, this is not all. Today, the citizens of the European Union have finally obtained a means to express their concerns directly in the European political space. One million citizens (Art I.47) can invite the Commission to present a proposal 'dedicated to matters in the merit of which those citizens consider a legal act by the Union necessary with a view to actualising the Constitution'. With this provision, the monopoly of the Commission to make legislative proposals is partly broken, and a link is created between the demands 'from below' of Union citizens and the concretisation of the constitution.

Beyond merely registering the increasingly problematic nature of positions that maintain that effective democratic power can only develop in 'closed Jacobin spaces' (Rodotà 2000), we also need to underline the diminishing centrality of the 'sociological truths' claimed by once determinative technocratic theories of European governance. In objective convergence with the 'sovereignist' conceptions of democracy, authors such as Fritz W Scharpf (1996, 2000 and 2001) or Giandomenico Majone (1996 and 2003) identified as one such a truth the ontological lack of trust and lack of preparedness for spontaneous and reciprocal dialogue that afflicts culturally heterogeneous populations. The unmistakable re-emergence of a Habermasian 'communicative' conception of the European demos nonetheless makes such claims less credible and militates against analyses within which the Union can only be predicated upon an 'output' legitimacy (Scharpf 2000).

THE INSTITUTIONAL COMPROMISE AND THE REFORMULATION OF THE VALUES AND OBJECTIVES OF THE UNION

Before examining the terms of the compromise reached in June 2004, an initial point of reference is given by the fact that the *acquis communitaire*, consolidated over almost 50 years of integration, has been confirmed by the draft. This long-standing normative and juridical corpus furnishes an existing and impressive level of Community penetration within national orders. According to some estimates, between 60 and 70 per cent of national norms already have a Community character even prior to reforms suggested by the Convention. To this we need to add the fact that the Amsterdam Treaty entered into force only a few years ago. Equally, the Nice Treaty has only been in force since 2003, such that the supremacy of European law over national law is bound to increase even without the draft's innovations. Further, the new 'open method of co-ordination', introduced in the chapter on employment of the Amsterdam Treaty (and extended in the Nice Treaty), represents, in addition to existing legal controls over national orders, a Community mechanism of 'soft law'. Current Union presence within national life is thus a political fact of such significance that no one dared to promote a campaign for the thinning out of the competences of the Union. On the contrary, the juridical origins of the principle of the prevalence of Union law over Member State law are consecrated in the final text. Together with the maxims of direct effect and state liability for non-implementation, this principle represents the most extraordinary contribution of the Luxemburg Court to the creation of a supranational juridical order (Cartabia and Weiler 2000).

Having said this, the most potentially significant innovations within the convention's draft lie in its affirmation of the principle of policy codetermination by the European Parliament (excepting specified areas) and of policy approval by qualified majority (majority of member states and at least 60% of the population). With this step, a major realignment to 'ordinary' constitutional arrangements has been made such that 'laws' without parliamentary approval, or laws founded within a unanimity principle, are now perceived as intolerable. The IGC considerably altered the criteria for the qualified majority (now 55% of the states and 65% of the population, with additional rules for the 'blocks' necessary to halt a policy proposal). The cases in which qualified majority voting applies were also further reduced, even though they are still doubled compared with the currently valid treaties. Furthermore, the work of 'clearing up' the corpus of European law has led to the distinction between 'framework laws' and 'European laws' and to a more neat distinction between competences (exclusive ones, parallel ones, and those of co-ordination) as well as to a merging of the so-called second and the third pillar of policy-making – to date 'sons of a minor god' – in the ordinary juridical discipline of the Union. In particular, with regard to the expanding area of 'liberty, security and justice' and of immigration policies, the unification of the pillars may lead to a – necessary – intensification of parliamentary and jurisdictional control.

Thus, a certain, if insufficient, simplification of the treaties has taken place, and the distinction made between a 'general' section and more specific ones is a positive step, as is the attribution of unitary legal personality to the Union. Certainly, if we adopt Thomas Paine's notion of a 'constitution' as 'something that you can carry in your pocket and quote, article by article', we are still far away from satisfactory results. A bridge towards the future, though, is the identification, at least as a matter of principle, of a common foreign policy with the creation of a unitary organ, the ministry of Foreign Affairs that is endowed with a double legitimacy (being nominated by the Council, but also acting as a vice-president of the Commission). In sum, the relations in the 'regulative quadrangle' of the Union do not seem to have been overturned. It seems that not only the Commission and the Council but also the Parliament and the Court of Justice have been strengthened. Potentially, these latter two organs can be considered the 'winners': the Parliament by virtue of the unification of the three pillars and by the sensible extension of the area of co-determination, and because of its power to nominate the President of the Commission and consequent degree of oversight over the Commission; the Court by virtue of the new system of competences, the inclusion of the Nice Charter into that constitution, and its potential power to constitutionalise the subsidiarity principle – in short, all the tools necessary for the evolution of the ECJ into a proper constitutional court.

The limitations within the document are serious ones and have already been widely denounced as such: the absence of effective economic government, even in relation to the Eurozone; the retention unanimity principle in foreign policy, fiscal policy and to some extent in social policy (that is, the 'red lines' that cannot be transgressed); as well as the confirmation of the hitherto observed unanimity rule for the modification of the 'Constitutional Treaty', the only exception to which are the few limited possibilities to extend qualified majority voting without a full scale treaty review (Art 26). Furthermore, the treaty recognises the right of negotiated secession from the Union, but does not allow for the expulsion of undesired states who may only be 'sanctioned' in cases of their violation of 'foundational' values of the Union. In the realm of justice and security, a single nation may evoke its own (further not specified) 'essential principles' in order to delay majority decision making, although the impact of this provision is mitigated by strengthened possibilities for co-operation amongst any group of countries wishing to do so.

It is thus true that the 'federalisation' and 'parliamentarisation' of the Union are not very pronounced. A long-term comprehensive interpretation of the text, which will also require the consolidation of opinions, however, will also be impacted upon by the revamping of EU objectives and the effects of the inclusion of the Nice Charter within the constitution. In this respect, it seems undeniable that the general part of the constitution has fundamentally altered the balance between social and economic objectives. Furthermore, the preamble, although a suitable subject for critique in its reaffirmation of old ethnocentric principles, does clearly proclaim the message that the EU was created to overcome conflicts between nation states and not was not merely directed towards the creation of a more appetising commercial space for business.

The rewriting of the values and the objectives of the EU is similarly to be appreciated. Article 1.2 states that the EU bases itself on 'respect for human dignity, freedom, equality, the rule of law and respect for human rights'. Further, it adds that these values are common to all Member States in a society 'based on pluralism, on tolerance, on justice, on solidarity and on non-discrimination'. Equality and human dignity have thus entered into the 'founding' EU values and are safeguarded by the competent organs which can resort to rather draconian measures in cases of 'evident risks of serious violation'. Similarly, solidarity and non-discrimination – without exception, thus not limited to sexual and racial discrimination – are now seen as foundations of the EU. In Article 1.3, it now even seems as if social objectives prevail over EU economic-functional purposes, an impression reinforced by the use of significantly innovative terms: 'The Union provides for its citizens a space of freedom, security, and justice without internal borders and a single market in which competition is free and undistorted', but it also commits itself to 'sustainable development, based on balanced economic growth and a highly competitive social market economy that aims at full employment and social progress, at an elevated level of protection and improvement of the quality of the environment'. With the use of the term 'social market economy', not any kind of economic growth is envisaged, but one that respects qualifications of an ecological and environmental, but most importantly of a social nature (for a more sceptical account, cf Joerges and Rödl 2004).

Objectives that are entirely derived from the principle of solidarity, which now is read in a postnational dimension, confirm this impression. The EU 'promotes economic, social and territorial cohesion and the solidarity between the member states' and, furthermore, it 'combats social exclusion and all discrimination and promotes social justice and protection, parity between men and women, and the solidarity between generations'. Although it could be further improved, a further positive point in the treaty is the definition of EU relations with the rest of the world, whereby the EU 'contributes to peace, to free and fair trade, to the sustainable development of the earth, to solidarity and mutual respect between the peoples and to the protection of human rights, as well as to the strict observance and the development of international law, in particular with regard to the principles of the Charter of the United Nations'. Thus, readers of the treaty can longer infer that the primary goals of the EU are of an economic nature. The Union seems to have a 'programme' that is very close to ones pursued by general political entities or states. Certainly, when one talks about the 'single market', the term 'provide' is used, whereas in other areas the EU only 'promotes', a term that refers to a programme rather than to a reality. The same article specifies that the objectives 'are pursued with adequate means'. And with regard to social exclusion and discrimination one affirms *sic et simpliciter* that the EU 'combats' them. It has been said (Shaw 2003) that those affirmations, unless connected to solid policies and practical processes of decision making, are bound to remain empty rhetoric. This may be true, but one should not forget that the general formulations of the future constitutional treaty will have a function of interpretative guidance for the European Court of Justice as well as for juridical debate among 'national' judges and lawyers who are called upon to assess the compatibility of national norms with EU law and, thus, must perform a hermeneutic operation on both in the light of the principles and objectives of the treaty. Just as in the past the limited nature of the objectives of European integration played a considerable constraining role in the jurisdiction of the European Court, and subsequently also limited national judges, one can now assume that a rebalancing between economic and social objectives – on the quantitative as well as on the qualitative level – should lead to decisions that are closer to providing complex legal guarantees to the citizens.

The constitutional recognition of the Nice Charter and European social policies

Finally, we turn to the inclusion of the Nice Charter within the constitutional treaty, both in its entirety (s 2) and in its initial first section recognition (Art 1.9): 'the Union recognises the rights, liberties and principles laid down in the Charter of fundamental rights.' During the Convention the political left, those of a federalist orientation and trade unions strongly demanded inclusion of the charter. Nonetheless, its status remained in doubt throughout the first part of deliberations, such that its final inclusions excited much interest. The significance of this historical transition is still difficult to assess, but the complex and tension-ridden elaboration of a European Bill of Rights, beyond its symbolic value, is destined to create a 'domino effect' that may profoundly change the nature of the European institutional constellation. Many authors already maintain that this inclusion will transform the individual national constitutions into 'partial constitutions' (Häberle 2002; Sorrentino 2003; Pace 2002). In any case, the thesis that the interpenetration of national and European arrangements will lead to a fusion of wider horizons, towards a 'union of constitutions or even towards a 'constitutional federation' (Pernice and Mayer 2003; Pernice 2002a and 2002b) now has a consistent counterpart in the treaty itself, thus rendering ever less convincing any position that insists on the primacy of national constitutions.

Even though the reach of the charter is limited to EU law, and to national law only in as far as it concerns the application of EU law, one may ask how much the states can persist in rejecting the obligation to respect, jointly with the EU, the norms of a charter that they have all approved. One may argue that the principle *patere legem quam ipse fecis* will now impose itself, at least *ex negativo*, preventing the states from shedding norms that imply the realisation of rights proclaimed in the charter. Thus, for instance, Italy cannot adopt an entirely 'liberal' dismissal policy in labour law, as the Italian Constitutional Court affirmed even on the basis of a truly merely symbolical document such as the preceding EU Social Charter.

The major rupture with the past consists in the fact that the charter includes the most significant socio-economic rights as well as many so-called 'fourth-generation rights', some of which are unknown to individual constitutions in Europe. Ever since the 1960s, the Luxemburg Court's courageous praetorian jurisprudence has affirmed that Community law protects fundamental rights as they are derived from the European Declaration of Human Rights and from the common constitutional traditions of the Member States. This formula has further been adopted in succeeding European treaties. Today, the incorporation of the Nice Bill of Rights not only finally provides for a detailed catalogue of these rights (a wider catalogue that might be inferred from the Court's jurisprudence), but also introduces a new dimension of guarantees. It finally overcomes what Massimo Luciani (1999) has lucidly called the 'reflexive' protection of socio-economic rights, whereby fundamental rights are not seen as judiciable prerogatives in their own rights, but are instead viewed as epiphenomena, an induced effect of the creation and maintenance of the single market. The first European labour law norms were of course adopted in order to combat forms of social dumping between states; that is why the Court often tried to limit the protection of fundamental rights to those areas and to those matters which were directly linked to the primary objectives of European integration. Today, in contrast, social and labour rights have the same status as first and second generation rights since the rights mentioned in the charter are explicitly defined as indivisible. Thus, a further step in the emancipation of Europe from its initial functionalist straightjacket has been accomplished.

Arguably, this equilibration has two consequences. It creates an obstacle to the infiltration of commercial law into other areas. European policies to promote the famous four economic liberties may not compromise other prerogatives defined as indivisible by the charter. Equally, national norms limiting certain free competition policies for social reasons can now be justified in the light of the charter, and thus even defy the criterion of supremacy of European law (De Schutter 2003). As is known, the British government succeeded in obtaining an additional 'horizontal' clause, not foreseen by the original Convention, which distinguishes in the ambit of the norms protected by the charter between rights and principles and limits full jurisdictional protection to the former. It is, however, highly unlikely that this clause will affect socio-economic rights, and this not only for textual reasons – social norms are always defined as rights – but also for profound systematic reasons. First, the last Convention stated that the distinction between principles and rights had in fact already been introduced by the first Convention, the one that drafted the charter, which had rejected any idea of 'downgrading' socio-economic rights. Secondly, given that the draft constitution obliges Europe to promote the respect for social rights in its relations to the third world, it would obviously be absurd if the EU demanded of others the respect of rights that it itself regards as mere principles. Thirdly, the concrete application of the distinction between rights and principles is a matter for the European Court, and it is not very likely, as some authoritative commentators have already underlined (de Burca 2003a), that this Court will ratify a distinction that had long been obscured within European jurisprudence. The European Parliament defined those amendments as 'unnecessary and of little juridical value'.

To conclude on this point, the constitutional elevation of the charter to full validity represents a decisive step in the process of relocating the welfare state to the level of the European Community. This relocation has been referred to by authors such as Jürgen Habermas (2003) and Ulrich Beck (2003) as the 'substantive' core of the federalisation of Europe and has incessantly been called for by authoritative continental labour lawyers (see the two manifestos 'For a social Europe' of 1996 and 2000). Even prior to Nice it was argued that the inclusion of the charter in the European Treaties 'would formalise the aim of the Union as a self-legitimating and self-constituting entity' (Luciani 1999; Pizzorusso 1999). In as far as this affirmation is correct, the inclusion of the charter is as such of an explosively federal orientation.

The analysis of the distribution of competence as foreseen by the constitutional treaty needs in turn to be radically critical. In the course of the work of the convention, some countries strictly opposed any extension of the social-policy competence of the EU beyond the boundaries defined in the Nice 'social chapter'. The number of areas in which the application of the majority principle was ruled out were multiplied in an alarming fashion. Furthermore, the traditional taboos in the 'social chapter' were evoked: wages, strikes and rights of association. Again, a frightening price had to be paid to the UK: the restraints imposed on the EU with regard to the regulation of compulsory collective agreements (right of association and labour disputes) determines that European requests for the effective trade union support on which such agreements rest are made in a vacuum. Again, in the absence of any compulsory object of negotiation at least with regard to minimum benefits, and given the volatility of the collective actors that might influence Member States, the open method of co-ordination seems equally ill suited to the comprehensive synthesis of economic and fiscal policy or social policy and labour law.

The albeit important improvement in the level of legal protection of individual and collective rights is insufficient for the take-off of a 'social model'. The lack of compulsory tools linking the various government levels makes any passage from a model of 'negative integration' to one of 'positive integration', from reactive harmonisation to cohesive harmonisation, difficult. Jealously guarding their own welfare models, the states aim to limit EU intervention to a secondary and non-original action thus translating the principle of 'subsidiarity' as one of 'subalternity'. Furthermore, the various governmental levels that the Convention also treated as distinct lend themselves badly to any attempt to address them separately exactly because of their interdependence. EU politics resemble a hydra with 1,000 heads but without any general sense of orientation. It is a machine needing permanent revision or, evoking another metaphor, a ship that must be repaired while at high sea. There is the danger that mechanisms such as the method of open co-ordination and the trilateral summit will worsen the situation by caging the unions into an institutionalised setting and thus denying them that autonomy without which there can be no genuine form of any kind of mediation that is meant to be broader than political representation alone. At the European level, the idea of 'regulation of self-regulation', raised by Gunther Teubner (1986) and his school of 'reflexive law', has not yet acquired any validity, because above the level of the state there is no self-regulation at all, and, in particular, not in the emerging sector of so-called atypical labour.

Two barely reconcilable perspectives are presently being debated. On the one hand, European trade unions aim clearly at a federal model that places its trust in institutional passage-points and categories that remain rather similar to the traditional ones, even though they are revised and of greater complexity: a federal parliament, the introduction of enforceable and legally deduced subjective rights (Pernice 1999). Collective negotiations would in this model be based on 'minimum' guarantees on the one hand, and on the legal recognition of their role, on the other (Mückenberger 2002; Leonardi 2000). On the other hand, a certain expansion of trade union powers has been justified in theories of new governance in which the 'supranationality' element becomes ever less legible in terms of the consolidated legal paradigms. Rather, it is expressed according to functional dynamics through technocratic 'networks' in which the trade unions are one of the many actors that aspire towards 'communicative' convergence with the organs of 'governance'. Labour unions move in such a context with much more difficulty than, say, non-governmental organisations, the visibility of whom does not correspond to any evident criterion of representation.

In the first perspective, one can easily see a European collective negotiation approach emerging, validated *erga omnes* and ratified by the Commission, while in the second perspective an uncertain and nuanced decisionality is brought forth by the experiences with open co-ordination methods and social summits. Even if it remains unaccomplished, in particular in its social dimension, the first view safeguards the idea of democratic participation, while the second reduces it to a kind of ex-post dialogue about the effects of social policies, as in Fritz Scharpf's thesis on output legitimacy (2000). On this point, which I consider as highly problematic, the new constitution leaves many questions open, to say the least. Thus, it will be left to the European public sphere, of which the labour unions are an essential part, to identify and strengthen the most appropriate spaces in which a diffuse social control over the policies of the EU can be anchored with a view to both integrating and transcending the sites of traditional parliamentary legitimacy. Even though the proposed constitution does not deprive the unions of their tools for intervening and for proposing objectives and programmes, it will, in my view, be vital for them in the meantime to demand and impose a drastic revision of the entire matter.

TOWARDS AN OPEN SOCIETY OF THE EUROPEAN CONSTITUENTS

The role that social movements and the critical public sphere can play in the constituting of Europe can hardly be overestimated, since 'it is juridical hubris to imagine that Constitutions really constitute' (Weiler 2003). The public sphere of the old continent will decide through the 'plebiscite of every day' of struggle and mobilisation whether and when a political Europe will come into being (Allegri 2003). This becomes even more true by virtue of the fact that, as even Giuliano Amato and Romano Prodi have admitted, it has been demonstrated that there is neither political leadership committed to Europe nor political groups that are able and willing to press ahead with the 'federalisation' of the EU. We lack figures such as François Mitterrand or Helmut Kohl, who at least had the courage to confront their citizens with difficult choices, such as the introduction of the euro.

That is why it is up to civil society, and not least its most critical and innovative components, to carry forward the 'mad flight' towards the construction of a political Europe. As we said at the outset, this suggests that democratic public opinion in Europe assumes a constituent character. Beyond merely using the noteworthy instruments of political action that already exist in the EU political space, such a constitutive character entails the attempt to widen the contours of this space and to fill the public agenda with contents, projects, needs and moments of the reappropriation of collective social wealth. As intriguing as some of those theoretical approaches may be that see in the 'citizens' the true interpreters – and thus, builders – of the constitution, the increasing consolidation of a continental 'modus vivendi', to use Habermas' words, cannot be envisaged in abstraction from the existing or evolving subjectivities. The institutional arrangements of the EU foresee large spaces for co-operative, associative, relational forms of all kinds. There, the so-called 'horizontal subsidiarity' is not frozen in the form of unionist neo-corporatism, and the fractures that have emerged in national pyramidal structures encourage a more open and less hierarchical dialogue between centre and peripheries.

Social movements and civil society actors with a participative attitude appear to have at least four major avenues for 'constituent action'. First, the 'struggle for rights' takes place in the European Court of Justice and in the national courts. A fact that has not yet been fully grasped is the reality that the potential impact of the charter will not be realised in the ECJ alone, but in all courts of Europe, to the degree that ordinary judges as functionaries of the EU are called upon to interpret EU rights as well as national rights in the light of the European Bill of Rights. In other words, the bill of rights has empowered a unitary circuit of jurisdiction which has the merit of being diffused across the continent and which can thus be penetrated by claims made anywhere in the territory and activated by any one. It is precisely the rather general formulation of the rights in the charter that favours such integrated 'construction' across the new continental fabric. Whereas many national systems, such as the Italian one, centralise the control of the constitutionality of laws, the European system allows the ordinary judge, unless he or she has radical doubts, to directly apply EU law (and thus invalidate contradicting national laws) that, in turn, now has to be coherent with the rights proclaimed in the Nice Charter. In as far as the EU has thus moved closer to the Anglo-Saxon model of 'diffuse' control compared to the 'verticalised' continental one, the former has proven in the past to be more sensitive – in particular in the US during the 1960s – to the claims advanced by social movements, specifically to those that practiced civil disobedience. As Roosevelt said: 'an amendment, like the rest of Constitution, is what the justices say rather than its framers or you might hope it is.' Furthermore, the multiplication of sites of jurisdiction is bound to increase the possibility of succeeding with social claims, at the very least with regard to making them widely public.

During its first few years of existence, and its uncertain status notwithstanding, the charter has already succeeded in asserting itself. It has been cited by various national constitutional courts; referred to systematically by lawyers; and mentioned in judgments of first-instance courts, in the Luxemburg Court of Justice and even in the Strasbourg Court of Human Rights. An increasing reference to the social rights in the charter by higher judges has been noted (we still lack studies of ordinary judges), and it seems reasonable to expect a further increase of such use with the inclusion of the charter in the constitution. Reading the charter and some recently approved directives and above all court judgments – with some recent ones about non-discrimination of precarious works being truly courageous – more closely, certain regulative lines of considerable originality and a high degree of innovativeness seem to emerge, which we will now attempt to reinterpret within an explicitly constitutional framework.

Assembling the three components of the mosaic – directives, judgments, charter – the slowly emerging model is one of an increasing adaptation of the welfare systems that relativises – in reception of the best of the social-democratic literature on such issues from Ulrich Beck to Anthony Giddens, from Zygmunt Bauman to Claus Offe – the centrality of dependent labour of the traditional type. The wise aim is to integrate the elimination of forms of contractual discrimination within the perspective of a far more complex reform of the very nature of dependency (a full scale reform whose day has perhaps yet to come (Roccella 1999; see also María Gómez Garrido, Chapter 6 in this volume)) with interventions that work against exclusion in markets, such as basic-income ideas, rights to continuous education, rights to parental leave. Taken together, the EU seems to have taken up – maybe short of any rigorous option and despite the policies and orientations of the individual governments – the suggestions of the Supiot report of 1999 on the future of labour law in Europe (Supiot 1999). This report defends a protective strategy of 'concentric circles' that aims at extending a basket of fundamental rights to all forms of productive activity, thus actualising a 'right to work' understood as an individual right to choose the times and modes of one's contribution to social productivity (Supiot 1994; D'Antona 1999), by means of, where necessary, an adaptation towards specific forms of contract telework and interim work.

This report, which certainly marked a turning-point, has sometimes been referred to as a 'constitution of postFordist labour'. It entails the identification of a core of social rights at the centre of citizenship and the conservation of a 'workerist' form of protection that is more stringent and demanding for those who work under conditions of particular heteronomy. However, this is not the only area in which the charter can be endowed with great significance. In a 'defensive mode', at the very least, it is possible to create jurisdictional 'counter-limits' of a European nature against national or also EU policies in matters of social security. And in a more prospective mode, the concept of 'citizenship of residence', which would substantively underpin the idea of Europe as a space of 'welcoming' is being discussed in various European societies (Dal Lago and Mezzadra 2002; Palma 2003). Until now, national jurisdiction has certainly not excelled in testing the legitimacy of laws that maltreat human dignity, such as the Italian immigration law knows as the Bossi-Fini law. Maybe the recourse to the higher authority of the EU is required to arrive at a return to elementary principles of juridical civility.

The second line of reasoning and experimentation proceeds along the path of the new municipalism. Horizontal interlinkages between town halls or larger territorial districts that co-ordinate their policies, communicate their experiences and experiment with new forms of social re-appropriation of norm-setting powers by means of 'participative accounting' are by now rather widespread. The emphasis on pluralism that can be found in the EU setting favours the formation of a non-vertical network of articulation of public powers that is in direct dialogue with the supranational institutions (McCormick 2002). In matters of structural funds, for example, the majority criterion is hardly ever applied in the negotiations. One aims instead at the integration of all concerned institutions and collective actors.

The third line concerns the procedures of the EU itself. Here, too, the point is to put pressure on those instruments that already exist, among which the 'directly-deliberative polyarchy' (Gerstenberg and Sabel 2002) seems an important mechanism in which non-representative organisations such as NGOs have found a very efficacious way of making their voice heard. The 'socialisation' of these procedures would mean their liberation from the technocratic flavour that accompanies them and their transformation into public arenas and *fora* of confrontation to which new and old trade unions, associations and non-profit organisations would have free access and which could, for instance, include widespread consultations about European public spending. Thus, the EU could be freed of its 'comitology' frameworks of policy co-ordination without however falling back into the sclerosis of national bureaucracies.

Finally, one would need to test the possibility of any direct use of the 'political' instruments that the constitution provides for the citizens. The most obvious example is the collection of signatures, accompanied by urban strikes and other means of struggle, for the institution of a European basic income that gives full substance to Article 34 of the Nice Charter. In such an effort to construct a different European society, the use of those concepts, suggestions, models and paradigms that the archipelago of the new constitutionalism has been elaborating over the past few years will be crucial. By this term we refer to a very mixed constellation of scholars with the most varied cultural backgrounds: from the pluralism and institutionalism of the early 20th century to Niklas Luhmann's systems theory to the postmodernism of Michel Foucault and of Critical Legal Studies, not to forget

Hans Kelsen's work, in particular in international law, the Frankfurt School and the incessant and masterly anti-nationalism professed by Jürgen Habermas or, in a more historical vein, by Eric Hobsbawm and his school of 'invented traditions'. All diversity notwithstanding, there is a point of convergence: the refusal of Schmittian decisionism and the intention to downgrade and redefine the concept of sovereignty (Bronzini 2003). Maybe this very mixed alliance will be capable to transform itself, by virtue not least of the push coming from social experimentation, into something that resembles, today, the laboratory of the 'Federalist', thus providing a more articulate and advanced, and also institutionally elaborate model for a more democratic and social Europe (Friese 2003; Wagner 2003; Negri 2003b).

References

Allegri, G (2003) 'I nuovi movimenti sociali nello spazio comune europeo: Primi spunti per una riflessione su alcuni nodi istituzionali', in *Democrazia e Diritto* n 12: 139–62

Beck, U (2003) 'Understanding the real Europe', in *Dissent* Summer

Bonacchi, G (ed) (2001) *Una Costituzione senza Stato*, Bologna: Il Mulino

Bronzini, G (2000) 'I diritti sociali nella costituzione europea', in *Democrazia e Diritto* n 5: 95–108

Bronzini, G (2002) 'La Carta europea dei diritti fondamentali: dal progetto di un *modello sociale europeo* alla costituzionalizzazione dell'Unione', in Friese, H, Negri, T and Wagner, P (eds) *Europa politica*, Rome: Manifestolibri 187–209

Bronzini, G (2003) 'L'Europa politica dopo la Convenzione: tra continuità e rottura', in Bronzini, G, Friese, H, Negri, A and Wagner, P (eds) *Europa, costituzione e movimenti sociali*, Rome: Manifestolibri 111–43

Bronzini, G (2004) '10 tesi sul processo costituzionale europeo', in Bronzini, G *I diritti del popolo mondo*, Rome: Manifestolibri 249–57

Cartabia, M and Weiler, JHH (2000) *L'Italia in Europa*, Bologna: Il Mulino

Cervati, A (2001) 'Il diritto costituzionale europeo e la crisi della dogmatica statualistica', Il diritto romano attuale n 6: 21–49

Dal Lago, A and Mezzadra, S (2002) 'I confini impensati dell'Europa', in Friese, H, Negri, T and Wagner, P (eds) *Europa politica*, Rome: Manifestolibri 143–59

D'Antona, M (1999) 'Il diritto al lavoro nella costituzione e nell'ordinamento comunitario', Rivista giuridica del lavoro n 3: 15–23

Dellavalle, S (2002) *Una costituzione senza popolo? La costituzione europea alla luce delle concezioni del popolo come potere costituente*, Milan: Giuffrè

de Burca, G (2003a) 'Fundamental rights and citizenship', in de Witte, B (ed) *Ten Reflections on the Constitutional Treaty for Europe*, 11–47, Fiesole EUI

de Burca, G (2003b) 'The constitutional challenge of new governance in the European Union', in European Law Review (December) 814–39

De Schutter (2003) 'La garanzia dei diritti e principi nella Carta dei diritti fondamentali', in Zagrebelsky, G (ed) *Diritti e Costituzione nell'Unione europea*, Bari: Laterza 192–221

Ferry, JM (2000) *La question de l'état europèen*, Paris: PUF

Fitoussi, JP (2003) 'L'ambizione di un nuovo contratto sociale', in Vacca, G (ed) *L'Unita dell'Europa: Rapporto 2003 sull'integrazione europea*, Rome: Fondazione Istituto Gramsci 61–77

Friese, H (2003) 'L'Impero e l'Europa a venire', in Bronzini, G, Friese, H, Negri, A and Wagner, P (eds) *Europa, costituzione e movimenti sociali*, Rome: Manifestolibri 59–77

Friese, H and Wagner, P (2003) 'Repubblica Europa', in *Global* n 2: 38–40
Gerstenberg, O and Sabel, CF (2002) 'Directly-deliberative polyarchy: an institutional ideal for Europe?', in Joerges, C and Dehousse, R (eds) *Good Governance in Europe's Integrated Market*, Oxford: Hart 289–341
Giubboni, S (2003) *Diritti sociali e mercato. La dimensione sociale dell'integrazione europea*, Bologna: Il Mulino
Häberle, P (2002) 'Dallo stato nazionale all'Unione europea: evoluzioni dello Stato costituzionale', in *Diritto pubblico comparato e europeo* n 2: 455–65
Häberle, P (2003) 'Il giurista europeo di fronte ai compiti del nostro futuro costituzionale comune', Incontro alla Luiss del 21 March 2003, available at www.luiss.it/semcost
Habermas, J (1996a) *Between Facts and Norms: Contributions to a Discourse Theory of Law and Democracy*, Cambridge, MA: MIT Press
Habermas, J (1996b) *Fatti e norme*, Napoli: Guerini e associati
Habermas, J (2003) 'Perché l'Europa ha bisogno di una Costituzione' in Zagrebelsky, G (ed) *Diritti e Costituzione nell'Unione europea* Bari: Laterza 94–119
Joerges, C and Rödl, F (2004) 'The "social market economy" as Europe's social model?', EUI Working Paper Law No 2004/8
Leonardi, S (2000) 'Diritto sociale europeo e dialogo negoziale', in Formula n 1: 1–10
Luciani, M (1999) 'Diritti sociali ed integrazione europea' in Annuario dell'Associazione italiana dei costituzionalisti 1999 *La Costituzione europea* 507–39, Padova: Cedam
McCormick, N (2002) 'European democracy – new directions in 2002?', in Diritto pubblico europeo e comparato 1526–32
Majone, G (1996) *Regulating Europe*, London: Routledge
Majone, G (2003) 'Deficit democratico, istituzioni non maggioritarie e il paradosso dell'integrazione europea', Stato e mercato n 1: 3–39
Mückenberger, U (2002) 'L'Europa senza regolazione sociale? Il dialogo sociale e l'importanza della sfera procedurale', in Friese, H, Negri, A and Wagner, P (eds) *Europa politica*, Rome: Manifestolibri 209–45
Negri, A (2003a) 'La frattura dell'ordine globale', in Global n 2: 32–36
Negri, A (2003b) 'Il governo e le prospettive di politica estera dell'Unione europea nel quadro globale', in Bronzini, G, Friese, H, Negri, T and Wagner, P (eds) *Europa, costituzione e movimenti sociali*, Rome: Manifestolibri 47–59
Offe, C (2001) 'Esiste, o può esistere una società europea?', in *Sfera pubblica e costituzione europea*, Rome: Carocci 95–121
Pace, A (2002) 'La dichiarazione di Laeken', in *Trimestrale diritto pubblico* 613–50
Palma, M (2003) 'L'Europa e l'ossessione della sicurezza', in Bronzini, G, Friese, H, Negri, A and Wagner, P (eds) *Europa, costituzione e movimenti social*, Rome: Manifestolibri 263–89
Pernice, I (1999) 'Multilevel constitutionalism and the Treaty of Amsterdam', in Common Market Law Review n 3: 703–50
Pernice, I (2002a) 'Elements and structures of the european Constitution', WHI Paper n 4
Pernice, I (2002b) 'The Charter of Fundamental Rights in the Constitution of the European Union', WHI Papers 14
Pernice, I and Mayer, F (2003) 'La costituzione integrata dell'Europa', in Zagrebelsky, G (ed) *Diritti e Costituzione in Europa* Bari: Laterza 43–69
Pizzorusso, A (1999) 'Il rapporto del Comitato Simitis', in *Diritto pubblico europeo e comparato* 559–70

Polanyi, K (1974) *La grande trasformazione*, Torino: Einaudi

Roccella, M (1999) 'Lavoro e mercato nella giurisprudenza della Corte di giustisia', in *Diritto del lavoro e delle relazioni industriali* n 1: 33–65

Rodotà, S (2000) 'Diritto, diritti, globalizzazione', in *Rivista giuridica del lavoro* 4: 765–79

Scharpf, FW (1996) 'Negative and positive integration in the political economy of European welfare states', in Marks, G, Scharpf, FW, Schmitter, PC and Streeck, W (eds) *Governance in the European Union* London: Sage 15–39

Scharpf, FW (2000) *Governare l'Europa*, Bologna: Il Mulino

Scharpf, FW (2001) 'Democratic legitimacy under conditions of regulatory competition: why Europe differs from USA', in Nicolaidis, K and Howse, R (eds) *The Federal Visions: Legitimacy and Levels of Governance in the United States and in the European Union*, Oxford: Oxford University Press 355–76

Scoditti, A (2002) *Costituzione Senza Popolo*, Bari: Dedalo

Shaw, J (1999) 'Postnational Constitutionalism in the European Union', Journal of European Public Policy, n 4: 579–97

Shaw, J (2003) 'A strong Europe is a social Europe', www.fedtrust.co.uk/uploads/constitution/05_03.pdf

Sorrentino, F (2003) 'La nascita della costituzione europea: un'istantanea', accessible at ww.associazionedeicostituzionalisti.it/materiali/costituzione_ue/interventi/sorrentino_nascita.html

Streeck, W (1999) 'Competing solidarity: rethinking the European social model', MPHG Working Paper No 8

Supiot, A (1994) *Critique du droit du travail*, Paris: PUF

Supiot, A (1999) (ed) *Au delà dell'emploi*, Paris: Flammarion

Supiot, A (2001) 'Diritto del lavoro in una prospettiva europea', in Derive e approdi n 19: 85–94

Teubner, G (ed) (1986) *Dilemmas of Law in the Welfare State*, Berlin: De Groeter

Torchia, L (2001) 'Una Costituzione senza stato', Diritto pubblico II 405–55

von Bogdandy, A (1994) 'L'Unione sovranazionale come forma di potere politico', in Teoria politica n 1: 133–51

Wagner, P (2003) 'La forma politica dell'Europa e l'Europa come forma politica', in Bronzini, G, Friese, H, Negri, A and Wagner, P (eds) *Europa, costituzione e movimenti sociali*, Rome: Manifestolibri 59–99

Weiler, JHH (2002) 'Introduzione', in Comba, ME (ed) *Diritti e confini: Dalle costituzioni nazionali alla Carta di Nizza*, Bologna: Il Mulino XIII–XXXIII

Weiler, JHH (2003) *La Costituzione dell'Europa*, Bologna: Il Mulino

ECONOMIC EFFICIENCY AND SOCIAL JUSTICE: A PRUDENTIAL APPROACH FOR PUBLIC ACTIONS[1]

Feriel Kandil

There are two types of arguments for considering the economy as a polity: on the one hand, the arguments relating to the embeddedness of the economies; on the other hand, the arguments relating to public action and the ruling of the economy. The former are descriptive while the latter are prescriptive. It is the latter on which I shall focus.

As the above chapters have shown, the stake with the descriptive arguments is to identify the different logics of co-ordination underpinning economic activities. These are either the logic of free exchange (price co-ordination) or of norm regulation (rule co-ordination). Therefore, as markets are dependent on social rules, they are identified as non-autonomous spheres of interactions (see Block, Chapter 1 in this volume). But then, what to think of state regulation? In the present context of market globalisation, should democratic states be economic regulators? Consequently, the question of public action arises.

The problem is the following: is it possible for modern states, in the context of economic globalisation, to achieve *good* public action, that is, to set the political conditions for satisfying the claims of the citizens regarding social justice and their expectations regarding economic prosperity? This is a crucial issue for it is at the heart of the political hardship encountered in modern democracies: under the pressure of market globalisation, governments concentrate on economic competitiveness and tend to neglect or even ignore their responsibilities regarding social justice. Significantly, this attitude of governments contributes to the weakening of their democratic basis, generating political and social instability and favouring economic malfunctioning. Therefore, it is necessary both for political and economic reasons to clarify how, in the context of modern democracies, good public action can be implemented.

My claim is that the conditions for good public action consist in promoting *prudential reason*. In contrast to the standard approaches to *public action*, which are either instrumental (such as the Rawlsian one) or procedural (such as the Habermasian one), the *prudential approach* argues for the indispensability of the implementation of public action aiming at *solidarity* in the context of modern democracies. The capacity of the public actors to make judgments and choices that

---

1   I am grateful to the contributors of this volume for their comments on earlier drafts. I have also benefited from helpful discussions during seminars I attended when I was Jean Monnet Fellow of the European University Institute.

are based on a *sense of solidarity* is called *prudential reason*. My argument is that for good public action to be actualised, it is necessary that decision makers, experts and citizens alike are able to exercise this capacity of reason. For the purpose of illustration, I shall base my argument on the European case.

THE QUESTION OF PUBLIC ACTION AS A CRUCIAL ONE FOR MODERN DEMOCRACIES

Caring both for social justice and economic efficiency

In the context of modern capitalism, it is common both among politicians and among social scientists to put the emphasis on the benefits of *economic liberalism*. It is frequent then to consider that the less the state interferes with markets, the better it is. Therefore, many people consider that the question of public action should be left aside, since they see the latter as related to dated and at bottom ideological debates. My argument is that this view is erroneous. I shall therefore use developments in contemporary economics (especially in welfare economics) to show that it is both politically and economically necessary that democratic states *actively* (that is, by means of *good public action*) care for social justice as well as for economic efficiency.

As Arrow (1974) explains, real markets are both impure and imperfect. This entails that actual economic exchanges cannot result from any theoretically unique and general price equilibrium that is actually reached. For real markets to be efficient it is necessary for them to be embedded in non-market forms of regulation. Therefore, for market economies to be efficient it is necessary that they be framed by social norms produced by social institutions. One resulting question is the following: what about the intertwining between price co-ordination and norm regulation? More specifically, how to conceive of the role of the state in such regulation?

The answer given by welfare economics is clear: modern states should play a large and active role within market economies. The argument is based on Pareto's analysis of economic efficiency. He has proposed the Pareto-optimality criterion as a standard for economic efficiency.[2] The basic theorems of welfare economics hold that an economy of pure and perfect competition is Pareto-efficient; conversely, all Pareto-efficient allocation can be generated as the equilibrium of an exchange economy. However, for a given economy, there are many Pareto-efficient equilibria, depending on the way the goods have been first distributed among exchanging agents. How to decide about the ex-ante distribution? Which rules of distribution should be favoured in a market economy? These are questions of social justice rather than of economic efficiency. Therefore, there are *two criteria* for exchange economies: efficiency *and* social justice. Then, the role of a democratic state should be to guarantee that both *criteria are satisfied*. The

---

2   An allocation is said to be Pareto-efficient if there exists no other allocation such that (at least) one individual is strictly better-off, and no individual is worse-off.

problem is the following: is it actually possible for democratic states, *in the present context of modern capitalism*, to deal with both criteria at the same time?

Three objections can be raised against the reasoning developed above, leading to a negative answer: the economic objection, the ethical one and finally the political one. They are all based on the same observation, namely that in the present context of global markets and of pluralistic societies, it is illusory for a democratic state to aim at implementing at the same time economic efficiency and social justice. I shall present the arguments and show that even if the premises are correct the conclusions are fallacious. However, my own argument is the following: it is all the more important for democratic states to care for implementing both social justice and economic efficiency since modern democracies are the object of conflicting tendencies of cultural fragmentation and of economic globalisation.

Three counter-arguments for leaving aside the question of a good public action

The economic objection is advanced by those who, as economic liberals do, insist on the global structures of the present markets and on the resulting effects on public action. In the context of economic globalisation, the economic constraints are so strong that the governments have no choice: either they concentrate on economic competition or they lead their countries to economic and social disaster. This is to say that competition in the context of global economies is so hard that favouring efficiency should be the main priority of any modern state.

The ethical objection is supported either by political scientists or by moral philosophers who insist on the fragmentation processes which are at the heart of the present pluralistic democracies. It consists in claiming that talking of a good public action entails some value judgment on the *good* and, in particular, on the principle of social justice that should be favoured: such condition is in contradiction with the pluralistic structure of modern democracies. More precisely, the latter are characterised by a plurality of cultural identities supporting different and even contradictory conceptions of the good. In such a pluralistic context, it is quite vain to aim at a public action which could unequivocally be recognised as *good*, that is, an action which could satisfy the conflicting claims and expectations of the citizens regarding both social justice and efficiency. All judgments about a *good public action* would entail metaphysical or even theological considerations on what the good should be and would contradict the modern and democratic consensus on ethical pluralism. Therefore, according to the tradition of tolerance characterising modern democracies, such an issue should be left aside. It is ethically more reasonable and it is politically more relevant to give an account of the complex functioning of modern political life than to aim at imposing some specific conception of social justice on the citizens.

The political objection is the one both ultra-liberals and Marxists would put forward. In the present context of modern capitalism, it is mistaken to assume that social justice and economic efficiency are compatible principles of public action.

They are not, since they are based on contradictory values, namely those of social equality on the one hand and of economic freedom on the other. For the ultra-liberals, public policies which aim at social equality lead to monetary redistribution: the latter provoke unwanted effects, favouring free riding, adverse selection, and counter-productive behaviour. Importantly, all these effects are also inefficient. Conversely, for the Marxists, public policies favouring economic freedom lead to increasing social inequalities, supporting and enhancing the domination of capitalists in modern societies. The following question arises in this context: which should be the priority for public policies? Economic freedom claimed by ultra liberalism or social equality sought by communism?

The arguments are fallacious

The economic and the ethical arguments rest on a present observation: modern democracies are subject to a tension created by two conflicting processes – one of cultural fragmentation and one of economic homogenisation. On the one side, citizens tend to withdraw into their cultural communities and their ethical identities. On the other side, with their open economies, modern democracies are under the pressure of global markets. This entails a homogenisation of their economic structures and of the individuals' economic behaviour.

However, this correct observation does not entail that there is no possibility for the implementation of *good public action*. On the contrary, the role of the democratic state consists precisely in responding, beyond such conflicting tendencies, to the common claims and expectations of the citizens. The former are claims regarding the basic democratic agreement and the way the basic principles of social justice, that is, liberty and equality, should be satisfied. The latter are expectations regarding economic wealth. In particular, the challenge for the governments consists in deciding to which extent the conflicting values of economic freedom and of social equality should inform public action. As Sen (1996) underlines, there is a spectrum of possibilities for public action between financial conservatism, giving all priority to economic freedom, and social reformism, focusing exclusively on social equality. The problem is: in a democratic state or in a democratic union, *who* should *decide* and *how*? The answer to this question is pivotal to the analysis of the conditions for good public action.

As ultra-liberals and Marxists argue, such a decision is indeed a normative one. It entails some underpinning engagement with the conception of the good to be publicly supported. Who should undertake such normative engagement? In a democratic state, the government as the representative of the will of the people should. However, for its action to be publicly legitimate, it has to meet the approbation of the people. In other words, public decisions bearing normative arbitrage should be under the political judgment of the citizens. Against ultra-liberals and Marxists, it is argued that the acknowledgment of the necessity of some arbitrage does not entail that these also have to be definitive. It is precisely the stake of a democratic state to consider all arbitrage between basic values as unfair unless it is seen as provisional and, thus, subject to possible democratic revision. The aim of a good public action consists precisely in identifying when and where it is required to intervene more or less either in favour of social equality or in favour of economic freedom. How to identify such conditions – the adequate moment and the adequate policy? My argument is that such identification is impossible without the *active participation* of the citizens and without recognising that, beyond the conflicts between economic freedom and social equality, public action should aim at *solidarity*. I shall base my argument on the European case.

THE CONDITIONS FOR GOOD PUBLIC ACTION: THE EUROPEAN CASE

The necessity of democratic control

In a democratic context like that of the European Union, the necessary condition for good public action relates to its being legitimate: it must be *publicly recognised as resulting from a democratic process of deliberation and decision.*

Then, as Habermas (1998 and 1999) emphasises, for a public action to be democratic it is necessary that it be under the control of the citizen's judgments. If such a condition is missing, as is presently the case for the European Union, then public action turns into technocratic policy-making, revealing significant institutional and political dysfunctions. Therefore, these are the arguments I shall develop:

(a) For a good public action to be implemented it is necessary that it be *publicly* recognised as an expression of the citizens' *collective autonomy*.

(b) For the citizens' democratic control to be effective, it is necessary that *an active sphere of public debate* be set allowing citizens to exercise their *capacity for voice*.

As Habermas reminds us, according to the republican tradition of political thought, the democratic people (or the citizens) manifest their collective autonomy while exercising their political will, that is, while giving themselves their own rules of collective life and their own principles of public action. In the context of the European Union, European institutions such as the Parliament and the Council represent indirectly the Europeans' will. However, for their actions to be publicly recognised as the expression of a European collective autonomy, it is necessary that they conform *continuously* to the will of the citizens, that is, to the expectations and the claims the European citizens manifest either through national or trans-national events (like, for instance, demonstrations against the Iraq war). However, such claims and expectations are heteroclite and even contradictory, since they combine competing interests and antagonistic values. For example, on the one hand, Europeans are attached to enhancing the European Common Market but, on the other hand, they are not willing to get rid of their existing welfare systems. This entails contradictions between the liberalisation of the markets and the reduction of public deficits on the one side and the improvement of public services and the maintenance of high levels of welfare expenditures on the other side. Because of such contradictions, there is a challenge for European public actors to help national states reform their welfare systems.

However, such reforms ultimately depend on some crucial arbitrage made between economic efficiency and social equality (see, for example, the difficulties with the pension reforms in France). The democratic control must be exercised precisely over such arbitrage.

In the context of the Growth and Stability Pact, national governments need some European support in order to keep some of the historical acquisitions of their welfare systems. Such a support cannot be delivered without the democratic consent of the Europeans, since it entails a crucial arbitrage between a liberal economy on the one hand and a social welfare economy on the other (see Stråth, Chapter 4 in this volume).

Social decision makers such as the Commission, the Council and the European Parliament are responsible for implementing public action. However, at the same time and as citizens, the Europeans are responsible for exercising their democratic control on the underpinning arbitrage. For such a democratic control to be effective, the existence of an active European sphere of public debate is necessary, where the citizens could exercise what Bonvin and Thelen (2004) call their 'capability for voice'.

For such a capability to be exercised, it is necessary: (1) that all the relevant information relating to European public action be available for all and every citizen; (2) that the citizens be educated so that they could form their own critical judgment; and (3) that the citizens be given the institutional means for their judgment to be expressed publicly, either indirectly (through parliaments) or directly (through unions, associations, media, etc). In sum, as Habermas (1998 and 1999) emphasises, it is necessary that all the institutional means be set for an active European sphere of debate to emerge.

Such an active sphere of debate is a necessary condition for the implementation of a good public action at the European level, but it is not a sufficient one. As we shall see below, the sufficient element for the implementation of a good public action is for the latter to aim at European solidarity.

From debates to solidarity

It is common, while referring to the so-called 'European democratic deficit', to regret the absence of a European sphere of public debate: European public actions do not proceed from public deliberations and they are not subject to public controversies.

The European Union's democratic failure is structural: its basic institutions are so organised that European citizens have very little room to express themselves, while they render impossible the emergence of a European sphere of public debate. In effect, European citizenship is merely passive, since it is reduced to a legal status dependent on national citizenship. On top of this, European institutions are fundamentally technocratic. The European Parliament's prerogatives are restricted compared with those of the Commission. This entails that public actions are the result of an occult game of strategic national interests. Neither the Commission nor the Council have to account publicly for their actions. Even the work of the convention was conceived in technocratic terms, consequently eluding all public debates, since the aim was to find a point of equilibrium between the different national constitutional texts (see Bronzini, Chapter 10 in this volume).

As a result, European public actions have little democratic legitimacy and the Euro-scepticism of the citizens is getting deeper. Indeed, European citizens are quite inclined to consider European choices as either unfair or inefficient. A good example is the imposed liberalisation of all European markets, including those related to public services. As Chorin (2003) illustrates for the French case, bringing about a structural change in national public services is the source of conflict between national and European economic interests. Such a conflict would not be problematic if it were played out publicly and debated democratically. Unfortunately, this is not the case: no European public debate was developed on either national or European public services. More generally, European governments have agreed on the Growth and Stability Pact in order to improve the efficiency of the Common Market. However, they are unable to respect their economic engagements and at the same time afford their welfare expenditures. Their inherited national welfare systems are then put into question. Many European citizens, such as the Danish people, consider that such an agreement is problematic: the cost for being a member of the Common Market is too high (Wind 2001).

Conversely, one can argue that even when the Europeans are given the means to express themselves on European matters they show little or no will to engage in European debates. The European Parliament elections of June 2004 are illustrative in this respect: any effort to base the electoral debates on European rather than national issues failed, while abstention rates were high in all European countries. Citizens need some motivation for exercising their civic responsibility. Therefore, the aim of public actors should be first to favour the expression of such responsibility. They should address the citizens as being endowed with the responsibility to achieve common ends and to participate in a common destiny. Citizens are concerned insofar as it is recognised as a political duty for the social decision makers to account publicly for their decisions. They are responsible for the common ends they pursue and for the reasons *why* they have implemented such actions and not others. It is on the basis of such justifications that democratic debate about public actions could take place and that public arbitrage can be legitimated democratically.

Political and social solidarity as European public goals

In order to resolve the European democratic deficit, it is necessary to proceed to institutional reforms that would yield the structural basis for an active sphere of European debate to emerge. However, this is not sufficient: for European citizens to engage actively into debates, it is necessary that they feel that their *common good* is at stake. Indeed, the sufficient factor would be the putting of the European collective choices publicly into question through both national and transnational debates. The question of the *ends* informing European public actions needs to be open to public debate among all citizens, social deciders and experts.

Putting the focus of the debates on the ends to achieve through public actions entails that European public actions are not under the complete control of technocratic organisations or of competing national state strategies. It further entails that European public actions are informed by that which makes members of a democratic union be more than just partners in a common market. Partners are self-interested in their mutual co-operation: if it is to their advantage, they are free to get rid of their agreement at any time. This is not the case with the members of a democratic union: as fellow citizens, they are engaged in a common destiny and they are responsible towards each other for their collective choices and for the common ends they give themselves. As fellow citizens, they depend on each other: their lives are woven together insofar as they depend on common ends. In other words, solidarity is what turns individuals into fellow citizens. A good public action should favour the participation of citizens in the governing of their lives while enhancing their sense of solidarity, that is, their being aware that they are dependent on each other and responsible for their common ends.

European solidarity is therefore what European public actors should focus on. Public actions should be a means for enhancing both the Europeans' political solidarity and their social solidarities. *Political solidarity* refers in this context to the awareness of Europeans regarding their sharing a common destiny ever since the adoption of the European founding fathers' project. This is the basis for acknowledging their commitment to the achievement of common ends and the undertaking of reciprocal duties. With the term *social solidarity*, I wish to designate the founding experiences and the common values they inherited from a common history. As Le Goff (1993, 1996 and 2003) argues, Europeans relate to a long history which goes back to Greek and Roman antiquity. Present-day Europeans emerged from a context of shared historical experiences of war and peace, of social struggles and political unifications, of artistic innovations and intellectual progress. Such European solidarity is the basis for their *common* claims and expectations to be formed, expressed and revised and for their common ends to be assumed as good and worthy. The resulting question is: what is the content of the ends the European would recognise as good and worthy? In other words, how can good public action in Europe be implemented? Answers to this question are given in the context of the European and republican tradition of political thought, which extends from Aristotle to Rousseau and Kant, or more recently to Leo Strauss and Hannah Arendt.

RENEWING THE EUROPEAN AND REPUBLICAN TRADITION OF POLITICAL THOUGHT

Solidarity in the European and republican tradition of thought

My argument is the following: as the authors from the European and republican tradition of political thought argue, for good public action to be implemented, it is necessary that they enhance solidarity between citizens. In the European case, public actors would reinforce European solidarity if their actions could reveal their substantial common good to the citizens. This entails that European public actors should abandon the usual ways of dealing with public choices, that is, both the procedural and the instrumental ones.

In effect, being solidly tied to a common destiny the Europeans are responsible for their common good. This is to say that they are politically engaged vis à vis one another in achieving good ends, that is, good for one and all. As authors such as Rousseau and Kant argue, a good public action will accomplish such ends. It will give citizens the opportunity to debate and reflect on their common good through their conflictive judgments regarding the achieved and future public actions. It will force the citizens to recognise that they are engaged in a process of identification of the ends that would be worthy for them both individually and collectively. Since this is a long process, it is impossible for citizens to engage in it without the existence of mutual esteem as Rousseau (1762) stresses and without reciprocal respect as Kant (1785) adds. Social feelings urge citizens to realise they are not strangers to one another but alter egos, that is, fellow citizens deserving respect and feeling affected by the injustices, the poverty and the sufferings befalling each other and responsible for improving the quality of their lives.

Therefore, a good public action should have two purposes. On the one hand, it should strengthen the legal system underpinning the democratic agreement, since by virtue of their legal entitlement citizens can experience political solidarity. On the other hand, it should favour the development and manifestation of social feelings of respect and esteem, which reinforce the sense of responsibility between citizens.

Two negative consequences can be inferred: first, a good public action should not favour values which are not *common* to all citizens; secondly, a good public action should not ignore the necessary process of the citizens' identification with a *substantial* common good. In sum, a good public action should neither be instrumental as Rawls and Harsanyi argue, nor procedural as Habermas advocates.

Avoiding the instrumental approach of Rawls and Harsanyi

According to the instrumental approach, public actions should result from the choices of a *rational* agent. However, as a *social* decision maker, one must decide according to public rather than private interests. How can such public interests be identified? By putting oneself under a veil of ignorance, argue both Rawls (1971) and Harsanyi (1976). Under such a veil, the social decision maker ignores both her interests and the conflicting claims and expectations of her fellow citizens. For Harsanyi, she can behave then as an impartial observer aiming at 'the interests of the society considered as whole'. As for Rawls, under such a veil, the social decision maker can behave as the fair partner in the 'original position': he or she maximises the general advantages that he or she and the other citizens can derive from their co-operation. What about those interests of the society as Harsanyi sets them? What about those mutual advantages mentioned by Rawls? They are what the social decider should identify as the public interest of the society. In

Harsanyi's theory, it is identified as the average utility. The resulting good public action is the one which conforms to the utilitarian device of average utility maximisation. In contrast, in Rawls's theory, improving public interest entails maximising an index of primary goods. This maximisation the social decision maker obtains when he subsumes his decisions under the two Rawlsian principles of justice as lexicographically ordered (liberty principle and difference principle).[3]

However, both in the Rawlsian and in the Harsanyian theories, the solidarity requirement is violated. Instead of considering his fellow citizens as engaged in a democratic process of identification with common ends, the social decision maker imposes a specific conception of the good, the common good being reduced, for rational purposes, either to utility or to an index of primary goods. This imposes a partial and anti-democratic conception of public action.

Indeed, public action is exclusively conceived as instrumental means for some given collective ends. The citizens cannot discuss publicly the ends at which the social decision maker should aim. Actually, the theoretician is the only one who can justify the rationality of the ends imposed by the social decision maker. Both in the Harsanyian theory and in the Rawlsian one, the theoretician draws on a specific moral argumentation for imposing a restrictive conception of the ends of a good public action: the moral argumentation of Harsanyi is utilitarian while, for Rawls, it is Kantian.

However, in the pluralistic context of modern democracies, a fortiori in the pluralistic context of the European Union, it is nonsensical to rely on ethical arguments for imposing a restrictive conception of the ends to aim at publicly. On the contrary, this is the purpose of public debates to put into question the common good and the ends that should be achieved publicly. Indeed, as Habermas and the tenants of the procedural approach argue, an active sphere of debate is a necessary precondition for the implementation of good public actions. However, as I shall argue now, this does not entail that public actions should be reduced to procedural ones, since the promotion of a procedural approach induces some violation of the solidarity requirement.

Avoiding Habermas's procedural approach

As Habermas (1998 and 1999) stresses, in the pluralistic context of modern democracies in general and in Europe in particular, public action is subject to conflicting critiques, justifications and debates. This happens because in a

---

3   These two principles are intended to apply to the basic structure of society – the fundamental political and economic arrangements – as opposed to particular actions by governmental officials or individual statutes. The liberty principle requires that the basic structure provides each citizen with a fully adequate scheme of basic liberties, such as freedom of conscience, freedom of expression, and due process of law. The difference principle requires that inequalities in wealth and social position be arranged so as to (a) to be connected to positions or offices or jobs in society that everyone has an equal opportunity to attain and (b) so as to benefit the worse-off groups in society. Rawls states that the two principles are lexically ordered, with the liberty principle taking precedence over the difference principle in the case of conflict.

pluralistic society a decision favouring some given ends and means will always contradict the interest or even the conceptions of the good of some interest-groups, some cultural community or some ideological collectivity. Therefore, instead of aiming at some impossible shared values, public actors should care to follow the accurate democratic procedures of collective decision, that is, bargaining, argumentation, voting, and so on. Then, the different decision procedures are evaluated according to their democratic characteristics: they must take fairly or equally into account the conflicting interests of the citizens as expressed by their cultural communities, their unions, their political parties, and so on and, finally, as expressed through public debates. Habermas insists on the importance of such debates for the testing of conflicting argumentations. This is a democratic test for him and the most accurate procedure for collective choice because it makes the debaters justify publicly their arguments and account for their reasons. Good reasons, those that should underpin public actions, are therefore the ones the debaters come to agree on.

However, in such debates, the agreement depends on the talents of the orator rather than on substantial conviction. Disputes and exchanges of arguments replace discussions and reflections on the common good. Procedural concerns for rhetoric replace substantial debates about common ends. Form prevails over substance: it is much less the very ends that matter than the formal characteristics of the procedure by which a decision is taken. How then could citizens feel responsible for their common future when this depends mainly on rhetoric? This rather leaves the door open to demagogy and to political disillusion.

The problem with the procedural approach comes from its blindness. It asserts that in modern democracies only procedural features could be identified as common. However, citizens need to share more than common rules of collective choice. They need to reflect on – and give meaning to – their collective and individual life. They need to reflect on the future they choose for themselves and their descendants and on the direction and meaning of their common life. As autonomous citizens, they have to assume their choices as resulting from their being committed to a common destiny and responsible for their common ends. How could they feel responsible for the ends which are imposed on them by means of formal procedures?

On the contrary, as Rousseau (1762) and the civic republican tradition insist, public action must be an expression of a *public reason*, that is, one which is shared by all and every citizen. This public reason must not be reduced either to an instrumental or to a procedural one. It must neither be conceived as favouring some substantial but partial conception of the good nor as promoting some formal conception of the good. In contrast, it must promote a substantial and overall conception of the good, yielding solidarity as a common end. How can public action underpinning such a public reason be implemented? Following Castoriadis's (1999a and 1999b) civic republican views, I shall show that such public reason should be a *critical* one and that the corresponding approach for public action should be a prudential one.

THE PRUDENTIAL APPROACH

Prudential reason for public actors

With the civic republican conception of public reason, the emphasis is put on the normative content of public action. For solidaristic public action to be implemented, it is necessary that public actors draw on a substantial conception of the common good. However, such a substantial conception is always partial and restrictive, favouring some specific values. Therefore, citizens are assigned to exercise their normative and critical judgment against the instituted values. Such public contestations are crucial for the inauguration of institutional reforms and historical changes. This is why Castoriadis calls the democratic and public reason a *critical* one, since it relates to the judgments citizens can make against their institutions and the actions of their representatives. Indeed, this critical reason is the cornerstone to the development and exercise of individual and collective autonomy.

Moreover, there are but two types of judgment they can formulate, namely determinative and reflexive ones. *Determinative judgment* underpins normative arbitrage. The judging person decides, that is, he commits himself to one public option, to one specific conception of the common good. Vested with political powers (executive, legislative and judiciary), public deciders are to exercise such determinative judgments. However, this is also the case with experts. The latter define the informational basis from which the alternatives of public choices are identified. However, such informational basis is evaluative and entails interpersonal comparisons. The standard for such comparisons is defined by the expert himself who decides on the elements of a social position to be positively evaluated. Depending on the standard employed, the evaluation of the needs and risks citizens are facing will vary, while their claims and expectations will be subject to different assessments. Therefore, when evaluating public decisions, experts exercise some determinative judgment, while favouring a given conception of the common good. Finally, when expressing publicly their claims and expectations, citizens manifest their commitment to the public promotion of some specific set of values, thus making some determinative judgment.

Reflexive judgment concerns deliberations and discussions. Active citizens exercise their reflexive judgment not only on the tested effects of public policies but also on public deliberations preceding collective choice. Such judgments put into question common ends, both those that have been achieved and those that should be pursued. A major democratic requirement is that social decision makers should submit their choices to such critical judgment, both during the deliberations preceding the choice and during the implementation of public policies. In both cases, the democratic legitimacy of the decisions is at stake. Finally, the very work of the experts must also be open to critical judgments for this is the way to revise their informational basis, that is, to take into account the citizens' diverse claims and expectations. Then the role of the experts should be to bring to light the citizens' critical insights which could subsequently be integrated into new public choices.

In order to designate the intricate and complex nature of the critical reason public actors should exercise, I shall call it *prudential reason*. Public actions should be prudential ones, since critical judgments employed by decision makers, experts and citizens alike put solidarity between them to the test.

Prudential reason and public action

Prudential reason allows citizens to reflect publicly on their common good. Not only can they question the set of public procedures but also the set of public values at which they should aim. They recognise that normative engagements are required. These favour some specific set of public procedures and of public values to which public action will conform. However, they also recognise that such normative engagements are contestable as they invite critical judgment and revisions.

Hence, the common good which is at stake in the exercise of prudential reason is neither reduced to a set of uncontested values as it is in the instrumental approach, nor is it reduced to set of formal procedures of collective choice as in the procedural approach. Rather, the *common good* consists in *a regulatory and critical idea underpinning the citizens' judgments*. It is a regulatory idea insofar as, with the employment of determinative or reflexive judgment, public actors aim at the realisation of common ends. It is a critical idea insofar as they put into question any definite and publicly established conception of the common good.

Thus, the employment of critical judgment allows citizens to reflect on the common good as a regulatory and critical idea necessary for their collective autonomy. While exercising their prudential reason, citizens enhance their solidarity and this is the reason why I argue that a good public action will favour the exercise of the citizens' prudential reason.

On the one hand, their political solidarity is given a concrete expression as they are encouraged to exercise their responsibilities towards one another. As determinative agents, they recognise each other as responsible for their normative engagements; as reflexive agents, they recognise each other as responsible for the revision of their engagements.

On the other hand, while exercising their prudential reason, they favour the development of their social feelings and the emergence of civic solidarity. Reflecting on their common good involves reflecting on the way their political commitment should be reinforced. This emphasises their responsibility to one another and their deserving mutual assistance.

In sum, the prudential approach for public action places the emphasis on the institutional means necessary for democratic deliberations framing public choices. In this respect, it favours political solidarity. The prudential approach also focuses on the importance of caring for social assistance as a necessary goal for modern democracies. In effect, this goal is as necessary as the preservation of liberties and the favouring of equality. In this respect, it emphasises the constitutive role of social solidarity either inherited or emerging. Indeed, the latter are the cement of a political community.

IMPLEMENTING PRUDENTIAL PUBLIC ACTIONS IN EUROPE

Overcoming the present anti-democratic inclination

Presently, European public actors are promoting both an instrumental and a procedural approach to public action. The result is a technical inclination leading to an increase of the European democratic deficit. On the one hand, the so-called 'European soft law' favours the instrumental approach. The member states at the European Council agree on some common goals, while they are to choose separately the means (that is, the national policies) for achieving such common goals (see Joerges and Everson, Chapter 9 in this volume). Take, for example, the Growth and Stability Pact, which is designed to give some leeway in relation to fiscal deficits in order to absorb the impact of outside shocks. Each member state within the Eurozone must communicate to the European Commission an update of its stability and growth programme, giving evidence of progress towards the goal of a balanced budget. The Commission imposes on the states penalties or rewards depending on their performance.

However, on the other hand, the procedural approach is also effective. The European authorities put the focus on the decision procedures that will guarantee the Europeans more agreement and co-operation. A good example here is the field of social legislation. Even if the legislative power is distributed among many European public authorities such as the Commission, the Council and the Parliament, the social partners play a decisive role, in particular with regard to social legislation. The latter is mainly the result of collective negotiations rather than public deliberations. As Supiot (2003) notes, in such negotiating procedures, the Parliament plays a very restrictive role. The Commission makes a proposal which is submitted to the social partners who are to negotiate the content of the proposition subsequently presented to the European Council. Depending on the national governments, the Council agrees with the proposition or not. Despite the diversity of national interests, a European social legislation could develop. Negotiating procedures are a guarantee for the fact that all European authorities, including national governments, will agree on the resulting decision.

However, irrespective of how instrumental or procedural European public action might be, the resulting tendency is that the European authorities account for their actions as if they were stemming from technical constraint rather than normative arbitrage. The growing power of the experts and the contractualisation of the law are testimonies for such technical inclinations.

Concerning instrumental public action, the agreed goals are very general and formal principles such as those pronounced in the Charter of Fundamental Rights. They cannot serve as precise guides for policy-making and it is up to the experts to plan the precise manner in which these principles must be implemented. Experts decide on the common understanding to give to the established common principle; they are the ones who decide on the effective common ends irrespective of the citizens' will. One could consider in this context the case of the 'open method of co-ordination' as applied to social policies, which is a good example of the anti-democratic consequences of such technical tendencies. As Maria Joao

Rodrigues (2001) reminds us, 'the concept was introduced by the Lisbon European Council of 23–24 March 2000 in order to better implement a long-term strategy for a competitive knowledge-based economy with more and better employment and social cohesion'. The Council has set very broad goals in different fields of public action, including the information society, enterprises, economic reforms, education and social inclusion. The Commission provides the states with tools such as indicators, benchmarks and exchange of the best practices for realising the European goals. Each state has its own action programme, the results of which the Commission has to evaluate. Such an evaluation is considered as mainly technical for it consists in improving the state's practices. There is always, however, normative judgment underpinning the Commission's evaluations. Some norms of public evaluation are imposed without being publicly debated or even explained. This is the case with the European Employment Strategy agenda, as Salais (2004) and Raveaud (2004) argue. The Commission uses the employability rate rather than the unemployment rate as a comparative indicator. The underlying ideology behind this is strictly liberal, since it encourages flexibility in the labour market and the weakening of the national systems of workers' rights. As Raveaud notes, the Council has mistaken the ends for the means. It would be most damaging for the European Union if it went on ignoring the normative aspects of public evaluations. Such aspects should be publicly identified and the choice of evaluation norms should be the object of public debate.

Now, from a procedural point of view, the technical inclination gives rise to another phenomenon: the contractualisation of European law. This is most effective in social legislation. As Supiot (2003) emphasises, the distinction between law and contract is gradually vanishing. The social law is, depending on the case, either a subsidiary norm for the social partners and their practices, or an incentive norm for the social partners and their collective conventions, or an induced norm resulting from the social partners' collective conventions. The result is that social legislation escapes from democratic control, as social partners do not represent the European citizens' will. Little by little, European social legislation is becoming a private domain under the influence of social bodies representing private competing interests.[4]

To sum up, however public decisions are taken (from a procedural or an instrumental point of view) their normative content is ignored. The sources of public action are considered as technical rather than political. From an instrumental point of view, public action is under the control of the technical evaluations of the experts, while from a procedural point of view public action escapes democratic control, especially in the field of social legislation. There is no way to assume publicly the normative choices informing public action and to develop a democratic critique. Facing such a situation, Europeans are condemned to turn to the European Constitution as the ultimate rampart for the future of a

---

4   Analysing such a tendency, Supiot argues that it is a resurgence of the feudalism underlying the Ancien Regime: 'the equilibrated representation of the different social bodies replacing the law of the greater number in the expression of a people's will' (Supiot 2003: 66).

European democracy (see Chapters 9 and 10 in this volume). The present text to be agreed on aims mainly at increasing the prerogatives of the European Parliament. However, it would be only a palliative if the Union kept on conceiving of public action either in instrumental or procedural terms. It is necessary that the Europeans recognise the normative dimension of their public action and, consequently, that the European authorities adopt a prudential approach to public action.

Implementing prudential actions

As discussed above, from a prudential point of view, the aim of European public action should be to favour the development of European solidarity. In other words, the aim should be, first, to place emphasis on the exercise of the responsibilities of public actors. Secondly, it should care for the cultivation of mutual assistance between Europeans. This entails, first, that the principle of subsidiarity should be reconsidered so that it becomes a juridical incentive for the exercise of political and social responsibilities and, secondly, that the social assistance the Europeans owe to one another becomes the main argument for social and economic reforms.

The subsidiarity principle of the Treaty of the European Union is the one whereby the Union does not take action (except in the areas which fall within its exclusive competence) unless it is more effective than action taken at national, regional or local level. Presently, with the open method of co-ordination, the subsidiarity principle serves as a justification for placing into competition national public action. The latter are compared according to evaluative norms which should be publicly debated. Unfortunately, they evade public debate and consequently the resulting evaluation processes escape democratic control. Such an effect is in perfect contradiction with the subsidiarity principle, since in its original formulation this principle was intended to ensure that European public action was planned as closely as possible to the citizens' experiences, their claims and expectations, their needs and the possibilities of action available to them at national, regional or local level.

The subsidiarity principle would achieve its primary aim only if it were reconsidered and reconceptualised so as to become the cornerstone of the arguments in favour of prudential reason. Therefore, the subsidiarity principle should be conceived as a legal tool forcing the European public actors (European decision making authorities, experts and citizens) to exercise their prudential reason. Social deciders should be legally forced to account publicly for their decisions, that is, in front of the European Parliament, and the experts should be legally forced to make all the available information public. This is to say that there should be European observatories on public action that provide public expertise. In their work, as the subsidiarity principle requires, the experts should care for the effective improvement of the citizens' lives rather than imposing normative judgments through the use of specific indicators. As Sen (1996) argues, one way to achieve this would be to base the experts' evaluations on information about capabilities. Capabilities are the personal and institutional means actually available to the citizens for improving their lives. Evaluating public action in terms of capabilities entails opening the evaluation to democratic control, for the citizens are expected to express their points of view as they strive to improve their lives. Furthermore, as their actions would be evaluated according to their consequences on the quality of life of the citizens (that is, on the achievement of their basic goods such as rights, liberties, health, education and wealth), the European authorities would be incited to put their choices under public debates.[5]

The second condition for implementing a prudential approach in Europe consists in putting the focus on the social assistance that Europeans as members of a democratic union owe each other. At present, the European systems of social assistance are under the control of national welfare states, but the latter are facing social and economic mutations that are too profound to be dealt with adequately at the national level. The nation states are thus in need of European support, this being the aim of public action of the prudential type. More precisely, the European welfare states are facing two difficulties, the first relating to the risk of a social and fiscal dumping, the second concerning the undermining of the European social and economic standards. The first difficulty stems from the fact that welfare states cannot easily co-ordinate their approaches as they represent specific and diverse welfare traditions. The second difficulty results from the European Growth and Stability Pact. The European Central Bank refuses to lead a less restrictive monetary policy as long as the national states do not balance their budgets. The national states are bound by the stability pact to lead restricted budgetary policies with adverse effects on growth. The result is that European social and economic standards are levelled from the bottom and future investments in research, education, infrastructures and so on, are insufficient.

Therefore, as the prudential approach stresses, it is decisive that European public action gives ample room to the expression and development of European solidarities. This is the indispensable foundation for the necessary European reform of the national welfare states. The basis for such solidarity is both inherited and emerging. Inherited from a common European history and emerging from common economic, political and social experiences such as, for example, the Common Market, demonstrations against the Iraq war, or the altermondialist manifestations of Geneva or Florence respectively (Delanty 1997).

A good public action should favour the development of European solidarity as based on cultural rather than national values. One can see the development of national solidarity as the various particular expressions the different European people gave to their common values. Additionally, one can see present-day Europe as an appropriate area for transnational expressions of such basic values. Without the public enhancement of such social and cultural values, the Europeans could not be autonomous because they could not give themselves the reasons for assuming their common future. Therefore, it is a political requirement for Europeans that they lead ambitious cultural policies. The latter would make Europeans aware of their participating in a common culture and enjoying a

---

5   For further considerations on Europe and the politics of capabilities, see Bonvin and
    Farvaques (2004); Kandil (2004); Salais and Villeneuve (2004).

common identity. This is the basis for giving a European rather than a national expression to feelings of solidarity among Europeans, while improving their democratic union and assuming the necessary reform of their welfare states.

CONCLUDING REMARKS: FACING EUROPEAN CHALLENGES

To break with both the instrumental and the procedural ways in which European public action is presently conceived is important because the anti-democratic tendencies resulting from such practices undermine the Union. In contrast, the prudential approach gives the Union the opportunity to deal with its present European challenges. It focuses on the importance of enhancing both political and social solidarity among the Europeans. In effect, in order to ensure economic growth and social progress within Europe, it is necessary that the competences of the inherited welfare states be revised. This redefinition is impossible without the exercise of prudential reason and the active participation of the citizens. At the same time, citizens cannot be active, responsible and critical, unless they share feelings of solidarity. The aim of public action of the prudential type is to favour the expression and the development of European solidarity. This consists on the one hand in institutional reforms so that all public actors be encouraged to exercise their political and social responsibilities. On the other hand, they refer to the cultural and educational policies that would favour the development and the expression of the Europeans' common values.

References

Arrow, K (1974) *The Limits of Organisation*, New York: WW Norton and Company

Bonvin, JM and Farvaques, N (2004) 'Employability and capability: the role of local agencies in implementing social policies', Eurocap Working Paper

Bonvin, JM and Thelen, L (2004) 'Deliberative democracy and capabilities: the impact and significance of capability for voice', Eurocap Working Paper

Castoriadis, C (1999a) 'Institution première de la société et institutions secondes', in *Figures du Pensable: Les carrefours du Labyrinthe VI*, Paris: Seuil

Castoriadis, C (1999b) 'Quelle démocratie?', in *Figures du Pensable: Les carrefours du Labyrinthe VI*, Paris: Seuil

Chorin, J (2003) 'Europe, marché intérieur et services publics: des principes à la réalité', 3 Revue de l'IRES.

Delanty, G (1997) 'Models of citizenship: defining European identity and citizenship', 1(3) Citizenship Studies 285–303

Habermas, J (1998) *Die Postnationale Konstellation: Politische Essays*, Frankfurt: Suhrkamp

Habermas, J (1999) 'Der Europäische Nationalstaat unter dem Druck der Globalisierung', 4 Blätter für deutsche und internationale Politik

Harsanyi, J (1976) *Essays on Ethics, Social Behavior, and Scientific Explanation*, Dordrecht-Holland: D Reidel Publishing Company

Joao Rodrigues, M (2001) 'The open method of co-ordination as a new governance tool', in Telo, M (ed) 2–3 L'evoluzione della Governance Europa, special issue of Europa/Europe 96–107

Kandil, F (2004) 'European social citizenship and the requirement of European solidarity', in Magnusson, L and Stråth, B (eds) *A European Social Citizenship? Preconditions for Future Policies in Historical Light*, Brussels: PIE

Kant, I (1981) [1785] *Grundlegung zur Metaphysik der Sitten*, Ellington, J (trans), Indianapolis, IN: Hackett

Le Goff, J (1993) *La vieille Europe et la nôtre*, Paris: Seuil

Le Goff, J (1996) *L'Europe Racontée aux Jeunes*, Paris: Seuil

Le Goff, J (2003) *L'Europe est-elle Née au Moyen-Age?*, Paris: Seuil

MacIntyre, A (1988) *Whose Justice? Which Rationality?*, London : Duckworth

Raveaud, G (2004), 'The European employment strategy: from ends to means?', in Salais, R and Villeneuve, R (eds), *Europe and the Politics of Capabilities*, Cambridge: Cambridge University Press

Rawls, J (1971) *A Theory of Justice*, Cambridge, MA: Belknap Press of Harvard University Press

Rousseau, JJ (1962) [1762], *Du Contrat Social*, Paris: Editions Garnier

Salais, R (2004) 'La politique des indicateurs. Du taux de chômage au taux d'emploi dans la stratégie européenne pour l'emploi', in Zimmermann, B (ed), *Action Publique et Sciences Sociales*, Paris: Editions de la Maison des Sciences de l'Homme

Salais, R and Villeneuve, R (eds) (2004) *Europe and the Politics of Capabilities*, Cambridge: Cambridge University Press

Sen, AK (1996) 'Social commitment and democracy: the demands of equity and financial conservatism', in Barker, P (ed), *Living as Equals: The Eva Colorni Memorial Lectures*, Oxford: Oxford University Press

Supiot, A (2003) 'Un faux dilemme: la loi ou le contrat?' Droit Social, 59–71

Wind, M (2001) *Sovereignty and European Integration. Towards a Post-Hobbesian Order*, London and New York: Palgrave Macmillan

INDEX